CHRIS McC

THE CRAFT AND THE CROSS

THE CRAFT
AND THE CROSS

The true story of the SUN OF GOD

CHRIS McCLINTOCK

First published in the United Kingdom in 2010 by

ÆSUN PUBLISHING

ISBN 978-0-9564598-0-0

A catalogue record for this book

is available from the British Library

aesunpublishing.com

Discovery is seeing what everyone else has seen,

and thinking what no one else has thought.

Albert von Szent-Gyorgyi

CONTENTS

Acknowledgements

This book has been eight years in the making, and has only been possible with the support and encouragement of many. Foremost among those who have given unstintingly of their support is my wife and soul-mate Yolanda, who lost me in a maelstrom of research many years ago yet never stopped believing in me. Many of the photographs herein are hers, and for that I thank her also. To my son Matthew and daughter Katherine, for putting up with my detachment from the real world this long time, I extend my heartfelt thanks too.

In the wider world especial thanks must be due to Robert Bashford, editor of the Irish Lodge of Research, who has accompanied me up hill and down dale, through bogs and over barbed-wire fences, in my search for answers in the often rain-drenched landscapes of Britain and Ireland. He too contributed photographs to the project.

To the reclusive genius David Alan Ritchie, who lives in an idyll on the Isle of Skye with his computer screens and his ducks, and who has helped in so many ways, I cannot thank you enough. You, David, know that this story is so much bigger than what is contained between these pages and will burn down many mansions when its fire gets fully ablaze. You have more to contribute than me and I'm just piling the kindling - the spark that will ignite the conflagration is yours. And to all those who attended the meeting of your fledgling Skythian Society in Edinburgh, your collective advice and encouragement was both timely and appreciated.

Posthumous thanks are due to Tony Batters for first encouraging me to write all those years ago. Thanks also to Martin Faulks of Lewis Masonic Publishers, who was the first in a professional capacity to tell me my work had merit. And to Ian and Viv. Robertson in Edinburgh, for their welcome and hospitality and helping me move along the path.

To my dear friend Bassam Dagher in Beirut, I owe you an immense debt for giving me freely of your Middle Eastern perspective on the Crusades, and introducing me to the Ikhwan el Safa.

To Josh Heller and Jay Hochberg for running the immensely informative Masonic Light web discussion group. And to Gerald Reilly from that same group, for ten years of his wisdom and philosophy. For support from within Irish Freemasonry, thanks are due to Trevor Darragh and Leslie McMullan who kept me right on the finer points of ritual, to my Provincial Grand Master Robert Quigley, and especially to the Grand Master, George Dunlop. Various members of the Irish Lodge of Research have taken an active interest in my research, including Robert Bashford, James Penny, Bill Howie, Peter McFadden and Martin Jackson – to all of them I extend my grateful thanks for their input. Further afield in Masonic research we have Trevor Stewart, Bob Mitchell and Alan Turton, all of whose encouragement was appreciated.

Special thanks must go to Simon Cox for seeing the potential in my work and rounding me up and pointing me in the right direction. And of the people he introduced me to Susan Davies must get particular mention. I first learned what an editor was with Susan, and her knowledge of the subject matter was exceptional. To Mark Foster too, I owe an immense debt of gratitude.

Closer to home I must thank Tom and Madeline McCully for their help with Gaelic; Dr. Bob Curran for his general advice, and Dr. Andy McCrae MBE, past president of the Irish Astronomical Association for his advice on the night sky. To Peter Gribben - my bulwark against the real world for so long; only he will ever know the debt I owe him. Perhaps more than any of the above, I thank Jonathan Wilson for keeping my stained glass business going these last years when I was mentally and often physically elsewhere.

Especially my thanks go to those many authors whose work inspired me. To fellow Irishmen Anthony Murphy, Richard Moore and I am particularly grateful. Thanks also to Martin Brennan for his pioneering work in ancient symbolism. And to Robert Lomas and Christopher Knight who inspired me to become a Mason in the first place. And lastly to everyone who ever expressed belief in my project and encouraged me to keep going over these many years, and to you, the reader, for making it all possible.

This

book is dedicated

to my soul-mate Yolanda,

without whose support this journey

would not have been

possible.

INTRODUCTION

THIS BOOK WILL challenge everything you ever thought you knew about Freemasonry, for it presents a radical new thesis on its origin, drawn from its symbols and rituals that has remained completely hidden until now. It also demands a reassessment of our current understanding of the development of Christianity in the British Isles, which, rather than replacing the paganism that went before, is proven to have simply absorbed and re-branded much of it as Christianity.

From the humble aspiration of research for a lecture on Masonic symbolism and ritual, the discoveries this study produced led outwards into other spheres, and backwards in time, to suggest a truly ancient origin of the concepts of deity that lie underneath the surface of the oldest and most misunderstood fraternity in the world. Those discoveries have huge implications not only for the date of the origin of Freemasonry, but demand a reappraisal of many fundamental symbols of the Christian Church – one of which is the Christian Cross itself. The national symbol of Scotland, the cross of St. Andrew also known as the Saltire, is found to lie at the very heart of the symbolism of the Craft, and is shown to be an ancient pagan symbol that was Christianised in the 12th Century. Over the course of this book I will demonstrate that the pagan derivation of the Saltire is not a singular aberration in the historical record, but is instead part of an immense trail of ancient sun veneration that started over five thousand years ago and remains to this day, lying forgotten in the rituals of the Craft.

Freemasonry describes itself as '*A peculiar system of morality, veiled in allegory, and illustrated by symbols*'. This description is very succinct, and highlights the problem for the historian. If the true message of Freemasonry is veiled in allegory and represented by symbols, it is because the architects of the fraternity, for whatever reason, did not want its message to be shown in a more conventional way. Following from that, it will only be by analysis of those symbols that we can discover their true meaning. Freemasonry uses, for example, the right-angled square as a metaphor for 'squaring' one's actions in life, and it is generally thought of as merely a tool of the stonemason that is suitable for the allusion. The square has, however, a far deeper meaning than being just a simple tool, and it is the discovery and explanation of that meaning that is the purpose of this book. Likewise the concept of the arch is central to the Craft. A well-built arch and the keystone through which it maintains its integrity are vital to the stability of a building, and the Masonic allusion is that God represents a metaphorical keystone in the lives of men. Both the square and the arch have other underlying meanings, however, that are much more archaic than the lessons Freemasonry draws from them. That meaning is revealed in this book for the first time ever, and is shown to have been sacred to an unseen tradition that has been active in the British Isles since at least the 12th Century.

The history of Freemasonry is inextricably mingled with the history of the stone-working industry. Those craftsmen who banded together in lodges and worked in stone in the Middle Ages are referred to as 'operative' masons, whilst the gentlemen who later joined their lodges, and who did not work in stone, are known as 'speculative' or 'accepted' Masons. Discovering the point in time and the purpose that lay behind the speculative aspect coming to dominate the lodges is the 'holy grail' of Masonic research. Current thinking regards the operative stonemasons as semi-literate, itinerant and simple Christian workmen, and takes the esoterica that can be found in lodge rituals today as being injected into the lodges by the speculative newcomers from around the 1650s. This book proves that this is not the case, and that the esoteric aspect was there for many centuries before the outside world took an interest in their lodges.

Freemasonry has no known beginning, and the many theories of its origin are fraught with difficulties and littered with enigmas. For every theory there is another one that contradicts it. Even the most universally acceptable claim - that educated gentlemen joined the work-squads of an industry in decline - has no plausible explanation as to why it would have happened. We also have London regarded by many as the place of origin, when much evidence points to Scotland as the true birthplace of the Craft. For many, the Knights Templar are an intrinsic part of the Craft's beginnings, whilst others scorn this as a fanciful fairytale, and regard the Craft as simply growing from the mediaeval guilds of stonemasons.

Similar contradictions are found right across the debate, with arguments raging about this or that possibility, and it was to unravel that tangled knot of disagreement that I decided to look at the problem from an entirely different perspective. In the absence of an agreed consensus I undertook an intensive examination of the rituals and symbols of the Craft in an effort to see if I could discern any vestige of ancient meaning. My reasoning was simple – if the Craft is as ancient as some claim, then the obscure, convoluted rites of the lodge room may still carry remnants of the past that if analysed on a minute level, may finally give up its secrets. If the past could be understood, then perhaps the path by which it became Freemasonry would reveal itself.

What I found did indeed illuminate what went before, and though the path was long, I was to eventually discover that the megalithic standing stones of the Bronze Age still cast the shadow of the rising sun across both the Masonic lodge rooms of today, and indeed, our Christian churches.

What I have uncovered shows that the deeply obscured esoteric references that differentiate Freemasonry from stonemasonry were not injected by the incoming gentlemen of the Enlightenment, but were there for many centuries before the 17th century, and that at least some aspects of them can be traced back a thousand years before that date. I have found that the rites and symbols of Freemasonry, almost without exception, refer to the sun and its yearly transit of the heavens. Newly discovered factors, revealed here for the very first time, confirm the true reason why it was Edinburgh rather than elsewhere that gave birth to the most ancient, misunderstood and enigmatic fraternity in the world, and why the Scottish landscape is host to a tradition, the symbolism of which can be traced from at least the 6th century. Uncovering that tradition also led to numerous discoveries that give form and continuity to other aspects of history that up until now have remained as mere legends, and form the skeleton of the thesis I offer about the origin of the Craft.

Masonic ritual is veiled in allegory. It is full of archaic practices that seem silly to non-Masons, and leave those on the outside wondering what it is that makes men take part in such curious behaviour. It is a common misconception, even within the order, that the rituals of the Craft are secret, but as early as the 1730s numerous 'exposures' had been published by disenfranchised Masons that revealed every word and gesture of the lodge room, so the idea that Masonic ritual is secret is nonsense. So why do Masons still cling to this illusion then, when this self-imposed aura of secrecy is responsible for so much criticism? Why be secretive, say non-Masons, if there is nothing to hide? I believe the reason Masonry retains arcane practices, and maintains the illusion that its ceremonies are secret, is because those rituals have deeply symbolic allegorical significance.

Criticism of the Craft does not stop at its secrecy. Another claim is that Freemasonry is a religion, and further, that it sets itself against Christianity. Masonic Temples are adorned with symbols like the Five-pointed Star, the All-seeing Eye and the constellations of the zodiac, which must mean that Freemasons are adepts in the Occult Arts. People who say that either forget, or are perhaps unaware, that symbols like these can be found in Christian churches too. They also say that the order's meeting places are devoid of ostensibly Christian iconography, a fact that draws criticism from fundamentalist Christians who question why it is God in general and not Jesus who is the focus of prayer. These same people see all sorts of dark references in the many strange pictograms that adorn thousands of Masonic centres across the world, and do not hesitate to proclaim that they 'know' what those symbols mean, when even Masons themselves do not.

This book is an attempt to give rational explanations for the curious symbols and rituals of Freemasonry, and in doing so, to present a hypothesis that accounts for many of the more obscure aspects of the Craft. Freemasonry itself is a philosophy for life, and its rituals are theatre, structured to impart that philosophy. The allegories they contain operate on many different levels, and they are not given with footnotes. Personal enlightenment cannot be given, it must be sought, and the reason the Craft veils its precepts in allusion is so that each Mason can come to his own understanding of what he is shown. This is why there exists no consensus of what Freemasonry is, for it means something different for every Mason who takes the time to look in depth at what it is. I use the word 'he' above, for although both male and female Masonic organisations exist, the three constitutions of the British Isles from which the Craft grew, and which are the focus of this study, were then and still are, male only bodies.

Since the symbols of the Craft are obscure, unexplained, and are non-specific about the nature of God, those outside the organisation ascribe all sorts of dark overtones to them. This obscurity about the name of God leads Masons to be regarded by some as quite literally devil-worshippers. As laid out in this book, the Craft's vagueness about the name of God is indeed quite deliberate, but has no sinister overtones whatsoever. Freemasonry, though based on religious principles, is committedly non-dogmatic, therefore rather than align itself with one particular section of society, it simply portrays God in symbolic form, without definition, so that each brother can carry his own god with him as he enters and leaves the lodge room.

It must also be noted that I am not a spokesman for the Craft, and that the observations outlined in this book are my own personal perceptions of the theatre of the lodge-room, and are simply the product of many years research into the essence of the Craft.

We tend to think of Sumer, Babylon, or Egypt as the first great civilisations, because they were the first to record their history, leaving their stories carved in stone or imprinted on clay tablets. I will show however that the observations about the heavens which are contained in Masonic ritual date from an earlier time, before history was recorded, when the sun-temples of the Boyne Valley in Ireland and Stonehenge on Salisbury Plain to name but two, were laid out.

What possible connection could mediaeval Christian stonemasons have with the builders of these ancient structures? If Masonry does indeed contain rituals that refer symbolically to the veneration of the sun's movements through the seasons, then how can we realistically think that semi-literate working men five thousand years later could structure their rituals around such archaic notions? It is the problem created by this difficulty that causes many academic historians to adopt the opinion that the esoterica that differentiates Freemasons from the working stonemasons that went before must have been introduced by the newcomers. What is contained in this book, however, proves beyond doubt that the esoterica was there long before modern Freemasonry came about, so the implication is that the original stonemasons did indeed carry arcane notions in their rituals.

But how can this be?

One possible explanation is that the knowledge was passed down from older sources and that at some point in the Middle Ages some organisation became aware of and revived those ancient secrets and devised a system of moral teaching in which they embedded that ancient knowledge. If this tradition then became enmeshed in the stone-working industry, that would account for the presence of arcane knowledge in the rituals of simple stone-workers. The labours of the lodge room having pre-existing esoteric rites would also explain why educated men completely unconnected with the craft of working in stone would have been drawn in later times to become members of that organisation, as we know they were.

Though the first connections I made were fragmented and seemed tenuous they gradually coalesced into a whole, with avenues of discovery diverging in many directions. The picture of the past that slowly emerged at first seemed incredible, particularly so because it was completely dissociated from any existing beliefs about the origin of Freemasonry that I had ever come across. A web grew outwards from those first discoveries that was intricate and far-reaching, and laid a definite, if unseen, path down through the years and set the knowledge of the sun squarely at the doorstep of those men who first sought membership of the stonemasons' lodges in the 17th Century.

From what I have discovered, Freemasonry preserves in its convoluted rituals and symbols a complete record of ancient Man's spirituality. Presented here for the first time ever is evidence of a veneration of the sun that started more than five thousand years ago, that rather than fading from the world, was preserved as allegory within Christianity until the Middle Ages when it became a secret tradition. Along the way we will encounter those who built Newgrange in Ireland and laid out the pyramid complex on the Giza Plateau. We will also look into the life of the Irish saint who brought Christianity to Scotland in the 6th Century, and by analysis of Greek and Celtic myth we will arrive at the ancient secrets of the cosmos that lie at the heart of Freemasonry.

And we will find those secrets hidden in the allegories of the death and raising of the candidate in the 3rd Degree....

THE CRAFT AND THE CROSS

PART ONE

VEILED IN ALLEGORY

THE CRAFT AND THE CROSS

CHAPTER 1

FREEMASONRY WAS BORN in the British Isles. It emerged in three separate countries at roughly the same time; England, Ireland and Scotland. On St. John the Baptist's Day, 1717, it emerged into the light when four London lodges banded together in public, elected a Grand Master and formed a Grand Lodge. It is a mistake, however, to think that this date is in any way the start of Masonry; it is only the day that a select few lodges chose to be less secretive about their existence and announced themselves to the world. There are many references to Masonry in the century before, indeed Sir Robert Moray, arguably the founder of the Royal Society, was initiated in Newcastle in 1641. Elias Ashmole the famous Antiquarian recorded in his diary that he was made a Mason on the 16th October 1646. It must be therefore presumed that Freemasonry up until the early 18th century had been a hidden tradition, existing in autonomous cells or lodges without any centralised, hierarchical structure, but due to some change in society it had decided that the time had come to emerge from the shadows and organise itself into the order we know today.

The operative craft of the stonemason has a very old recorded history. The earliest British lodge is documented as having worked on the building of Kilwinning Abbey in Ayrshire, Scotland as early as

1140, and the development and existence of these lodges is well documented. The most important documents that attest to this are the Regius Poem c1390, the Cooke Manuscript of c1450, and the two Schaw Statutes, drawn up in 1598/9 by William Schaw, 'Maister of Works' to King James VI of Scotland. The Schaw Statutes are couched in terms similar to modern Freemasonry and set out a fulsome code of conduct for the operative masons under his authority. One of his innovations was the keeping of minute books, and by the year 1600 seven of the lodges under his control were keeping a record of their existence for the first time ever. Those seven lodges were the very first to become speculative, and are universally accepted as being the oldest Masonic lodges in the world. They are found mostly in the vicinity of Edinburgh, and already we are starting to see evidence for Scotland's claim as the birthplace of the Craft.

The London lodges went public in 1717 with the formation of their Grand Lodge, and eight years later the Irish Craft in Dublin followed suit. Scotland formed its Grand Lodge in 1736 and within a few years Freemasonry had spread around the globe. On the Continent, the Craft was enthusiastically embraced by the upper echelons of society and quickly developed a superstructure of higher orders and degrees. France, in particular, took to the new fraternal society with gusto; it is presumed because of what is known as Ramsay's Oration, a speech that whilst not actually given, was widely distributed in written form in Paris in the 1730s. Andrew Michael Ramsay, also known as Chevalier Ramsay, was a Scottish Freemason, and held the post of Grand Orator in the fledgling French Craft. In his oration he claimed that Masonry had originated in the Holy Land with the re-instatement of the ancient mysteries, and was carried to Scotland by returning Crusaders. This oration was the first record of anyone suggesting that the mediaeval knighthood had a connection to the Craft, and many point to this recent date as proof that the Templar link is a modern invention that was too readily believed by those who wished to ascribe a glorious history to their new order.

In his Oration, Ramsay claimed the descent of Freemasonry from the mysteries of Ceres at Eleusis and other similar cults in Classical times. It is largely because of this notion's antiquity that his Oration has always been regarded as fanciful. Following from that, his claim that Crusaders played a part in the origin of the Craft is another idea for which there is scant and contradictory evidence, and so is similarly dismissed.

Until the last few decades the rituals of the Craft were, like the mystery cults of the Middle East, a strictly oral tradition, it being anathema to write down even the slightest detail of its rites. As a result, we do not know precisely what rituals existed during the purely operative times. Whatever rituals the accepted gentlemen Masons inherited, however, it is an established fact that during the earliest days of speculative Masonry there was a certain de-Christianising of them. This suggests that the earlier rites of the lodge room were Christian, and is a central plank of more conservative theories as to the origin of the Craft. What I offer in this book, however, suggests another, altogether different reason for that de-Christianisation, suggesting that the earlier Christian element was a public façade, similar to the outer aspect of the pagan mysteries, and was simply discarded as the Craft developed.

There were also other instances of changes to the rituals - quite fundamental changes, as we will see when we look at the esoteric significance of them in a moment. In most cases the changes took the form of removing elements of the ceremonies because they appeared to be meaningless mumbo-jumbo to those who modified them. When I demonstrate how vital some of what was removed was to the original meaning of the labours of a Masonic lodge, it will be evident that by the 1700s the true meanings had been lost to those who undertook the alterations.

There was one body of Freemasons however, who seemed to have retained a clearer understanding of the past than those who altered the rituals, and who openly challenged those changes. That body - the Grand Lodge of the Antients – was a second Grand Lodge set up in London thirty-four years after the original one and its purpose will be examined later, when we better understand the nature of the tradition that became Freemasonry. For now, we will move on to look at the present-day rituals of the lodge room, and see why the allegorical references contained within them must be truly ancient.

For Masonic readers, I should point out that all references to ritual contained in the next chapter are, unless stated otherwise, from Irish ritual, and may vary from other jurisdictions.

CHAPTER 2

THE WORD ALLEGORY will be mentioned often throughout this book. Some allegory is by nature obvious and is merely used to illustrate a point. Allegory of this type only requires a modicum of intelligence to penetrate the veil, and examples of these are the parables of the Bible. However there is another use for allegory, and that is as a device to disguise something completely and utterly, so that its true meaning is hidden from all but those who have been taught to see it. The purpose of such allegory is to make a point or record a detail without directly alluding to it. Robert Burns the Ayrshire poet shows this perfectly in his poem, *To a Mouse*. The narrative takes the form of his apologising to a field mouse for cutting its nest in two with his plough and scattering its family. Burns was a truly compassionate man and the depth of his regret shows through in every word as he speaks personally to the mouse.

There is an underlying subtext however that is not directly mentioned at all, but is the true meaning behind the poem. Burns championed the common man, and hated the power and privilege of the landed classes because of the way in which they abused that power. He lived through the earliest of the Highland Clearances, when the lands were cleared of people to make way for more profitable sheep - when entire communities were forced off the land they had worked as tenants for generations simply to enable the gentry to show a better balance sheet at the end of the year. The true message of Burns' lament to the wee, sleekit, cowrin, tim'rous beastie was to highlight the injustices heaped on the common man by those who, whilst serving themselves generously from the platter of life, could so callously upend the lives of others. Those human sentiments are not expressed directly in the text at all however, but are there nevertheless, expressed through his apology to the mouse, and represent the true meaning behind the poem.

The allegories of Freemasonry are identical to the above, and whilst appearing as one thing, they will be shown to carry a much deeper, unstated message. Though never referred to directly, there are unspoken, underlying references that are the true focus of the metaphors. Deeply buried allegories like those in Burns' poem saturate early Masonic imagery, though they are not immediately obvious unless looked at with a specific mindset.

The most effective use for such allegory is in subtle alterations to well known images, thus the hidden message can reside in plain sight, shouting its significance to those who have eyes to see, yet remain invisible to those who haven't. As such, many of the symbols of the Craft appear as simply being drawn from Classical or Christian sources, but underlying the obvious, however, is an altogether deeper layer of meaning that is unstated, and is the true meaning of the symbol's use. The difficulty that arises from a word, movement, or gesture having such an allegorical, hidden meaning is that many centuries later, when its original meaning has been forgotten, we can only speculate as to its true import.

From the moment I was myself initiated into the Craft eighteen years ago, I had been intrigued by the preponderance of compass directions and times of the day with particular reference to the sun within the ceremonies, and it was in an effort to understand the meanings of these references that I first started the quest to discover their origins. After much head-scratching it was when I happened across the book *Uriel's Machine*, that what I saw before me started to make sense. The aforementioned book by Christopher Knight and Robert

Lomas shows how the ancients kept track of the movements of the sun through the seasons of the year, and drew my attention to the behaviour of the sun in northern Britain, and immediately I saw the significance of at least some of the rituals of the lodge room.

This is the first time ever that the interpretations laid out here have been put before the world, and as such, new ground must be broken. The breaking of this ground, in this chapter, will perhaps therefore seem over-laboured in its continual references to the same themes. Such is the nature of the beast however and cannot be avoided. The succeeding chapters will, I hope, clear the fog in which this one will envelop the reader.

The All Seeing Eye

The All Seeing Eye is perhaps the Masonic symbol that most plainly suggests the sun. It has been a symbol of deity in many cultures, and in many eras, and is thought to have been derived from the sun's passage overhead each day. As it traverses the heavens we are always in its view, so the metaphor of it being God's eye, watching us, is quite plain. Not only is it an ancient notion, but it is an intellectually primitive one, and as such has survived to the modern day not as reality, but merely as a symbol of God. It is a powerful allegory that links God and the sun, and it is telling that it is such a popular Masonic motif.

The picture on the right is a close-up of the top of the arch on a stained glass window in the Masonic hall in Portrush, Co.

Antrim, Northern Ireland. The All Seeing Eye is a very common Masonic symbol, and is often placed as it is here on the keystone of an arch. It has rays of light emanating from it, so the sun-allusion is considerably strengthened.

The right-angled square

The right-angled square is considered so important in Masonry that it is half of that best-known emblem of the Craft, the Square & Compasses. Though not so immediately obvious as the All Seeing Eye, I believe the sun still lies behind the meaning of this symbol. We talk of the sun rising in the east, but in actual fact that only happens on two days in the year, the 21st of March, and the 21st of September – the equinoxes. On these two days the sun rises precisely due east, sets due west, and is directly overhead at noon at the equator, giving a night and day of equal length. Because of the tilt in the earth's axis as it revolves around the sun however, on every other day the sun rises either left or right of due east, giving us our seasons. Over the summer the sun is in the northern hemisphere so rises to the left of the east-west line, moving northwards until the summer solstice where it changes direction. From then until September it moves southwards, reaching due east again on the autumnal equinox, at which point it passes into the southern hemisphere where it spends the winter months.

When the sun reaches its extremity to either left or right, it gradually comes to a stop before changing direction. This happens twice a year on the solstices, the word meaning 'sun standing still'. This gives four special days, the equinoxes and solstices, equally spaced on the calendar, which divide the year into four quarters. The marking of these four days was of enormous significance to the ancients, as their main religious observances of the year hinged around them. The summer solstice represented the sun at its strongest, the highest it reached in the sky, whereas the winter solstice signified the sun, not at its weakest, but rather as the day it started to turn towards the north again and triumphed over winter. The winter solstice therefore was regarded as the rebirth of the sun.

The sunrise on the equinox is due east regardless of where it is viewed from on the surface of the globe, but the positions of the solstice sunrises depend on one's latitude. The further north the viewer stands, the further those special sunrises are from due east, the further south, the closer. At Cairo, for instance, the separation of the sunrises from the winter to the summer solstices is roughly 54 degrees, whilst at Stockholm it is 101 degrees, and therein lies the significance of the square to those who recorded the sun's movements.

Peculiar to the latitude of southern Scotland, both solstice sunrises are separated by exactly 90 degrees. In other words, sunrise on the summer solstice is 45 degrees north of east; referred to specifically in Masonry as the northeast corner, and on the winter solstice is exactly 45 degrees south of east, being the southeast corner. The angle between these sunrises is precisely 90 degrees, and in the northern hemisphere this precision only happens at the latitude of southern Scotland. I was alerted to this fact by Christopher Knight and Robert Lomas' book *The Second Messiah*, which noted that the solstice sunrises at Rosslyn Chapel formed a square. They did not develop this notion as I have into the origin of the Craft, however, for as I was to discover, this is singularly the most important factor in Freemasonry's beginnings around that same geographical location. Though at this point I only offer this fact for consideration in our appraisal of the rituals of the lodge room, the rest of this book will explain why I believe the square formed by the sun in Scotland is central to the Craft.

The ancients who tracked the movements of the sun they worshipped were so aware of its movements that they aligned their henges and standing stones towards its rising and setting on the solstices. They are unlikely, therefore, to have been ignorant of the fact that at only one latitude does the sun's movements create a 90-degree alignment from mid-summer to mid-winter. Whilst the line of latitude where this happens extends right around the globe, across Denmark, Russia and Canada, we will limit ourselves to the British Isles, where it passes through southern Scotland. Presuming the ancients were indeed aware of this phenomenon, would it be rash to assume that they would have regarded this area as being in particular favour with God, and that the term *square* would therefore have had sacred connotations for them?

Since similar connotations exist in Freemasonry today, I would therefore suggest that the true, allegorical meaning of the square in Freemasonry does not end with the tool used to square stone, but refers directly to the 90 degrees between the winter and summer solstices In Scotland. We will further develop this idea later but for now we will simply note the fact that Edinburgh, where the oldest Masonic lodges in the world are to be found, lies in the middle of this area.

Another time we see the right-angled square associated with the sun is in the location in which the candidate is placed when he first enters the lodge room. He is blindfolded before being admitted, and as such can be regarded as being received in darkness, and before the ceremony starts he is placed in the northwest corner of the lodge room. The significance I attach to this is that it is where the sun sets on the summer solstice, so perhaps the lack of light then, is equated with the setting of the sun and the onset of night. Once initiated and having obtained 'light,' as Masons term the first introduction to the craft, the candidate is then specifically placed in the northeast corner, which I suggest is symbolic of the sun's rising point on the same day. The 90-degree angle between these two compass-points gives rise to the Masonic notation of being received upon the square.

Further references to the solstice points in Masonic ritual are the peculiar stances the candidates adopt whilst giving the salutes of the various degrees. In the 1st Degree, the right foot is placed in the hollow of the left forming a 90 degree angle and is known as *Standing to Order*. If this is done while facing due east, which is precisely what the candidate is doing during this part of the degree, his right foot will point to the southeast corner, or the rising point of the sun on the winter solstice. This means that the candidate outlines the same corner of a square on the ground as the sun does at the particular latitude that interests us.

First Degree	Second Degree	Third Degree	
Winter Solstice	Summer Solstice	Both Solstices	
SE corner	NE corner	NE	SE

In the 2nd Degree the position is reversed, pointing the left foot towards the northeast corner, which is the sun's rising point on the summer solstice. The 3rd Degree is different again, with both feet being placed heel-to-heel forming a right-angle on the ground that points to the two places marked by the sun.

The compasses

From the right-angled Square that forms half of the Masonic logo we will now turn our attention to the Compasses that complete the emblem. Whilst in England there is no standard angle for the compasses to be set at, there is a strong tradition in Ireland that the proper angle for the Compasses is 60 degrees. Can we find any solar significance in the choice of 60 degrees?

The maximum height achieved by the sun each day changes from winter to summer. It achieves its zenith at noon when it passes the mid-point of the sky in the south - the meridian, a place that is referred to often in Masonry and indeed in astronomy generally. The meridian is of enormous significance to any celestial body, because it is on crossing it that the object reaches its zenith, or as the ancients perceived it, the object's most powerful. The height the sun reaches also depends on latitude; the farther north one goes, the lower the angle, whilst the nearer the equator, the higher the angle. Again we find a notable angle in the middle of the British Isles, being precisely 60 degrees on the summer solstice at the latitude of Dublin. This perhaps lends credence to the suggestion that the 60 degrees refers to the altitude of the solstice sun, when we consider that it is only in Ireland, out of the three founding Masonic Constitutions, that the compasses are traditionally set at that angle. In London the sun achieves 61.54 degrees on the solstice, and in Edinburgh 57.31. If only Irish Masonry regards the proper angle of the compasses to be 60 degrees, this surely hints that the sun lies behind the allusion.

Another time we see a similar angle is at the moment the lodge is both opened and closed with the coping of the deacons' wands over the altar. Each lodge has two deacons who are equipped with long poles with brass tips, called wands, similar to those used in church services. To cope literally means to tilt at an angle, and at the moment the lodge is both opened and closed, the deacons cross the tips of their wands over the altar at the centre of the lodge room floor. The fact that they specifically cross the tips instead of merely touching them will become important when we get deeper into the allegorical meanings of the movements, but the reasoning is complex and needs to be seen in a context that we will look at shortly. Whilst obviously not precisely 60 degrees, the coping can nevertheless be seen as symbolic of the sun's rays over the altar, particularly since the tips themselves are brass and therefore mimic the colour of the sun. This may seem an irrelevance at this point, but Masonry will be shown to be overflowing with little instances similar to this one, all of which have deeply significant, allegorical meanings that are not immediately obvious. There are many depictions from Ancient Egypt that show the Aten, the sun disc, casting its rays over the proceedings in a similar fashion to the symbolism I believe is included in the coping of the wands over the altar.

In the Square & Compasses therefore I believe are encoded the two solstices, represented in the 90-

degree Square, and the angle of the noon-day sun on the summer solstice represented by the Compasses. Further evidence of the veracity of this claim is that while the Square in the emblem is more often than not depicted in silver, the Compasses are usually in gold, which is again symbolic of the golden rays of the sun.

Placing the letter G in the centre of the Square & Compasses identifies the knowledge contained within the symbol with God, and indicates that the amalgamation of these references was considered sacred. There is also another part of the ritual that involves a golden square, which in its context can also be specifically linked to the sun, but will be left until we better understand the nature of the ritual.

Squaring the altar

The altar, which traditionally was a square cube, sits in the very centre of an Irish lodge room and always has done, a situation which is not necessarily 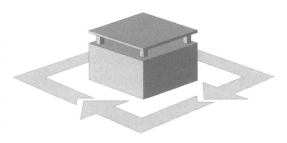 so in the other Constitutions. As the officers move around the floor conducting the business of the meeting, they are not permitted to pass the altar on the left, and must always move around the room in a clockwise manner, or sun-wise, keeping the altar on the right at all times. If we consider the altar, or indeed the lodge room as a whole, as a representation of the square formed by sun on the solstices, then the officers of the lodge mimic the sun's clockwise passage around that square by similarly moving clockwise around the altar. Not only must the altar be kept to the right at all times, but those crossing the floor must 'square the floor' by only turning in 90 degree increments. The movement therefore squares the centre of the lodge room, strengthening the allusion that the sun and its square is indeed being referred to.

Black and white

We also see squares on the black and white chequered Masonic pavement, and there too we can identify astronomical significance. The black and white pavement is one of the aspects of the order that hints at a link with the Knights Templar since their battle flag, the Beausant, was a black square over a white square. Traditional Templar lore will suggest that the black and white signifies dark and light, good and evil, night and day. That is undoubtedly so on a simplistic level, but I think there is also a hidden, allegorical meaning much deeper than this, because the equal sized squares on their flag suggest nights and days of equal length, and that only happens on two days in the year; the equinoxes. Does the Beausant therefore allude to those equinoxes, and by extension therefore does the Masonic Pavement do likewise? You may ask why either the Beausant or the Masonic Pavement should allude to the equinoxes, and the answer to that question, which forms the second half of the book, goes to the very heart of Masonic symbolism.

A point within a circle

 A point within a circle between two parallel lines is one of the better-known and more enigmatic Masonic emblems. Yet again it can be seen as an illustration of the solstices, and is closely allied to the feast days mentioned above. The point within a circle is nothing more obscure than the universal astronomical symbol for the sun, but what then are the two parallel lines that touch it? I would assert that they are simply the Tropics of Cancer and Capricorn - the furthest points the sun travels from the equator. The days on which the sun reaches these extremities are the solstices, and so yet again a Masonic emblem can be read as referring to these special days. The dot

at the centre of the circle then becomes the sun at the centre of its travels, or in other words over the equator on the equinoxes. Yet again an emblem of Freemasonry can be seen to show appreciation and an understanding of the workings of both the solstices and the equinoxes.

The parallel lines have also been linked to the Masonic pillars Boaz and Jachin, that William Preston, an early commentator on Masonic symbolism, suggested were identified from the earliest times with St. John the Baptist and St. John the Evangelist. In their earliest depictions, the parallel lines are not merely straight lines but have serifs or tails top and bottom, as in the illustration above, making them into the Greek Iota, the capital letter I that is the initial for Ioannes, the Greek for John. We will next look at the likelihood that those two saints are linked to the solstices, and in this emblem we see why that allusion is made.

Feast days

The two feast days of the Craft are those of the two saints John; that of the Baptist on the 24th June, and the Evangelist on 27th December, referred to earlier as twin parallel lines. Why are these two saints regarded as patrons of the Craft when the order is universal and specifically makes the point that it is not a Christian organisation? I suggest it is the dates of their feast days rather than the saints themselves that are important here, and again the significance is pre-Christian. As Christianity rose to prominence in the 3rd and 4th Centuries, it was impossible to dissuade people from worshipping their old gods on the ancient holy days, so the ancient pagan festivals were allowed to remain but given Christian names. The ancient world venerated a god of the summer solstice known as Oannes, thought to be the origin of the association of the name John with Midsummer's Day, and it is now widely accepted that the two St's. John days are really the pagan celebrations of the solstices. The dates today do not fall exactly on the solstices, but that can be attributed to the various calendar changes causing the dates to drift over the years, and to the Church wishing to distance its celebrations from the pagan past. So here too we find solar significance in Masonry's two most important days.

Lodges also install their Master on St. John the Evangelist's day or as soon after as is practicable. If we equate this date with the winter solstice, then his elevation to office can be seen as the return of the sun and the birth of the new solar year. I discovered near the beginning of my research, however, that up until the middle of the 19th century a new Master was installed for only six months at a time, and that one was installed on St. John the Baptist's day and another on St. John the Evangelist's Day. Though initially confused by this, I eventually realised that this was in direct reference to the two saints John and the solstices to which those days refer.

Venus

The planet Venus, known throughout history as the five-pointed star, holds a particularly strong position within the symbolism of Freemasonry. It could be argued that outside the Square & Compasses, the five-pointed star is the most important emblem of the Craft,

In simple terms Venus has a rhythm to its movements that repeats every 584 days, which is known as its synodic period. If its position is noted once every 584 days, over five of these periods, which totals almost exactly eight years, the planet has traced an irregular five-pointed star in the heavens. The five-pointed star derived from this rhythm has been a sacred symbol for many thousands of years, and is seen often on Ancient Egyptian and Sumerian temples.

In Masonic terms, Venus is seen on many early objects that carry the symbols of the Craft. In the earliest days lodges met in tavern back-rooms and as the lessons of each degree were taught to the candidate certain symbols were drawn on the floor in chalk. Through time these symbols were formalised and painted on boards known as Tracing Boards. The 1st Degree board has a chequered pavement strewn with various symbolic objects. Central to the montage is a stairway that leads up to the sky. Though both the sun and the moon are present, it is

Venus that stands at the head of the stair, suggesting the importance of that planet to the Craft.

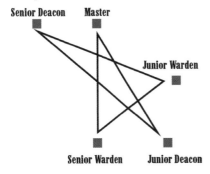

More obtusely but even more significantly perhaps, it is also traced on the floor as one progresses through the offices of a Masonic Lodge. The figure opposite shows the position of the officers within the lodge room, and how the progression through the offices outlines the five-pointed star on the floor. Starting with the first office, that of the Junior Deacon, then the Senior Deacon, Junior Warden, Senior Warden, Master and finally back to the Junior Deacon, the officers have physically traced the five-pointed star on the lodge room floor.

Five points of fellowship

During the 3rd Degree initiation, the candidate symbolically dies and is later raised. On being raised, the candidate is placed in a strange position called the Five Points of Fellowship, where he is placed in contact with the person giving him the degree in five deliberate places, being foot-to-foot, knee-to-knee, breast-to-breast, cheek-to-cheek, and hand over back. It is at this moment, with a word whispered in his ear, that he becomes a Master Mason. It is the defining moment of his Masonic

career, and the inclusion of the five points of Venus indicates surely, how important the planet is to Freemasonry. Yet again, then, we have astronomical significance in an aspect of the Craft.

33 Degrees

Another interesting fact about the sun in northern Britain is that on the equinoxes, when it passes along the celestial equator, its angle above the ground as it reaches its highest point in the sky on the meridian is 33 Degrees. This happens at the latitude of Aberdeen, a location that will shortly be shown to have significance to our thesis, and brings to mind the 33 Degrees of Freemasonry. Yet again, then, we have what can be seen as a link between Freemasonry and the equinoxes.

Marking the solstices

A traditional Irish lodge room and the officers' positions within it are as this sketch. The room itself is oblong in shape, a double cube in fact, and is orientated along an east-west axis, and with a raised platform at the eastern end. On this is placed the Master's chair, from which he directs the proceedings on the floor in front of him. Beside him on his right is the Senior Deacon who carries his wand with him at all times. In the centre of the floor is the altar where the Bible lies open during the proceedings. Towards the west end of the room sits the Senior Warden,

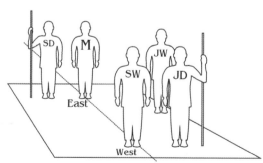

the lodge's second most important officer, with the Junior Deacon at his right hand, also equipped with his wand. The last remaining officer, third in seniority, is the Junior Warden, who sits to the south of the altar, half way along the southern wall of the room, and has no deacon in attendance. The importance of these positions will be demonstrated in a moment, but for now we will forget the modern lodge room and imagine it is a time before the Pyramids were built and the sun is about to rise over the eastern horizon. The senior priests of one of the temples of the sun get ready to perform their three daily tasks, which are to record where the sun rises, where it sets, and precisely when it reaches its zenith on the meridian. By recording these details, they would be able to pinpoint exactly when the significant days of the solstices and the equinoxes occurred, and by noting when the sun reached its highest point in the south, they could also pinpoint the moment of noon and initiate whatever ceremony they had for that occasion.

The marking of the sunrise required two men and was achieved with the use of a solar gnomon, which is a complex name for what amounts to a straight pole. By setting that pole vertical against the sunrise, as can be seen in the first part of the above sketch, the shadow it cast on the ground could be marked with a chalked line. One man was required to hold the pole that casts the shadow, the other to make sure it was vertical using a square, and then chalk the shadow-line when the sun first breaks the horizon. The reason this was done was because the solstices occurred when the sun reached the extent of its migration across the horizon during the year. The shadow line would get closer and closer to the previous days, until eventually the shadow stopped moving altogether and the sun literally stood still. In similar fashion, two men were also required for marking the angle of the sun as it disappeared from view in the evening.

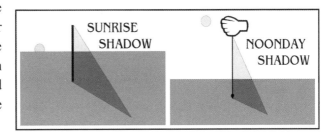

The other daily task is depicted in the second part of the sketch above, and was to mark the moment the sun reached its highest on the meridian in the south. Only one man with a plumb-line was needed for this. Holding the plumb line over a north-south line drawn on the ground, he knew the sun was exactly in the south when its shadow fell along the line, indicating noon. By noting the length of the shadow against the height of the plumb line, the angle of the sun could also then be observed. The shortest shadow would be on the day of the summer solstice, the day coinciding with the standing still of the sun's shadow in the morning and evening; whereas the day of the longest shadow, when the sun was at its lowest, was the winter solstice.

That was many thousands of years ago. We will now apply the methods of those ancient ritualistic observances to Freemasonry in the twenty-first century.

The three principal officers of the lodge occupy positions in the east, the south and the west. The Master presides in the east of the room, the Junior Warden stands in the south, and the Senior Warden stands in the west. Each wears a collar from which hangs an emblem called a jewel, which is the symbol of the respective offices. The Master's jewel is a 90 degree square, the Senior Warden's is a level, and the Junior Warden's is a plummet with plumb-line affixed. All of these emblems are tools for laying out and checking the vertical or horizontal. The two deacons who stand beside the Master and the Senior Warden are equipped with wands, which are really nothing more than long poles. Though now purely symbolic, the significance of the officers' insignia becomes apparent when considered alongside the ritual recording of the sun's movements thousands of years ago.

The Master's place is in the east, to mark the angle of the sun as it rises. Behind him, or further to the east, between him and the rising sun, is the Senior Deacon with his wand that doubles as a gnomon for casting the shadow. Why do I say closer to the east? Because in the precise wording of Irish ritual the deacon sits 'at the back of the chair of the Worshipful Master, or at his right hand if so permitted'. This indicates the deacon's place to be behind the Master, and since the Master sits in the east of the Temple facing inwards, this places the deacon further east than the Master, or between him and the rising sun. They are both therefore properly positioned to use the shadow-stick carried by the deacon in the form of his wand to mark the angle of the sunrise. For the utility of the lodge room they sit side by side, but nevertheless the deacon's proper place is enshrined in the wording of the ritual. The Jewel around the Masters neck is a square - the square he needs to place against the deacon's wand to ensure that it is a true vertical. Close at hand, among the Working Tools that lie on the altar, is the skerrit or chalked line with which he marks the shadow-line, to record the position of the rising sun.

We also have the Senior Warden who stands in the west, with his assistant in the form of the Junior Deacon, whose place is similar to the Senior Deacon's, and is 'at the back of the chair of the Senior Warden or at his right hand if so permitted,' so is therefore between the Senior Warden and the setting sun. So both of them also, are fully

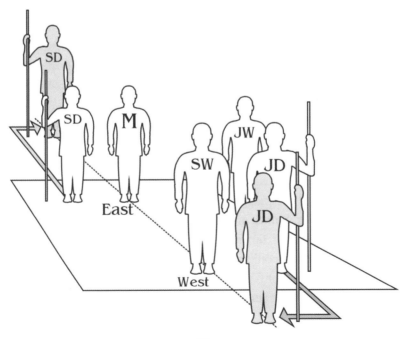

equipped, and are in precisely the right positions, to mark the angle of the sun as it disappears from view.

Then in the south we have the Junior Warden, whose symbol of office is a plumb-line with plummet affixed. This is precisely the tool he would require for marking the moment the sun reaches its zenith on the meridian. He needs no assistant to perform this task, so has no deacon in attendance. He alone marks the sun at its zenith on the meridian, and gives the signal that noon had occurred. His duty, when asked in the opening ritual, is 'to observe the sun on the meridian. To call the Brethren from labour to refreshment, and on again to Labour...' In doing so he performs a similar function to the muezzin who calls the faithful to prayer from a mosque's minaret. So as well as having the tool needed to perform the function of the Temple in the south, his true role is enshrined in the wording of the ceremony.

Could it be coincidence that the principal officers of a modern Masonic lodge are of the right number, have the right tools and are in precisely the right positions to carry out the duties of the ancient priesthood? There is even a place in the ritual where a square is placed against the Senior Deacon's wand, thereby introducing the notion of squaring the wand/gnomon, when the 2nd degree candidate is having his obligation to the Craft explained during his initiation. At that moment he has his left arm upraised and squared at the elbow, and held squarely against the wand by using a square. When seen against the veneration of the sun by the early peoples of these islands, the symbolic use of their methods in the labours of

modern lodge-rooms is surely proof that Masonry centres its rituals on the sun. If we look to Ancient Egypt where the sun was all-important too, we see exactly the same right-angled gesture represented by the arms in this statue of Ka.

As laid out here it appears that the deacons perform an absolutely critical symbolic role using their wands in the rituals of the lodge room, even if that original function has been so deeply buried in allegory that its original purpose is now virtually invisible. We earlier briefly mentioned the second Grand Lodge in England, the Grand lodge of the Antients that was formed to counter the changes the first Grand Lodge introduced. One aspect of those changes was the deacons, which, whilst they remained an intrinsic part of both Irish and Scottish ritual, were removed from English lodges. When we see how pivotal a role they played in the symbolic meaning of the proceedings, we can see why those who understood the nature of the ceremonies would have been outraged at the change.

Marking the equinoxes

As well as the solstices, the equinoxes would also have been marked using the same methods, because on the equinox the sun rises due east and sets due west. The shadow cast by the Senior Deacon's wand in the morning therefore, would lie on the same line as that of the Junior Deacon's in the evening. This would only happen on the days of the equinoxes, and by using the primitive tools that are still present in Masonic ritual, those special days could be identified.

By starting with a true east-west line from the shadow of the sun on the equinoxes, simple geometry using the 3-4-5 right angled triangle will then give a north-south line, the only one which cannot be found from the sun itself, but which is vital for marking the sun on the meridian. The tool needed to convert a true east-west line to a north-south line is the 90-degree square that hangs around the Master's neck and is another possible reason for its importance in Freemasonry. High Twelve (noon) would have been enormously important to anyone who venerated the sun for it was then that the sun reached its most potent. As pointed out earlier, the sun reaches its highest when it is due south from the observer. Having a true north-south line on the ground would be imperative for finding the sun on the meridian, so that a line suspended vertically over it would cast a shadow along it when the moment occurred. At this stage of the research I thought that perhaps the special veneration of the equinoxes was that by giving an absolutely accurate east-west line, and by extension a north-south line, those two days provided the priesthood with the means to identify exactly when noon happened, but I was later to discover that the importance of those days went much, much deeper than that.

The Agnus Dei and the Scales

Whilst on the subject of the equinoxes, there are two prominent Masonic symbols that also allude to the equinoxes - the Agnus Dei and the Scales.

The Agnus Dei, the Lamb of God, is a well-known Christian icon. Perhaps less well known is that the symbolism it contains is based on the zodiac, and refers directly to the spring equinox. From a pictorial point of view it is a lamb that has its foreleg crooked around a pole that can either be the long tailed Cross of St. John, or a flag with an equal-armed cross or in some instances both. This symbol had been associated

with that time of year since antiquity, and therein lies its significance for us. Easter is linked to the sun crossing from the southern hemisphere to the northern on the spring equinox, evidenced by the front leg of the lamb being crossed over the pole. This gesture, of crossed legs, will become a dominant theme as we progress through the book, and the argument as to its meaning will become clear later.

In pagan times the lamb would simply have represented Aries, the zodiacal sign that ruled the two thousand years before the Christian era, and gave way to Pisces at around the time Jesus was said to have been born. It must be remembered that the starting point in the zodiac, both in space and time, is known as the First Point of Aries. This refers to the sun being in Aries on the first day of spring, as it did when the zodiac first came to the fore in the Bronze Age, so the first linking of a lamb with the spring equinox long predated Christ. It is also interesting that the cross used in the emblem is the long-tailed cross of St. John, which in itself can be seen to indicate the upcoming summer solstice when the sun is higher in the sky than during the winter solstice. So in this emblem we have one of the Christian symbols that originally had pagan astrological significance, and which was later converted for Christian use. We will encounter many other instances of this duality of meaning later, indeed it will become the foundation on which the thesis of the book is built.

At the other end of the year we have the autumnal equinox. The date on which the sun passes back into the southern half of the sky is around the 21st of September. The astrological sign of Libra starts at that time, and is represented by a set of scales. The autumn equinox was seen as the end of the light half of the year, when the sun passed below the horizon for the six months during which night was longer than day. This time of year was therefore a time of balance between light and dark, so the use of the scales becomes obvious. Scales are a very common symbol in Masonry, and though they are generally taken to mean the scales of justice, the deeper allusion is to the autumnal equinox. Both equinoctial symbols – the Agnus Dei and the Scales are therefore complementary to one another, and are indeed often found together in Masonic symbolism.

In conclusion, the foregoing reading of the symbolism of the Craft suggests that the ritual of the lodge room is structured around the marking of the sun's progress through the year, and identifying when noon happened in a time when clocks as we know them were many thousands of years in the future. In addition to the many references dotted through the procedures, I have also shown that the insignia of the officers and their positions in the lodge room, taken in conjunction with the wording of the ritual, indicates that they are symbolically equipped and positioned to measure and record the sun's movements. The purpose of this is that by doing so they would have been able to pinpoint the four important days of the solar year - the solstices and equinoxes. At the early stage of my research when I discovered these references I had no idea why these days would have been important, but having found them, I knew I had at least taken my first steps on the voyage of discovery to explain the arcane mysteries of the Craft.

The above points are by no means the only links I made with the sun and its position on the days of the solstices and equinoxes, but they are the most obvious. In truth there were few aspects I was unable to link with the sun in some way. The role of the deacons is perhaps the most potent indicator of this, and it is interesting that by the time the London lodges formed their Grand Lodge in 1717 the deacons, who remained elsewhere, had been removed from their rituals. This can only be because they were by then seen as superfluous and therefore not needed. This is surely proof that by the 18th Century, knowledge of the allusions contained within the rituals was already in the process of being lost.

The appraisal of the Craft's nuances as laid out above is far too all-pervasive for them to be coincidences, so I moved forward with the premise that the sun did indeed lie at the root of the Craft's symbolism. This immediately raised two fundamental questions in my mind. How does this affect existing perceptions about the beginnings and purpose of Freemasonry? And more importantly, from where could such arcane knowledge have come?

CHAPTER 3

FREEMASONRY COULD BE described as a moral philosophy that teaches its members uprightness of character, social responsibility, and to be charitable towards the less fortunate. It also divides its teachings into hidden grades or degrees, and screens its esoteric teachings under layers of allegory and symbolism to obscure it from the outside world. Whilst Freemasonry was singularly unique in the 18th Century Age of Reason, similar institutions existed in abundance in ancient times in the pagan mystery schools of the Middle East and Asia Minor. In dividing its teachings into separate layers that required initiations for each grade or level of knowledge, Freemasonry was merely copying the pagan mystery cults that flourished two thousand years ago around the eastern end of the Mediterranean Sea. The lands around Palestine were peppered with a variety of cults such as those of the gods Osiris, Mithras, Bacchus, Adonis, Dionysus and others, which were not only similar to each other, but also have intriguing parallels with Freemasonry. Where they differed from Freemasonry was that they were fully-fledged religions that centred around a titular godhead and promised salvation, whereas Masonry offers no access to the afterlife. Once this major difference is set aside, the similarities become obvious, if not even overwhelming.

The pagan cults that proliferated in the East in the centuries before and after the time of Jesus were called 'mystery schools' because their true nature was not immediately obvious to those on the outside. They operated on two separate levels and had two distinct sets of teachings that satisfied the spiritual needs of different audiences. There was an outer mystery that was for all adherents of the faith, and there were inner mysteries for those who sought deeper understanding. In Christianity, two things are needed for salvation; a well-lived life, and belief in Jesus as the saviour of mankind. In the mystery schools a blameless life was also needed, but in place of faith was gnosis, or sacred knowledge of the divine. Gnosis was a mixture of self-awareness and an understanding of the cosmos and can almost be seen as the antithesis of faith. Where faith by definition demands acceptance of that which cannot be proved or even properly comprehended, and can denigrate the search for scientific understanding as an affront to God, those who seek gnosis believe that since God made the laws of nature, any enquiry into those laws is bound to bring one nearer to Him.

The aspect of the mysteries we are most familiar with is the outer mystery, because it was not secret and would have projected itself openly to the people as a straightforward religion, and would have appeared much like the Christian faith today. Where it differed from Christianity, however, was that there was another, hidden side to it that one could only access from the inside. If one wished to progress into the inner mystery, one did so by passing initiations similar to those of Freemasonry, that introduced the acolyte to deeper and deeper knowledge and understanding.

The most important aspect of this process, that guaranteed the preservation of the cult's secrets, was that the pupil would swear not to divulge to the uninitiated, any of what he was about to learn. This is the first similarity with Freemasonry, because even today, when the rituals of the lodge room can easily be found on the Internet and in books, each candidate swears on pain of symbolic and horrible death to keep the secrets of the Craft. The three degrees in modern Craft Masonry are now purely symbolic and are given as a matter of form to those accepted into the order, but the underlying principal is still the same.

The second notable link between the mysteries and Freemasonry is that neither institution actively sought members. The mystery schools did not proselytise, because they believed that a pupil who was coerced into joining would never freely conform to the doctrines of the order. The whole purpose of joining was self-improvement, and they rightly believed that to improve oneself the individual had to want to do so, so it was left up to him to approach the mysteries seeking membership, and in Masonry today it is the same. In fact, on entering a lodge room for the very first time, the candidate is asked to confirm that he seeks membership of his own free will and accord, unbiased by improper solicitation. While the inclusion of the word free in Freemason has various claims on its origin, I tend to favour the simplest one of all; that all candidates approach of their own free will, and are Masons because they choose to be so.

With each successive level, the pupil in the mysteries was given more information about the nature of the cosmos, by which he would progress towards the ultimate goal, which was gnosis. During his initiations, the secrets that lay at the centre of the cult were passed from teacher to pupil, behind closed doors, carefully guarded from the uninitiated. Although Freemasonry is a purely symbolic rendition of this, one of the most vital parts of Masonic ritual is to ensure the lodge is free from outsiders and eavesdroppers; a process known as tyling. In opening the lodge it is the Master's first responsibility to ensure that there is no one present who shouldn't be there. Before he can open the lodge he must instruct the deacons to take a password from everyone in the room. In addition, he also instructs the Inner Guard, who is responsible for securing the door from the inside, to ensure that the lodge room is also guarded against eavesdroppers by the outer guard known as the Tyler. All Craft lodges open on the 1st Degree, but when a 2nd or 3rd Degree is being given to a candidate, the lodge is 'called up' or 'raised' to those levels in preparation. Each time the lodge is raised, the Master must ensure that each brother present is entitled to participate in those degrees. This ensures that everyone present has already been given the secrets that are about to be imparted to the candidate as he is taken through his obligation and instruction. So in respect of this ritual securing of the lodge from those who should not be there, Freemasonry can be said to be identical to the pagan mystery cults.

Another similarity is that the pagan mysteries were a strictly oral tradition. The writing down of any aspect of their teachings was totally forbidden; a stricture that ensured that none but the initiated could ever learn their secrets. Like those mysteries, Masonry in its original form also strictly forbade the writing down of even the slightest detail of the rituals of the lodge room – a situation which persisted right up until the last few decades. In the earliest days of the modern Craft, when meetings were held in the back room of a local tavern, the symbols of the degree were chalked on the floor whilst an initiation was taking place. When finished, it was the candidate's job to wash the symbols he had just been shown off the floor with a mop and bucket, and so leave no trace of them whatsoever.

When we look at the pagan mystery traditions of the Middle East it is clear that they all share a common root in what can be called the myth of Osiris-Dionysus, the dying and resurrecting god-man.

Greek civilisation flourished from about 800BCE and its arrival revolutionised the way Man looked at the world around him, for it was they who first sought to explain the laws of nature, however primitive some of their ideas may now seem to us. They were first to separate the causes and effects of nature from religious belief, and sought rational explanations for what they saw around them. The word pagan means '*rustic country dweller,*' and was a disparaging term used by the more sophisticated, city-dwelling priesthood of the Olympian gods, who regarded their country cousins as uncouth, primitive and superstitious. It is one of the great ironies of history that some of the greatest minds that existed before the Enlightenment, pagan sages like Socrates, Aristotle and Pythagoras, were dismissed as rustic country-dwellers by people who themselves passed unnoticed into historical oblivion.

Pythagoras, traditionally the greatest of all the pagan sages, was believed to have been born on the Isle of Samos, south of Troy. He travelled widely, and studied the wisdom of Egypt, Persia, Palestine and beyond. In Egypt he was initiated into the mysteries of Osiris, where at huge, yearly festivals, a ritual was staged representing the death and rebirth of the Egyptian God. On his return, he settled in the Greek community of Croton in southern Italy around 531BCE, where he established his Pythagorean School and started to expound the wisdom he had learned on his travels. His teachings soon captured the imagination of his own people and a cult formed around him - his disciples creating a Greek version of the Egyptian mystery around the local God Dionysus. So popular was this new mystery religion that it rapidly spread to surrounding cultures, each one adopting the principle and adapting it to include elements of their own pre-existing gods. Thus the deity who had been known as Osiris in Egypt, and had been conflated with Dionysus in the Greek world, was replicated again and again across the Mediterranean Basin. In Syria he became Adonis, in Italy, Bacchus. In Asia Minor he was known as Attis, whilst in Persia he became Tammuz. There were many more, and in every case the cults had the same structure; an outer mystery which was open to all, and an inner mystery which preserved sacred knowledge imparted through powerful initiations. The number of levels varied, but the basic principals were the same.

The individual details differed from one God to another, but the various stories loosely converged on certain points. These were that the God's son, be he Horus, Mithras or whoever, was born to an earthly existence, to a virgin, in humble surroundings. His birth, around the winter solstice, was sometimes portended by the appearance of a star or other significant celestial event, and after reaching maturity he initiated a ministry that only lasted a few years. Falling foul of the religious authorities he was tried and found guilty, and after suffering a squalid death, was in some of their stories entombed for three days before ascending into heaven to rule with his Father for eternity. All these god-men lived virtuous lives and through their sacrifice exhorted the faithful to do likewise, and by believing in him the reward for them would be a place with him in the afterlife.

The stories were a construct, to satisfy the spiritual needs of the general populace who needed guidance in their lives, and also to offer them the comfort that there was a greater power that watched over the minutiae of their humdrum existences. The vast majority of believers never looked past this literal truth and remained satisfied to accept it as given. There are obvious similarities between this perennial myth and the story of Jesus which sometimes shock those who have never looked at the origins of Christianity in comparison with that which the Christian Fathers dismissed as pagan religions. Without labouring the point here, there is little if anything in the story of Jesus that cannot be identified within earlier pagan traditions.

There are obvious parallels between the stories attached to the pagan gods and those of Jesus of Nazareth, which beg the question, how can the Jesus narrative be unique when it is seemingly a carbon copy of many god-men who went before? Both Jesus and the likes of Dionysus, Mithras *et al* apparently shared a similar life story, and whilst no single god-man has precisely the same narrative as Jesus, almost all the elements of the Christian message were present to varying degrees in the others.

In their book *The Jesus Mysteries*, the authors Timothy Freke and Peter Gandy put it like this... 'The stories told about Osiris-Dionysus will no doubt sound familiar. He is the Son of God who is born to a virgin on the 25th of December before three shepherds. He is a prophet who offers his followers the chance to be born again through the rites of baptism. He is a wonderworker who raises the dead and miraculously turns water into wine at a marriage ceremony. He is God incarnate who dies at Easter, sometimes through crucifixion, but who resurrects on the third day. He is a saviour who offers his followers redemption through partaking in a meal of bread and wine, symbolic of his body and blood. The Jesus story is a synthesis of the Jewish myth of the messiah Joshua (in Greek Jesus) with these pagan myths of the dying and resurrecting god-man.'

How is it possible that a real flesh and blood god-man could have arisen in the midst of so many similar allegorical ones? The early Christian Fathers were forced to confront this very problem, because there were questions from pagan sages asking why Jesus should be regarded as different from their own gods. *Is it not more likely*, they would have asked, *that Jesus too is mythical*? The answer from the Church Fathers was ingenuous and worthy of note. They declared it 'Diabolical Mimicry,' by which the Devil knew that Jesus was to come, and seeded impostors in advance to deflect people from the truth.

Modern Christian commentators often make the point that there is only fragmentary evidence about these pagan god-men, and what little there is dates largely from the 1st and 2nd Centuries CE. They thus argue that the transfer of ideas may well have been from Christianity to paganism and not the other way round. The reasons why so little evidence exists of these cults is because of their hidden, esoteric nature, and the fact that the Christian Church itself, on being promoted to state religion of the Roman empire in the 4th century, set about the eradication of all its opposition, burning books and libraries and tearing down temples or converting them to Christian use. Further to this, their own argument of diabolical mimicry indicates that the early Church Fathers accepted that the pagan gods did indeed predate Jesus, because had the pagans borrowed their ideas from the Christians there would have been no need to claim diabolical mimicry in rebuttal of pagan criticism. Another stumbling block in the Christian argument is that the story of Jesus as we know it today was not formalised until the early 4th century at the Council of Nicea, so by the time the currently accepted story of Jesus had coagulated from the miasma of early beliefs about him, the pagan mysteries were already fading from the scene.

Today we can point at countless elements of the Jesus story that are purely pagan in nature, such as the birth on the 25th of December which has previously been identified with the yearly rebirth of the sun, and the death and resurrection at Easter which had been honoured for the rebirth of vegetation since time began. Many pagan gods from around the time of Jesus also died on a cross - the symbolism of which can be traced directly to the movements of the sun and its rebirth on the equinox – the day when light becomes longer than dark. Even the three days in the tomb was an ancient pagan tradition associated with the sun, and this too will be examined in more detail later.

Christians today set great store in pointing out that many of these details are not actually in the New Testament and are only later traditions, and therefore whether or not they are of pagan origin is of no consequence. But Christians still commemorate Jesus' birth at Christmas, celebrate the Passion at Easter - the date of which is still today linked directly to the spring equinox, and the cross is still the defining symbol of the faith. The sun, too, died in ancient times when it 'crossed' into the underworld for the winter months. As this study will show, this cross of the sun is the original meaning of death on the cross, and is the reason for venerating the cross in the first place. Although these things are acknowledged as pagan by Christians themselves they still form at major part of the faith, and if stripped away would leave precious little behind.

It is not the scope of this book to pursue the above argument beyond making the point that modern scholarly thought tends to see Jesus as an allegory identical to the pagan mystery schools of the eastern Mediterranean which flourished around the same time. In 1970, John Allegro, one of the original Dead Sea Scroll scholars, suggested that Christianity grew from a shamanistic sect who used mushrooms as an hallucinogen to transport them to another plane. Earlier, Max Muller, the 19th Century German philologist proposed the idea that Mankind's need for myth caused him to transform spiritual concepts into personalities and tales. From this background, they suggest, Jesus was created in an identical fashion to figureheads of the pagan mystery schools mentioned above.

It is this fact which is instrumental to arguments put forward in the succeeding chapters of this book, in which I will argue that those who devised the philosophical school that became Freemasonry were cognisant of this and instituted a new mystery to reinstate the pagan aspects of Christianity to their position prior to being enmeshed with the story of Jesus. It must be stressed however, that this mystery was not meant to be an adversary of the Christian Church, nor its rival - rather it was intended to complement it and indeed all the worlds' religions, in the way the original inner mysteries complemented their outer aspects.

From the above, it appears that there is a definite inspiration both for Christianity itself, and Freemasonry, in the structure of the outer mysteries of the ancient world. Whilst we in the modern world tend to think of the word myth as being an untruth, it was not so in ancient times. For them a myth, while not strictly true in a literal sense, had the truth buried deep within it and was seen as a legitimate part of the process of enlightenment, if used to introduce the novice by stages to complex ideas. This process has a direct parallel in modern Freemasonry, even if it is now only symbolic, in that the 1st Degree candidate is not told everything at the start. It is only as he progresses that more pieces of the picture are added, giving him a deeper understanding of the Craft and ultimately of himself. It is because of the subtle distinction between the ancient meaning of myth and its more modern connotation that modern critics of Freemasonry claim that the initiate is deliberately lied to, to deny and obscure the true nature of the order. It is perfectly true that Freemasonry becomes clearer at higher levels, but the lower degrees should be seen as allegorical myths of the old sort that lead the candidate towards the deeper understanding offered in the higher degrees. To label it as a deliberate deception is to miss the point entirely, and demonstrates ignorance of the subtleties involved.

By the time the candidate in the pagan mysteries had attained the highest level he had learnt that the outer mysteries were not the literal truth but were merely allegories, and that God was not an external entity but dwells within, to be found through self searching and improvement. He learnt that the father-figure of human likeness offered as literal in the outer mystery was an allegory, and that his veneration was to be directed instead to the laws that governed the cosmos - the laws of what we now know as chemistry, biology and physics, the colossal forces beyond human comprehension that created and moved the heavens, which in their turn drove the cycle of the seasons and from which all life emanated. These are the very same forces that are venerated in Freemasonry by marking the seasons of the year, though now in a purely symbolic way.

Whereas the pagan outer mystery was a simplistic rendering of the more complex knowledge held at the heart of the inner mystery, it would still have served to introduce the newcomer to what was to come later. Whilst we do not know precisely what exact form the rituals of the outer mysteries took, it is generally accepted that their sacred words and movements contained elements of the deeper knowledge contained within the inner mysteries. The followers of the outer mysteries then, in taking part in those ceremonies, still participated in the truth, even if they did not fully comprehend that fact. The rituals they learned and repeated by rote still brought them close to the truth, however, without them realising how deeply symbolic their actions were.

There simply couldn't be a better description of Freemasonry than the above, both in the purpose, structure and ethos of the organisation, and in the vehicle of allegory used to perpetuate the knowledge. It is my contention that those who formulated the philosophical mystery in the Middle Ages that became Freemasonry utilised a structure identical to the ancient pagan mysteries. Although the Craft emerged from the shadows in the 18th century with no outer element that offered a symbolic saviour, that does not preclude the original mystery that existed before that time from having one, and that is a possibility we will come back to later.

CHAPTER 4

WHEN ONE SEEKS Freemasonry's possible inspiration among the ancient mysteries, the one mystery cult that stands head and shoulders above all others is Mithraism, and it is only in the last few decades that the Cult of Mithras has been truly understood. Mithras was one of the many dying and resurrecting god-men whose stories were told to the faithful in the Middle East and Europe in the years around the birth of Jesus. The earliest written evidence for Mithraism is when Plutarch recorded that in 67BCE the cult emerged from Cilicia in Asia Minor and was spread westward by the pirates who infested the waters of the Eastern Mediterranean. As a brief aside here, a newly made English Master Mason is told he is now brother to pirates and corsairs, an enigmatic phrase that has no obvious derivation. Could that enigmatic phrase allude to the fact that it was the pirates of Cilicia who first introduced Mithraism to the west? This may also explain the name of one of the tunes used during Masonic Labour, namely 'Sicilian Mariners,' a corruption perhaps of the long disused word Cilician?

The cult of Mithras gained popularity among the Roman garrisons who carried it with them to all corners of the Empire. From Palestine in the east to the Antonine wall in the extreme north-west, Mithras was worshipped wherever Roman soldiers were billeted. The cult reached a peak of popularity around the middle of the 3rd Century of the Christian era, before it was subsumed like the other pagan cults in the rising tide of Christianity. Like modern Freemasonry, Mithraism separated its teachings into layers, having seven known levels of initiation. The new believer was first initiated into the lowest level or degree, which was known as the outer mystery and was open to all comers. Only seekers after gnosis, who committed themselves to the necessary study, were initiated into the inner mysteries.

The inner mystery

As stated before, the mysteries of Mithras were an oral tradition, so no record of the detail remains, but it is generally accepted that like the other pagan mysteries, the candidate would learn progressively more about the nature of the cosmos at each successive initiation. This information was what we would now regard as basic science, and although science is nowadays often seen as God's adversary, in those times it was seen as bringing a deeper understanding of Deity. Each initiation brought more knowledge, which in turn brought salvation closer to the individual. It was within those levels that they would learn that the outer story was an allegorical myth and not the literal truth. Once the initiate had reached the highest level, the greatest secret in the universe was entrusted to him, after which he was known as Master. Due to the work of David Ullansey and his recent, groundbreaking book *The Origins of the Mithraic Mysteries*, we now know that at that highest level of Mithraism the pupil learned of the phenomenon known as the precession of the equinoxes.

From when Man started to quantify the movements of the heavens it was thought that the sun made one revolution of the earth every 360 days, which formed the basis for dividing the circle into 360 units or degrees. During that time period the cycle of the moon occurred roughly twelve times, around which the year was divided into twelve months, the word month being derived from the word moon. The sun was known to pass along a particular path through the stars during the year, known as the ecliptic, and the groups of stars that lay on that line were given special significance. As there were 12 moon-phases in the average year, twelve groups were chosen, one to denote each of the months. Each was given an identity of beast or man, and collectively they came to be known as the signs of the zodiac.

The twelve lunar cycles linked the sun, moon and stars together into what was considered a sacred synchronicity, and the sun's route through the star-signs gave rise to the tales of the earliest gods. The passage of the sun through these constellations also coincided with the seasons of the year, in particular the growing season that was all-important in the existence of Man, and so humanity came to be linked to the stars through this system. In trying to understand the forces that drove the heavens, then, the ancients believed they better understood God.

The ancients' perception of the cosmos was based on the two known heavenly forces mentioned earlier - the apparent daily revolution of the sun, and the yearlong passage of the sun through the zodiac and the seasons that it gave. These visual movements came from the earth spinning on its axis, and its rotating around the sun once each year. But around 150BCE the certainties of the ancient world were shattered by the discovery of a third, hitherto unknown force. Although earlier peoples had observed the phenomenon, the Greek astronomer Hipparchus was the first to explain, from the close scrutiny of the movements of the sun through the year, how the entire celestial sphere was moving very slowly. The effect of this was that if recorded on the same date each year, the sun was moving backwards through the signs of the zodiac at an infinitesimally slow rate, hence the name precession. This movement is due to a wobble in the earth's rotation similar to the way a spinning top shudders as it slows down, and takes approximately 26,000 years to make one complete revolution. It was called the precession of the equinoxes because it was the spring equinox that formed the zero-point for the measurement of the astrological year, and from which all other timings were taken.

The ring of constellations on the ecliptic appears to rotate endlessly around us, and in the way that we use midnight as a base-point to take our daily clock timings from, a single point on the zodiac had to be chosen to become that base point.

The two fixed points in the sky are the places where the planes of the zodiac and the celestial equator intersect, these being on the equinoxes, six months apart, one each side of the year. These two days unite the geography of the heavens with the passage of time, and are the only two days when this happens. Since spring was associated with the rebirth of vegetation and therefore the beginning of the year, it was the March equinox that was chosen as the zodiacal equivalent of midnight on the clock and became the single point from which all measurements of the heavens were taken. Because the sun was in Aries on the spring equinox when the zodiac in its present form was first devised, this meshing of time and place became known as the First Point of Aries.

Hipparchus discovered the phenomenon of precession when his calculations showed that by his day the sun was moving out of Aries on the spring equinox, and would shortly be in the next sign along which is Pisces. As far as the Greek–speaking world was concerned this meant that there was a third hitherto unknown force that controlled the heavens, moving the entire universe around an axis, and this discovery led to belief in a new deity.

This new God, more powerful than any that had gone before, came to be known as Mithras, and formed the focus of a new mystery cult that arose in Cilicia, an ancient state that lies between Turkey and Syria. The most well known manifestations of this cult are its temples, known as Mithraeum, and the various items of furniture that adorn them. Central to the temple was the Tauroctony, a tableau of figures - the centrepiece of which was Mithras killing a bull.

As the new God was given the attributes to be able to move the entire heavens, there was no better way of showing this power than by having him kill the Bull of Taurus, the sign that Aries had replaced as a result of precession. In being shown displacing Taurus to make way for the next sign on the zodiac, the immense power of the new God was thus demonstrated perfectly. The Tauroctony here is a typical example, and shows a collection of animals that surround the bull killing. For many years these other symbols defied understanding, but they are now known to be the constellations that lay on the celestial equator rather than the zodiac itself during the Age of Taurus, and so can be seen as a visual record of the moment Taurus was displaced. The constellations in question are Taurus itself, Canis Minor the dog, Hydra the Snake, Corvus the Raven, and Scorpio the Scorpion. In the standard relief common to all Mithraic Temples we find the above creatures either observing, or participating in, Mithras' slaying of the old constellation.

For countless thousands of years the one single immovable truth was that the stars remained fixed, revolving endlessly around the earth's axis, the Axis Mundi. When it was discovered that there was another, greater force than this that caused the entire heavens to move, this was sacred knowledge indeed. Not only was knowledge of precession sacred, it was also a difficult concept to comprehend and was beyond the average person's grasp, so the secret was preserved at the core of an initiatory cult where possession of the secret guaranteed access to the after-life.

Mithraic Temples were generally single story buildings with barrel-vaulted stone roofs, mostly sited in hollows or even underground to mimic the legendary cave of Mithras' birth. Mithraism was the most popular of all the pagan religions around that time and was Christianity's biggest rival for the hearts and minds of the people, and were it not for Constantine's political manoeuvring; we might today see bumper stickers proclaiming 'Mithras Loves You'. Whilst the secrecy and the initiatory nature of Mithraism has undoubted parallels in modern Masonry, it is also interesting because of the knowledge of the workings of the cosmos which are represented in the Tauroctony. Flanking the main scene are the two standing figures, Cautes and Cautopates, one of whom

carries his torch aloft, the other lowered. The picture here is of one of the torchbearers in a Mithraeum near Hadrian's Wall, just outside the Roman fort of Brocolita, near Hexham, Northumbria. The position of the feet with one leg crossed over the other is of particular interest to our quest, as it is has a very specific corollary within Freemasonry, but we will come to that later.

The torches are thought to refer to the two solstices; the raised one signifying the sun high in the sky in summer, the lowered one, winter. From this we can already see that the movements of the sun throughout the year were, just like the rituals of Masonry outlined earlier, important to the cult of Mithras. The crossed shins are further thought to refer to the crossing of the equinoxes, and represent the cross of the sun's rising and setting points on the solstices.

Central to the concept of precession is the axis about which the panoply of Heaven turns. This axis passes through the earth's north and south poles and was thought of as supporting the roof of heaven. Known as the world's axis, it was seen in many ancient societies as either a

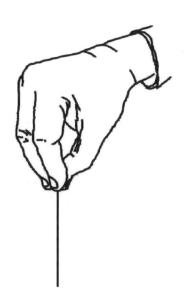

pillar or a tree. In Norse Mythology it was known as Yggdrasil, the World Ash, and it found its way into Christianity as the Tree of Life, without reference to its original meaning. This axis lies at the heart of the beliefs of the cult of Mithras, and I believe finds artistic expression in Masonry in the holding of a plumb-line between the fingers and allowing it to hang vertically - a gesture that forms part of the ceremony of installing a new Master in the chair of a lodge, and is seen often in Masonic symbolism.

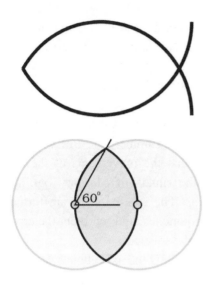

The precession of the sun through the signs of the zodiac results in one sign after the other dominating the skies for one twelfth of the precessional period of 25,920 years, which is 2160 years, or 2000 in round terms. Around the time of Jesus, the sun moved out of Aries and into Pisces, where it has been ever since, slowly moving through the individual stars of that sign. Today we stand at the dawning of the Age of Aquarius, although because the signs vary in size and the gaps between them vary considerably, no definitive date for the start of the new age exists.

Central to the claims laid out in this book will be the proposition that Christianity, in its earliest form, grew out of exactly the same allegorical symbolism as those pagan mystery cults - the very same symbolism which I believe still lies at the heart of Freemasonry. Few Christians see more in the pictorial images of the stained glass in their churches depicting Matthew, Mark, Luke and John as a lion, an ox, a man and an eagle, and little realise that the origin of that imagery lies in the zodiac. In similar vein, that other powerful Christian icon, the Icthys, the Sign of the Fish, is derived from the intersecting lines of the Vesica Piscis, an emblem that has its roots in the constellation Pisces and in the

sacred number mysticism of Pythagorean thought. Whereas the Church has since turned its back on the true origins of these icons, however, Freemasonry has not undertaken such a purge, leaving its symbols to retain their original message.

It is one of the ironies of the anti-Masonic movement that many of the very same pagan symbols that are regarded as occult when displayed in a Masonic hall are also to be found in Christian churches without any pagan associations whatsoever. The Vesica Piscis is one such example, for in addition to being the basis of the Sign of the Fish, its form is used in both the crest of the Grand Lodge of Ireland, and that of the Church of Scotland. The root of the symbolism in both cases is the same.

So the inner mysteries, at least that of Mithras, seem to have been structured in such a way as to preserve sacred knowledge of the cosmos in general and the precession of the equinoxes in particular. This knowledge was buried at the heart of an initiation process because the science involved in its understanding was complex and could not be explained other than in an environment such as that which the graded initiations supplied.

The similarities in the structure of the pagan mysteries and Freemasonry are too strong to ignore, so it would be, perhaps, fruitful to look further at the possibility that the former inspired the latter. The major argument against this is the fact that the mysteries faded from the world around the 6th Century whilst Freemasonry did not appear until the 17th. The second problem is geographical – for the mysteries flourished in the Middle East, far from the British Isles, and their more local equivalents had been extinguished in Europe since the 7th century. Assuming that Freemasonry was indeed a modern mystery school, and that it had been derived from a European endeavour of the Middle Ages, how then, can we seriously believe there to be a link when we consider how remote those mysteries were from the Craft, both in time and place? If we are to pursue the possible link between the pagan mysteries of the Middle East and Freemasonry in the British Isles, we must look at a time in history when Europeans could have been exposed to those ancient traditions, and there is really only one occasion when that is likely to have happened. The Crusades of the 12th century!

CHAPTER 5

CHRISTIANITY WAS BORN in Palestine, but that is not where it grew to manhood. It divorced from Judea not long after the Crucifixion, and grew to maturity in Europe. This left the locations of Christ's Passion far from the centre of Christian power, sites that had been under the control of Arab Muslims since the 7th century. Due to the tolerant attitude of the Muslim rulers Christian pilgrims had more or less unhindered access to the sacred sites and shrines, but in the 11th century all that changed. In 1071 this amicable situation took a turn for the worse with the invasion of the area by fierce Seljuk Turks from Central Asia. These Turks were Muslim also, but had been only recently converted and were full of militant zeal so were not disposed towards compromise with other religions. In an effort to exclude faiths other than Islam from the area, they made it increasingly difficult for Christians to travel to the holy places under their control.

In 1095 the Byzantine Emperor, Alexius Comnenus, wrote to the pope, Urban II, for assistance in fighting these Turks in the East, highlighting the fact that the holy sites were no longer accessible to Christians. Urban was outraged that Christian pilgrims could no longer make the pilgrimage to pay homage where Jesus had walked the earth, and felt he must respond to the Byzantine request. In the autumn of that year he invited the Frankish nobility to a church council at Clermont,

France, to ask them to undertake a crusade to free the Holy Land, promising a powerful indulgence that gave full absolution and remission of sins past or future to those who placed their lives in jeopardy in the name of God. Thousands flocked to the papal banner and a massive army was mustered to win back the sacred land where the defining moments of the Christian message had been played out.

Whilst piety and the promised spiritual reward undoubtedly drove many to leave all they held dear in Europe, there were also baser motivations for some of those who pledged themselves to the endeavour. The lands of the East were there for the taking, by anyone with the strength of arms to seize them once Jerusalem had been wrested from Seljuk control. The pope was well aware of what would motivate his audience and gilded the lily somewhat, exaggerating the behaviour of the Turks, and painting a picture of Palestine being a veritable Promised Land, and indeed promised the land itself to those who answered his call.

The Crusaders reached the walls of the Holy City in the summer of 1099, taking six weeks to bring it under their control, with such violence and mayhem that it was said the blood ran ankle deep to the horses. The carnage was unspeakably horrendous, and was one of the darkest episodes in the entire history of the Christian Church. Aware that Jews who comprised a large section of the population of the city sometimes swallowed their gold to protect it in times of crisis, and not knowing Jew from either Muslim or Christian, the invaders killed all, and slit their victims' bellies open, ferreting through their spilled entrails lest the smallest bauble be lost. One can scarcely imagine the horror of the mounds of eviscerated corpses, bloated and stinking in the heat of the Levantine sun. Did some of those wonder if God really intended that such deeds be done in his name?

Most Crusaders considered their vows fulfilled once Palestine was in Christian hands and returned to their homes, but some remained as part of the new administration. Jerusalem had a Christian king for the first time in history, in the person of Godfroi de Bouillon, who had left his Dukedom of Lorraine behind to serve God in the East. Horrified at the blood which had been shed to found his new realm he refused the crown, instead taking the title Lord Protector of the Holy Land. Within twenty years Godfroi was dead and had been succeeded by his brother Baldwin, and the states of Antioch, Tripoli, Jerusalem and Edessa had been established, leaving a sizeable European satellite state in the midst of a sea of Muslims.

The Europeans who chose to live on in the Holy Land took on a vastly different lifestyle than they had left back home, and it must have been an enormous culture shock to move from Europe, which was just awakening from the intellectual hibernation of the Dark Ages, to the East where Greek philosophy had survived intact. Whereas Christian dogma frowned on the use of reason, Islam was awash with offshoots that espoused scientific enquiry, sought understanding of the cosmos, and embraced deeply esoteric Sufi philosophy. It cannot be overstated how different this world must have been from the one the Europeans left behind, for they had come from countries that were primitive, deeply superstitious and intolerant of other faiths, and the Muslims they now governed would have seemed urbane and cultured in comparison to their own simple, poorly educated subjects back home.

Although the First Crusade had been a triumph, inasmuch as it achieved its objective, the following seven crusades were largely ineffective, and the Muslims slowly but surely reclaimed the lands held by the West. Even so, and vitally important to our quest, the European presence in the Holy Land was to last for almost two hundred years, which is certainly long enough for a certain cross-pollination of ideas to have taken place. Although the eventual loss of the Holy Land in 1291 also has implications for our quest, the politics of the Crusades are not of paramount importance to us at this point. What is important is to look at the situation in Outremer - the 'far side of the sea,' as the area of European influence came to be known, to see whether or not it was possible that any vestiges of the pagan mystery cults could still have been present during the time the Crusaders were there.

As will become apparent, rather than the pagan mysteries being forgotten relics of the past, there were several groups which still followed similar tenets flourishing right in the heart of the area of the Crusader occupation. Three groups are of particular interest to us, being the Druze, the Alawites, and a semi-secret brotherhood called Ikhwan el Safa, the 'Brethren of Purity.' What is particularly interesting for our story is that these groups regarded their holy book, the Qur'an, as being allegory. Europeans who spent time among these groups may well have come to view their own holy book the Holy Bible as allegory too, providing the impetus for the creation for the mediaeval mystery that I suggest came into existence then.

In the following pages we will look at each of the three groups in turn, but it is the last group, the Ikhwan el Safa, which most closely resembles Freemasonry, and in my opinion there is no doubt that those who instituted the new mystery in Europe were exposed to the teachings of this learned brotherhood. Before we begin to look at the groups contemporary with the Crusaders' presence, it may be useful to summarise and reiterate the relevant observations we have noted to date.

Modern Freemasonry is a philosophy that urges its members to look inwards to improve themselves, and though it demands belief in a Supreme Being, no individual God is specifically identified as being 'the' God. The thesis of this book is that Freemasonry grew from a new, mediaeval version of the ancient mystery schools, but even by the early Middle Ages, the mystery cults had been defunct for close on a thousand years. If the thesis is to be advanced, we must discover not only if the teachings of those cults could have survived, but also how they would have become available to the Europeans who would then carry them to the British Isles. In other words a credible link has to be established which brings together the ancient wisdom of pre-Christian teachings of the Middle East and the stonemasons' lodges of 17th and 18th century Britain. The obvious place to look for that link is the Middle East itself where the pagan cults had existed, and the most obvious era in which to look is the time of the Crusades, when for the first time in history Europeans had a large presence there.

CHAPTER 6

THERE WERE THREE groups extant in the Holy Land that could have inspired some of the European Crusaders and alerted them to the existence of the mysteries. The first of these is a closed sect that is still in existence today, and is so protective of its teachings that we in the West can only guess at what their doctrines actually are.

The Alawites

The Alawites are an offshoot from mainstream Islam, founded around the 9th century, and are still a small but politically powerful sect in Syria who tend not to read the Qur'an literally but from a more esoteric slant. They are secretive about their faith; so secretive in fact that little is known for sure about their innermost teachings. They do not accept converts, nor do they commit their sacred beliefs to writing, instead passing their knowledge down orally from scholar to scholar. In this last point they are identical with the earlier pagan mysteries. From the little that is known by the outside world, it appears that their teachings are loosely based on the writings of the pagan philosophers, particularly those of Socrates and Aristotle. Astronomy too plays an important part in their teachings.

As a people they keep themselves very much to themselves, and believe that it is more important to worship Allah in their hearts than make a public show of their faith. It appears that most Alawites today know very little of the inner theology of the faith, which is carefully guarded by a select group of male initiates. Without having direct knowledge, which is obviously impossible to obtain under the circumstances, we as outsiders have to assume that the core knowledge is protected by layers of initiation, and this assumption is central to the debate about Masonic origins. If the mystery tradition in Europe was indeed structured along the same lines as groups such as the Alawites, which consciously set out to leave no record of their beliefs for outsiders to see, then would we really expect to find record of a western version of this esoteric tradition? The question we must ask is whether or not Crusaders would have had the opportunity to mix with the Alawite sect, and therefore be in a position to absorb any of their teachings?

In fact this is not in question, because although the Crusaders attacked them in 1097 before the fall of Jerusalem, the two groups later formed an alliance against the Ishma'ilis, the largest grouping of Shia Muslims during the early Crusades. This alliance obviously placed the two groups in contact with one another, making possible the transference of ideas between them. Though such a clandestine meeting of minds would not appear in the historical record, the possibility that it did nevertheless exists. In any case we are not reliant on this connection, because the Alawites were not the only group active at the time that could have influenced the Crusaders and opened their minds to alternative spiritual paths to approach deity.

The Druze

Like the Alawites, the Druze too are still with us today, and are another closed sect like the Alawites that may have had an effect on the Crusaders. Writing in the first quarter of the 20th century the highly acclaimed Masonic historian JSM Ward suggested there were close ties between the Crusaders and the Druze of the time, who he refers to as Dervishes. He also identified one secret sign, and at least one initiatory degree as being what he termed Masonic. Today found mostly in Lebanon, they also exist in the Golan Heights in Syria and inside the Northern borders of Israel. Formed in the 9th century around the same time as the Alawites, they refer to themselves as '*Mowahhidoon,*' which translates as monotheistic. Like the Alawites they also do not accept converts, nor marry outside their faith. Estimates of how many Druze exist today vary between two and seven hundred thousand, a task made difficult because of the aura of secrecy with which they cloak their faith, and their practice of '*Taquia*'.

Taquia is a concept by which the Druze hide their true beliefs by feigning conformity to another faith, and is not an idea that is readily understood in our western tradition. It must be seen in the context of the Middle East where the geographical situation between Europe and the Orient has produced a turbulent and volatile history. On numerous occasions invasion by outside peoples dictated religious change, and the practice of taquia came about to enable one's own faith to continue in the background, irrespective of what belief was expected in public. This was only possible because their faith was very personal and involved no public show of piety. Christianity involves many public acts, which fact alone would make impossible the feigned participation in another faith. With the Druze however, the outward participation in mainstream Islam was not only acceptable, but was seen as a valuable contribution to the maintenance of their own secret beliefs, in fact it was a central part of their doctrine, and involved lifelong commitment to religious practices that were often at considerable variance with their own.

This need to hide their true faith from the authorities who would have considered their practices heretical was undoubtedly responsible in part for the dense cloak of secrecy with which they surrounded their beliefs. The idea of initiations to protect the innermost teachings had existed since ancient times, and would have been eminently useful as a method of ensuring that only the select few ever knew the whole truth. Such a practice is followed by Freemasonry to this day. Due to the similarity in the concept of taquia and the cloaking of the teachings of Freemasonry, I think it reasonable to consider the possibility that knowledge of the practice may have played a part in the structuring of the esoteric tradition in Europe that I suggest was the precursor for the Craft. If Crusaders were in a position to discover the fact that certain groups in the East read their holy book as allegorical and sought to copy that practice, it is also likely that they would have understood the concept of taquia.

The Druze hold the Qur'an sacred, but regard it as being only an outer shell, needing to have hidden, sacred knowledge applied to it to be fully understood. In this respect at least, their sect can be seen as a mystery religion. Among the prophets, they revere Adam, Abraham, Moses and Jesus, although they regard the idea of Jesus being born to a virgin as an allegory. They do not believe in a literal Heaven and Hell, rather seeing them as a state of mind which is generated by being either at one with God, or not. Their community appears to be based on the model of the philosophical school that grew around Pythagoras on his return from Egypt. The leaders are known as '*Uqqal*,' ascetic sages of the same kind as Pythagoras, who is particularly highly regarded in the faith. The ordinary members are '*Juhaall*,' and do not generally concern themselves with the study of religious texts, rather leaving such learned matters to the Uqqal. In this they are identical to the mysteries of the ancient world, and perhaps this also gives us a glimpse of how the mediaeval mystery was structured. To become one of the Uqqal, the pupil has to show extreme piety and devotion, and demonstrate that he has a suitable disposition to be entrusted with the sacred knowledge. Whilst the passing of the initiations in Freemasonry is today a matter of form, it is not hard to imagine that in the past, the passing of the degrees took a similar level of commitment, and a certain demonstration by the initiate that he was made of the 'right' stuff.

Another similarity with the ancient mysteries is that the Druze have no unified, central hierarchy to rule and govern their faith, rather keeping to cell-like units centred on select groups of Uqqal, who alone hold the truth. In relation to Freemasonry, there are also several basic principles central to both doctrines. The Druze are expected to be charitable to their fellow man, particularly if he be Druze, to be guarded in what they say to outsiders, to respect others, and to believe in a Supreme Being. All these aspects of their doctrines can be seen as defining the ethos of both the ancient mysteries that went before, and modern Freemasonry that came after.

Having looked briefly at the beliefs of the Druze, we must now turn to any possible influence they could have had on the Crusaders who occupied their lands. Although they fought against the Europeans several times, it is a matter of record that in 1305 the Sunni Mameluk Sultan of Egypt punished the Druze for supporting the Crusaders before their expulsion in 1291, so as with the Alawites the possibility of interaction between the two cannot be ruled out. As noted before, there was a European presence in the Holy Land for almost two hundred years, during which time the fortunes of the invaders waxed and waned, and it is known that the Europeans formed many clandestine alliances with different groups as and when it suited them, even utilising the services of the Assassins in their political struggles. It is unthinkable that at least some of the Christian knights who lived in the dry heat of the Levant did not learn from, and take on board, esoteric wisdom from those they ruled.

As previously mentioned, it must have been an incredible culture shock to leave behind an illiterate, superstitious Europe ruled by a single, inalienable religious doctrine, for a culturally far more advanced land where various spiritual paths co-existed. I suggest that at least some of the Crusaders must have looked at the mystical teachings of these other doctrines and seen merit in them. It is also possible that they were exposed to the stories of the Osiris/Dionysus god-men who so closely resembled the story of their own saviour, and to the writings of the Greek philosophers who had openly questioned the literal truth of Jesus' divinity.

We have seen how the two groups, the Alawites and the Druze, did not take their holy books literally, but viewed them as allegories that held deeply significant hidden truths within, which were only understood by adepts who had passed strict initiations and proved their desire to understand. The teachings of these two groups were inaccessible to those who did not offer themselves as eager pupils, and who pledged to keep secret all that they learned. It is perhaps arguable therefore whether outsiders would have been invited into the bosom of those faiths, but the possible contribution of the above-mentioned sects pales in comparison to the third grouping that we will now examine.

This group, known as Ikhwan el Safa, the Brethren of Purity, is so significant to our search that they warrant an entire chapter of their own. They were a major influence in the Islamic world that the western knights found themselves inhabiting, but unlike the Druze and the Alawites, the Ikhwan were not secretive about their faith to the same extent as the others, in fact they existed primarily to spread their knowledge outside their own group. Unlike the other two groups mentioned the Brethren of Purity no longer exist, but in terms of the philosophy they espoused and the knowledge they imparted, they were a significant part of the history of how the wisdom of the East came to fill part of the European intellectual void left by the Dark Ages.

CHAPTER 7

IN EUROPE DURING the Middle Ages the Bible was considered the sacred word of God, divinely inspired, and therefore not open to interpretation. The same could perhaps be said of all holy books, but in Europe the Church took steps to maintain the sanctity of its sacred writings. To ensure the populace didn't try to read its own significance into the words, the text of the Bible was kept in Latin, a long-dead language that only the priesthood of the Church understood. It therefore fell to the priests to extract the stories which best illuminated the Christian message and pass them on in their sermons, thus preserving the Bible from unwanted interpretation.

The situation in the East however was somewhat different in that the Qur'an was freely available to all, and various groups, like those in the last chapter, had arisen which interpreted its sacred writings esoterically, mixing the teachings of the holy book with the mystical thinking of the Greek philosophers. These groups came to see the Qur'an as a repository of hidden knowledge, veiled from all but the adepts who had been taught to see it. Isma'ili philosophy was the first to develop this system with the *Umm al-kitab,* the Mother of Books, written in the 8th century. By their very nature these interpretations of the Qur'an were esoteric, and so those who followed this path kept their knowledge hidden under layers of initiation in groups such as the Alawites and the Druze.

Then there arose an altogether different movement, which did not secrete its teachings away for the benefit of the few but sought to spread its wisdom freely to all. The name '*Ikhwan el Safa,*' which translates as the 'Brethren of Purity,' was adopted by a group of free-thinkers from around Basra in modern day Iraq, and although the date of their founding is not known, their teachings were freely available by the year 983. They distributed their collected wisdom in the form of open letters, or epistles, called '*Rasa'il*', which, taken in their entirety, give an encyclopaedic record of the scientific knowledge of the time. The Brethren believed that while the Qur'an was the most sacred of all books, the hidden wisdom it contained could only be extracted by the application of the philosophy of the Greeks and an understanding of the most up to date scientific knowledge available. Although their over-riding passion was to seek understanding of the cosmos, it was not merely for the sake of possessing knowledge that they studied. They believed that knowledge was of no use unless it was then used to further man's quest towards the ultimate goal of salvation. The following summary of the epistles is largely drawn from '*The Epistles of the Brethren of Purity*' by Asghar Ali Engineer.

To the Brethren of Purity the exoteric or outer meaning of the Qur'an was a lower level of knowledge which was meant for the '*awamm*' or common people, who preferred '*taqli'd*' or blind imitation of ritual. The higher knowledge, the '*batin,*' which was hidden from the uninitiated, was meant for the '*kwass*' or elite members of society. Epistle III p 379 states that 'Among people there are groups of intellectuals who would not be satisfied with 'taqli'd but would demand proofs and 'haqa'id,'(the uncovering of truths), and the seeking of 'illah,'' (the purpose of religious law). Since they themselves derived their spiritual outlook from seeking deeper meanings in their holy book, the purpose of their Rasa'il was to educate others to the point where they too could avail themselves of the same esoteric understanding.

These Rasa'il would have been easily obtained by the western invaders, and may well have influenced their thinking.

The Ikhwan had a particularly liberal attitude to their faith. In Epistle III p 538, they say 'Acquire knowledge, any type of knowledge, philosophical, legal, mathematical, scientific or divine. All that is nourishment for the soul and life for it in this world and the hereafter'. If the Brethren of Purity sought to educate people to the level where they could interpret the Qur'an esoterically and thereby reach a deeper understanding of God, then might some Christian Crusaders not have thought there was wisdom in doing likewise with the Holy Bible?

The teachings of the brotherhood were not a religion; rather they were an addendum to faith that provided its adherents with an additional way in which to approach God. In simple terms, they exhorted their followers to practice whatever faith they wished, and to do it to the best of their ability. Although the Ikhwan regarded no one religion as perfect, they nevertheless urged their followers to select one of them. They reasoned that it was better to have an imperfect faith than none at all, as there are elements of truth in all religions. This plank of their 'manifesto' if it could be called such, is identical to Freemasonry's attitude to religion, in that whilst it demands that its members believe in a supreme being, it makes no enquiry as to what constitutes a supreme being for the individual, leaving it up to his own conscience.

Not regarding any one religion as perfect, they forged their own path among them all, based on scientific understanding of the laws of nature and the complexities of the human mind. They studied all religions in order to discover what was good about each one and adopt it into their own philosophy. They said in Epistle III p 501 'Know that the truth is found in every religion and is current in every tongue. What you should do, however, is to take the best and transfer yourself to it. Do not ever occupy yourself with imputing defects to the religions of people; rather try to see whether your religion is free from them'. If Freemasonry were to espouse any religious teaching – which it doesn't – the above is exactly what it would offer.

Newcomers were recruited through personal contacts and recommendations, and were introduced to the fraternity by initiation. Freemasonry does likewise, only accepting candidates of good repute from the same community from which the lodge draws its membership, and who are well known to at least two existing members of the lodge they seek to join.

There were 53 Rasa'il in all, 52 of which are still extant. They run to thousands of pages, which astound modern researchers as to the depth of knowledge available at the time. It took until the Enlightenment of the 18th century for reason to break free in Europe, but even a brief reading of the letters shows that five hundred years earlier the Arab intellect was far ahead of that of their European invaders.

Not only did they know that the earth was a sphere, they knew that at the North Pole the sun didn't set at all throughout the summer. They divided the earth into three kingdoms, consisting of elements, plants and animals. They reasoned that the mineral kingdom must have been in existence long before the plants, and that sea animals, which they regarded as less developed than land animals, must have existed first. They further surmised that the animals must have existed long before Mankind, and that the ape was closest to man in its development. It would have been an easy mistake for them to conclude that as the most developed of all the animals, mankind must have been around the longest, but they identified the correct order of things eight hundred years before Charles Darwin set off in the Beagle.

Their knowledge also extended to the heavens, which they calculated to possess 1092 objects, which were as many as could be seen with the naked eye. They distinguished between the moon and the celestial objects because it alone gave off no light of its own and merely reflected that of the sun. They had calculated the year to be 365 ¼ days long and identified the orbital time of the planets to be more or less what we know them as today. They even tried to calculate the volume of the universe, and though completely off the mark, the fact that they even attempted to do so illustrates the scope of their thinking.

Among their more astounding doctrines was that the stars were without weight. Weight, they said, was merely the attraction of bodily masses for one another. Although they presumably did not fully understand the complexities involved, they had effectively described gravity six hundred years before Isaac Newton expounded his theory to the world. In saying that the stars were without weight because their attraction towards one body was cancelled by their attraction to another, they had precisely described an object in orbit, because when one body is in orbit with another, the gravitational pull of the host is exactly balanced by the centripetal force of the orbiting object's forward momentum, and the body can very precisely be said to be weightless in space.

Whereas the Druze and Alawites were and still are extremely secretive about their membership and teachings to the point that even today outsiders cannot tell for certain whether an individual is a member or not, the Ikhwan el Safa were not so guarded. Where the Druze held their beliefs in private and did not want the outside world to know of their membership, the Ikhwan were more akin to modern day Freemasons who, though they do not shout their membership from the rooftops, also do not take much trouble to hide it.

The Brethren were a small grouping holding no political power, so were unable to change society through politics. They believed that if they could influence the individual to make him a better member of society, they could spread their philosophy through society from the bottom up. They did this through education, and by encouraging their membership to think for themselves.

Whilst Freemasonry cannot claim to bring the most up to date scientific knowledge to the public, the underlying ethos of the Craft is nevertheless identical to that of the Brethren of Purity; the betterment of society in general by improving the individual in particular. In the earliest days of the Craft many Freemasons were prominent among the intelligentsia that drove forward the Age of Reason in the 18th century and did indeed bring the most up-to-date scientific knowledge of the age to the people, so in that respect those first Freemasons could be said to be very much the spiritual descendants of the Ikhwan.

The Ikhwan promoted the idea that if an individual could harness his own passions and reflect inwardly on his existence, then he could make himself more useful to society. Whilst it would be foolish to suggest that all modern day Masons are such paragons of virtue, the underlying aspiration of the craft is to promote exactly such an attitude in its membership. From that point of view I suggest that Freemasonry can find in the Ikhwan el Safa an earlier incarnation of itself, and a likely candidate for providing the template for the formation of the mystery in the Middle Ages.

Let us for a moment accept that some of the crusaders did indeed adopt the Ikhwan's philosophy. From the fall of Rome in the 5th century until the end of the Dark Ages, learning faded in Europe, with writing being kept alive only in the remote monasteries in the far west. As the continent rubbed the sleep from its eyes in the 10th and 11th centuries, scholarship was still in its infancy when the First Crusade took place. The culture shock must have been enormous for European citizens to find themselves in an alien culture that was in possession of knowledge such as that expounded in the Rasa'il of the Brethren of Purity. What effect must they and other philosophical movements have had on these ignorant newcomers from the west?

On the most basic level it would have made them question the uniqueness of their own faith. They would also have learned from the Qur'an that Jesus was regarded only as a wise prophet in the land of his birth and not as divine. They would have discovered that although the Jews, bearing in mind this was Jesus' religion, held him in high esteem as a prophet, they did not regard him as the divine Son of God. Both the Muslims and the Jews revered Jesus as a wise man who imparted timeless wisdom to his followers, but they did not see him as the redeemer of all mankind.

The crusaders may have learned that the early Christians were criticised for believing that their god-man Jesus was real, when his story was no different than that of many other pagan god-men who were allegorical constructs. From that they may have discovered that almost every aspect of the story of Jesus had existed in the outer mysteries of the Osiris/Dionysus template centuries before his supposed birth. They could also have learned that the date of Jesus' birth was the pagan celebration of the rebirth of the sun, and that his cruel death and ascension at Easter was replicated over and over again in the pagan world, its timing due to the spring-time regeneration of all things on earth. His baptism, the Last Supper, his Ascension to Heaven to rejoin his Father, his appellations of the 'Way,' the 'Vine,' the 'Lamb of God' and the 'Son of Man,' had all been attached to other dying and resurrecting god-men before him - gods which were acknowledged to be allegorical.

No one can tell how much of this knowledge was absorbed by the crusaders, but even a little would have been enough to open their minds to dramatic possibilities. This information was intellectual dynamite, and Palestine was where it was to be found, and it would simply not have been available back in Europe. Europeans lived in the Levant, far from the watchful gaze of the Church for almost two hundred years. If there was a time in history for Westerners to develop an esoteric understanding of God it was in Palestine during the Crusades.

Added to the above, we have the fact that Jerusalem was won from the Muslims in 1099 with dreadful bloodshed and mayhem. Whilst it was one of the vilest incidents in human history, it was not the depraved, squalid bloodlust of Vlad the Impaler or the unbridled ambition of a Genghis Khan or a Hitler – it was done for the glory of God, and was sanctioned by His most senior representative on earth. It was religious intolerance on a monumental scale, and may well have sowed the seeds of discontent that the knowledge learned from the Ikhwan later fertilised. If some became disillusioned by the killing done in God's name, did they, on being introduced to the Ikhwan's attitude to other faiths, resolve to institute a similar philosophy themselves?

From that was born a new, western esoteric tradition in the mould of the Ikhwan el Safa. Like the doctrine of the Brethren of Purity and its esoteric reading of the Qur'an, the new Christian movement would have regarded the Bible narrative as allegory. The Mystery of Christ, as we will call it, would transcend religious dogma and offer an alternative spiritual path that, because it was non-dogmatic, removed the need to quarrel over the nature of God. Dogmatic faith was replaced with gnosis, and like the Ikhwan, the philosophy was based on scientific understanding of the cosmos, rather than superstitious belief in miracles that override the laws of nature. From what I have discovered about that which lies below the surface of Masonic symbolism, and which we will cover later in the book, there can be no doubt that Freemasonry emerged from exactly such a philosophical mystery school as I suggest here.

For such an endeavour to survive in the Middle Ages it would have had to exist in complete secrecy. If the Church authorities got even the slightest whiff of such unorthodoxy, its adherents would have been burned as heretics. If traditional history does not record the formation of such a mystery school in Europe, we should not therefore be surprised.

To fulfil its true purpose the tradition would need to function in the open, for hiding it away from the world would have negated its purpose. If it was to make a difference in people's lives it had to be available to the world. How could it exist, and yet not be seen to exist? The answer to that was to follow the structure of the pagan mysteries of old, and have both an outer and inner aspect. The outer mystery was simply Christianity, whilst the inner mystery with its esoteric teaching could rest behind that façade, veiled in allegory and illustrated by symbols. Under the guise of a regular Church body, a cabal within that grouping could promote the mystery in a safe environment, free from any suggestion of heresy.

Jesus was the figurehead of this new tradition, so he would be venerated as normal. It would be in the higher levels of initiation, when outsiders were ritually excluded, that more esoteric notions could be introduced. The original mysteries, and latterly the Druze and Alawites had gone to great lengths to maintain an oral tradition, and they committed nothing to writing – ever. In its pre-Grand Lodge years Freemasonry too was incredibly successful at guarding not only its teachings but its very existence from the outside world, so would the historical record really show the existence of the earlier tradition?

Whilst the mystery would have been in no way against Christianity, such was the paranoia of the mediaeval Church that it would never have been tolerated. In the early 13th Century the Church tightened its grip on any deviation from accepted dogma. As we will see in later chapters the Inquisition was created under the auspices of Pope Gregory IX in the 13th Century specifically to discover and eradicate heresy. Though it took until the 16th Century for it to reach its full zeal in Spain, the earlier Inquisition was a formidable foe, and its vicious suppression of heresy would have ensured that the tradition maintained itself in absolute secrecy. It is for this reason that the historical record is quiet about the mystery's existence. That some form of mystery tradition existed simply isn't in doubt, because the deeper analysis of the rituals of Freemasonry that conclude the book will prove that a conduit to the past simply has to exist.

In conclusion, what I have suggested in this chapter is that remnants of the pagan mysteries survived in the Holy Land in groupings like the Druze, the Alawites, and the Brethren of Purity, and that some of the Crusaders who made their home in the East were exposed to the esoteric teachings of these groups. I have also suggested that during their sojourn in an alien environment far from home, some of the Westerners adopted the esoteric outlook of their subjects, and instituted a mediaeval 'Mystery of Christ', that grew from seedling to sapling in the Levant before being transplanted to Europe as a western esoteric tradition.

Opinions on the origin of Freemasonry tend to fall roughly into one of two camps. On one hand we have the medieval guilds of stonemasons, and on the other is the Knights Templar. Earlier chapters indicated that though lodges of stonemasons did indeed play a part in the pre-1717 development of the Craft, there was an esoteric side to their rituals that was unlikely to have originated with them. The last few chapters suggest that these pre-Christian ideas had originally resided around the eastern end of the Mediterranean Basin and Asia Minor. The first occasion on which Europeans would have been exposed to these teachings was in the years following the First Crusade, and that having learned them in the east, some of the crusaders then carried them back to Europe.

It is a simple fact that when one thinks of the people involved in the Crusades, one of the foremost groups that comes to mind is the Knights Templar. It is no surprise, then, that that order of fighting monks is widely believed, in popular imagination, to have played a part in the origin of Freemasonry.

It is also a fact that the Knights Templar had been closely associated with operative stonemasons from the earliest days of the Crusades, and indeed would remain so throughout the entire existence of the order. Perhaps the transition of this knowledge from the Holy Land into the rituals of the stonemasons was via the close working relationship between the Knights Templar and the men who built their castles and churches for them. Perhaps instead of trying to prove whether it was either the stonemasons' guilds or the Knights Templar that provided the basis of modern Freemasonry we should look at the possibility that it was a mixture of both organisations working as one, which provided the origin of the Craft.

What we must do now therefore is look at the established history of the Order of the Knights Templar, and see if there is anything about them or the symbols they used that would indicate that they could have been party to the development and promulgation of a new mystery that based itself around the figure of Jesus.

So who were these enigmatic Knights, and what is it about the order they instituted which still holds an air of intrigue seven hundred years after their destruction?

CHAPTER 8

FEW ORGANISATIONS IN the history of the world have gathered such an aura of mystery as the Knights Templar. Many histories of those enigmatic knights exist, some very serious affairs indeed, scorning any heretical possibilities, and drawing only on documented records of their existence to reiterate the view that they were nothing more than a monastic order dedicated to the service of the Papacy and ultimately therefore the promotion of Jesus as the one true Saviour. This is not an unreasonable position to adopt, because being based solidly on documented evidence the image that emerges cannot be proved to be wrong. The reality of history, however, does not start and end with what can be proved.

In terms of their being possible forerunners of the Craft, the foremost counter argument is that no one has yet offered a sensible reason as to why the order would wish to have continued as a clandestine brotherhood after its official dissolution by the Church. Perhaps if a reasonable, un-sensational motive was advanced which suggested that it was not the order as a whole that survived the purge in the 14th century but only the teachings of the mystery of Christ, then a different picture would emerge.

Many theories already exist about the Templars' relationship to Freemasonry. The thesis presented here is completely dissociated from all of them, so we will ignore them and forge our own. First, though, we will briefly recount their history as accepted by mainstream historians.

Formation in the East

Sometime between the taking of Jerusalem by the Crusaders in 1099 and the official sanction of the new order by the Pope in 1128, the Knights Templar came into existence. The consensus of opinion tends to place their formation in 1118. The first report that mentions them is not until more than fifty years after their foundation, when the chronicler William, archbishop of Tyre writes about their foundation. In his book, *Historia rerum in partibus transmarinis gestarum*, translated by James Brundage, the archbishop tells us that nine French Knights led by Hughes de Payens from Champagne presented themselves to the King of Jerusalem and offered to protect the highways and byways for the safe passage of the pilgrims who toiled along the dusty routes to the holy sites. Those knights were given a wing of the Royal Palace near the Dome of the Rock in the al-Aqsa Mosque. As this building stood over what were thought to be the massive underground stables of King Solomon, they assumed it to be the original Temple of Solomon and took their name from it.

William further writes that for the first nine years of their existence, until their official sanction in 1128 they had enlisted no more recruits and still stood at nine members. This curious fact is the first of the enigmas about their early existence, because so few knights would have made little impact in protecting the thousands of pilgrims who criss-crossed the landscape around Jerusalem. Another detail which is perhaps strange is that although there was an official scribe at the court of the King of Jerusalem during that nine-year period up to 1128, he makes no mention of their existence at all, nor of any armed force for the protection of Christian wayfarers during the time when they were supposed to be performing such a task. Many ascribe this to a conspiracy of silence, but the truth is likely to be that they did nothing during those years outside their own closed group. What is certain, however, is that if the founding date of the Templar order was indeed 1118, and few dispute this, then it was almost twenty years after Jerusalem was taken, and this was plenty of time for a certain cross-pollination of ideas with the esoteric Muslim sects, as suggested in the last chapter, to have taken place.

It must also be remembered that it was the nine knights themselves, without sanction from anyone, who instituted the order unilaterally, and then presented the pope with a *fait accompli*. It was not a case of the pope or the Lord Protector recognising the need for such a force and directing that one be instituted from the ranks of the available Europeans in the Levant, rather, the new order was from the outset in the control of those who stepped up to the plate and offered their services. By the time the pope was asked for his blessing they were already up and running as an independent order. In this respect at least, while it does not prove an ulterior motive, it certainly leaves the door open to the possibility that the formation of the new knighthood was an orchestrated strategy by a certain group wishing to place themselves in such a position.

The case for their formal recognition was made to the pope on their behalf by Bernard of Clairvaux, a giant within the Church and arguably the most influential prelate of his day. He had joined the Cistercian Monastery at Citeaux as a young man, and had gone on to found his own daughter house, the Abbey at Clairvaux. He was uncle to one of the nine knights, Andre de Montbard, and possibly had family connections to two of the others, which gives reason for his involvement in the setting up of the order.

Formal Acceptance

Bernard praised the new knighthood highly, and urged the pope to honour them for their sterling work in the Holy Land. Pope Honorius was suitably impressed by his accolade, and agreed that the Church should indeed formally institute the knights as a military wing of the Church. Taking the official name of the '*Poor Fellow-Soldiers of Christ and the Temple of Solomon,*' the brethren of the new knighthood swore to live by a monastic rule similar to that of the Cistercians, both rules drawn up by Bernard. They pledged to live chastely in commune with their brothers, to hold no personal property and to surrender everything to the collective ownership of the brotherhood. So whilst the individual members could technically be classed as poor, the brotherhood as a whole had no such restraint, but there was nothing strange in that, as other orders operated along similar lines.

On being formally instituted in 1128 they saw a huge influx of new members and donations from all over Europe. Hughes de Payen, the first Grand Master, immediately set off on a grand tour, accepting gifts of land and money to help the movement in its noble endeavour. Importantly for our enquiry one of the first donations of land was from the Scottish King David I in that very year of their inception, 1128, who granted them lands at Ballantrodoch on the lower slopes of the Pentland Hills just southeast of Edinburgh. Ballantrodoch, now known as the village of Temple, became their Scottish headquarters. This establishes right from the earliest days of the order a connection with Scotland in general, and in particular with the region wherein lie the oldest Masonic lodges in the world. This geographical link may seem superfluous at this point, but as I was later to find, it would be one of the most telling facts of all.

Growth

As the new knighthood grew it turned its attention with gusto to the task it had been founded to do. As its numbers swelled and its coffers grew full to bursting with donations, the burgeoning organisation formed itself into chapters and started to patrol the highways and byways between Jerusalem and the coast. It soon became the most important organisation in the new kingdom of Jerusalem, far outstripping other orders like the Knights Hospitallers. The knights immediately set about an aggressive campaign of castle building and the rebuilding of fortified towns seized from the Muslims, which in addition to the construction of their own preceptories and chapter houses would bring them into close communion with the stonemasons who carried out this work. Besides their security role they also assumed responsibility for overseeing the building of an infrastructure of roads and bridges to facilitate the better government of the land, and in this capacity became ever more closely aligned with the stonemasons who carried out the work.

The Templars did not just build castles in the Levant of course, but also across the length and breadth of Europe; indeed by the end of their existence they possessed no less than 900 Commanderies and an estimated 10,000 castles of various sizes and importance. No institution in the Middle Ages could lay claim to such a prodigious appetite for construction as the Templars, even surpassing the Church itself. By far the craft at the forefront of this programme was that of the stonemason, so we can readily see how closely the Knights Templar must have worked with the operative masons in their employ during the roughly two hundred years of the knights' existence. The two were so closely associated with each other that the Templars sometimes even acted as agents, supplying stonemasons from their own sites for projects other than their own.

Besides their work overseeing their building projects, the security of the remote kingdom was the Templars' chief concern and they maintained a sizeable army of mounted knights and sergeants at arms to keep the Saracen hordes at bay. Outremer was an isolated outpost, far from the security of Europe, and was surrounded by a sea of hostile forces. The situation was not one of constant warfare however, and diplomacy and bargaining played its part in the maintenance of the status quo. There were many instances of deals done to avoid the unnecessary shedding of blood, with towns exchanged, cities spared, prisoners treated with respect, and battles called off at the last moment when compromise had been reached. Many uneasy truces were upheld between the King of Jerusalem and the rulers of neighbouring lands, and at the forefront of this politicking were the Templar Knights, who had many contacts with the enemy and developed a great skill in diplomacy that would assist them in their other sphere of influence back home in Europe.

Influence

The Templar legacy goes far beyond their original purpose, in that at the height of their powers they were at the forefront of many aspects of European life, and contributed substantially to the development of the modern world. As a by-product of their work towards the safe passage of pilgrims within the Holy Land, they also assisted those pilgrims to make the arduous and dangerous journey from their own lands to the coastal ports of Palestine where their grand tour of the sites would start. The Mediterranean Sea was infested with pirates and brigands who would all too readily prey on vulnerable travellers whom they knew to be carrying money. The Templars organised the whole enterprise for the pilgrim, using their fleet of ships to ferry their charges in safety to and from the Levantine ports. They also kept rooms in their secure chapter houses for the use of travellers, and in these endeavours became the world's first travel agents. All this came at a price of course, and the brotherhood grew wealthy on the commerce.

They also introduced the notion of banking and cheques to the world, in that they would accept money in one of their treasuries near the pilgrim's home and issue a letter of honour against it that could be redeemed at any other treasury along the route. Not having to carry gold was obviously advantageous to the traveller, and yet again the fees charged for this service added considerably to the Templars' wealth.

In addition to their work in the Levant the Templars became major landowners in Europe, accepting gifts of manors and huge tracts of land that they administered to produce revenue to finance their work in the Holy Land. From around 1140 a succession of papal decrees exempted them from many of the normal constraints on business enterprise, and largely made them an autonomous organisation that could trade freely anywhere in Europe without paying taxes to local kings and princes. Whilst this undoubtedly assisted the meteoric rise in their fortunes, it did little to endear them to those rulers in whose territories they operated, nor indeed to the clergy who saw no tax revenue from the Templar lands within their dioceses.

Largely because of the Templar structure as a commune, their monopoly in the pilgrim trade and their freedom from taxation, their wealth was free to grow without hindrance. With generous gifts from benefactors, and estates signed over when landed nobles joined, they soon found themselves arguably the wealthiest organisation on earth. They put their money to good use, lending it to monarchs and nobles throughout the continent, and in so doing made many rulers dependant on them and often deeply in their debt.

In their dealings with the various Arab groupings in the East they had learned to be consummate negotiators, and became valued emissaries for many of the royal houses of Europe in their diplomatic negotiations with each other. Their skill in money matters placed them at the very centre of European finance in general and in that of France in particular, where they actually ran the exchequer for the French king. Being widely travelled and experienced in the ways of the world, Templars were much sought after as advisors at royal courts and even had influence in the papal Curia. Such was their prestige in the Church that the Pope bestowed extraordinary privileges on them such as granting them superiority over all laws both ecclesiastical and secular, and making them answerable, through their Grand Master, to no one but the Vicar of Christ himself.

Throughout their existence they must have seemed an unstoppable military and financial force in the Christian world, so how did it all go wrong? How did such an illustrious organisation fall from grace, and why was that descent so dramatic?

Downfall

The brief facts regarding their suppression are that at dawn on Friday 13th of October 1307, agents of the French King descended on their Commanderies and chapter houses within France and placed everyone they found under arrest. The plan worked like clockwork and the knights were caught off guard and put up no resistance. They were charged with ten counts of heresy, including denying Christ, trampling on the Cross and worshipping a head they called Baphomet. The torture started immediately, and within a few weeks the confessions started to appear. The case of heresy against them was eventually declared proven, and the order was officially suppressed in 1312. The Templar Grand Master Jacques de Molay was burned as a heretic along with the Preceptor of Normandy Geoffrey de Charnay outside the Cathedral of Notre Dame de Paris in March 1314, bringing a final end to the order of the Poor Fellow-Soldiers of Christ and the Temple of Solomon after one hundred and eighty four years.

So how reliable were the confessions of heresy? In light of my portraying the Templar Knights as promoters of a mystery tradition that would have been regarded as deeply heretical by their masters in the Church, it is tempting to say that the charges against them prove the case. In fact it would suit the thesis presented here very well to suggest that their heresy had been uncovered and that they had to be eradicated by the church at all costs; but it is highly unlikely that there was any substance to the charges at all. They were in fact nothing more than the standard heresy charges of the day that were rolled out to marginalize the accused and make pariahs of them.

The early Middle Ages were not like today where we can expect fair treatment by our rulers and where if it is not forthcoming we can appeal to the newspapers, the courts, or bodies like Amnesty International or the European Court of Human Rights. At the time the Templars were suppressed, individuals, institutions and even entire races only existed with the blessing of those who ruled them, be they king, emperor or pope. If the powers that be decided that an institution was an obstruction to their ambition then that institution was in deep trouble. Nowhere is the fragility of existence better demonstrated than what happened to the Templars after the loss of the Holy Land in 1291, for to compound the troubles of the order which no longer had a Levant to defend, there was an on-going situation between the French king and the Pope which was ultimately to bring the once noble order to its knees.

The story that the Templars became embroiled in started many years before their suppression, and involved another heretical group, which spanned the region from the Spanish Pyrenees, across the ancient land of Gaul and into the mountains of northern Italy. Although this heresy, which vied openly with Catholicism for the hearts and minds of the people came to the fore in the early 13th century, it was violently suppressed and was all but extinct by the 1250s and set the stage for what would later happen to the Templars.

In the next chapter we will leave the demise of the Templars for a time, to examine this other heretical group and see how its rise to prominence and brutal suppression laid the groundwork for the ultimate downfall of the order of the Temple, and gives us an insight into the world in which the mystery tradition would have had to exist.

CHAPTER 9

AT THE END of the 12th century, a hundred years before the demise of the Templars, the then king of the Franks only ruled over the top half of what is now France. To the south of his domain lay the land of the so-called heretic people known as Cathars; *le pays du Cathare*, which extended from the Pyrenees in the west to Italy in the east. The extent of the Cathar region was denoted by its language, which was not pure French but a dialectic mixture of French, Catalan and remnants of Latin from the time of Roman occupation. The name of the region, Occitania, came from the dialect's word for yes, which was *'oc'* rather than the more familiar *'oui'* used in the north. Though the name Occitania is no longer in use, the difference still lives on in the modern name of the area - Languedoc - which translates literally as the 'language of yes,' and that region was the very heartland of the heresy. Even to this day the inhabitants are fiercely independent and proud of their tradition of non-conformity.

There arose from this area the heresy known as Catharism, which whilst heretical in the eyes of the Church, was still nonetheless Christian. The leaders, known as Bon Hommes or 'Good Men,' tried to emulate Jesus in their lives, living as simply as they could, eschewing all material possessions and living off alms donated by those they ministered to. They felt they must lead by example, not by diktat, and were particularly scathing of the Roman Catholic clergy, whose lavish lifestyles and moral bankruptcy contrasted strongly with the harsh, ascetic lives the Good Men chose for themselves. The ordinary people were drawn to these men, disillusioned by the corruption and worldliness of many of their Christian priests.

The rise of this heresy was to prove a boon for the French King whose lands bordered the northern marches of Occitania. Its brutal suppression saw unprecedented violence by Christians against Christians over a thirty-five year period, laying waste the countryside and ultimately dispossessing many southern nobles of their lands. It was no quirk of fate that within a few years of the cessation of hostilities the seized lands were in the hands of the French king, who benefited by ridding himself of hostile lords, consolidating his position, and enlarging his country as a result.

A gentle people

Catharism, from the Greek word *katharos* meaning pure, was a form of dualist Gnosticism which had grown from the much earlier Manichaeism and the more recent Bogomilism of Bulgaria, and took root in the fiercely independent region around Toulouse where it flourished openly under the patronage of the local nobility. Groups showing similar beliefs to the Cathars had started to appear as early as the year 970, and by the 1140s, fully developed Catharism as we know it was established throughout the region. Whilst history doesn't suggest any direct link between the faith of the Cathars and the Mystery of Christ as suggested here, the two doctrines appear to have shared certain similarities that warrant mention. In the first place the Cathars regarded much of Christian dogma as allegorical, including Jesus' divinity. Their existence therefore demonstrates that there were, at that time, heretical groups questioning the authenticity of the Jesus narrative as presented in the New Testament, and further, that those groups were proliferating in approximately the same part of the world where the original nine Templar Knights originated, and were spreading and multiplying at precisely the same time in history. There were several similarly heretical groups extant at the time of the First Crusade; at Ravenna, Orleans and Arras, and within fifteen years of the formation of the Knights Templar in 1128, a fully developed Catharism appeared in the Languedoc. The belief system of the Cathars is complex and would deserve an entire book of its own and even a full chapter here would not adequately tell their story, so the briefest outline will have to suffice.

They believed that there was not one God but two, a good one and an evil one, hence the dualism of their faith. The Good God was a purely spiritual being who was beyond comprehension, intangible, and dwelt in perpetual light, playing no part whatsoever in the world of Man. Like many deeply religious peoples, the Cathars struggled in their own minds to explain how the evil they saw in the world around them could emanate from a completely pure source, so they came to believe that another God, the Rex Mundi, the god of the World, had created the physical world and all that was in it. This second God was intrinsically evil and therefore all aspects of the material world that he had created were considered evil also. The Cathars believed their souls belonged to the intangible world of the god of Light, but that their physical bodies were of the evil God, made by him from the mud of the earth. They believed in re-incarnation, and the aim of their faith was to free themselves from their earthly prison, which they achieved by leading totally blameless lives and thereby ultimately attaining an entirely spiritual existence free from the body.

The followers of the faith were divided into two distinct groups. The Bon Hommes travelled the country in pairs, preaching wherever they found an audience, whilst the rest were known as 'credentes', or believers, and lived ordinary lives, not pledged to the ascetic existence of the Good Men. These credentes took little or no interest in the theology that underpinned the faith, but looked up to the Good Men because of the example they set to others. In eschewing all material possessions and pleasures, the Bon Hommes had bound themselves to an incredibly harsh existence devoid of all selfish pleasure, which they saw as the only way to become truly spiritual beings, and thus break free of the cycle of human reincarnation and move on to the afterlife.

They saw themselves as faithful Christians who were true to the simple doctrines of Jesus, but abhorred the decadence of the Church, which they saw as corrupting the simple Christian message. Although they venerated Jesus above all others, they regarded him as a purely ethereal manifestation of spirit. He could not therefore have been born of a flesh and blood woman, and hence they regarded that claim as an allegory for the simple-minded. Taking this to its logical conclusion they deemed that he could not therefore have died on the Cross. The worship of Jesus as having sacrificed himself for the redemption of mankind was anathema to them and they believed that the Catholic Church, in worshipping a torture implement as an icon, placed itself in the service of the Evil God. They also rejected the veneration of relics and dismissed the need for a hierarchy of priests to interpret the Holy Scriptures for the common man. It was perhaps this last belief which the Roman Catholic clergy regarded as most worrying, as it diminished their role as mediators between God and Man, and therefore lessened their power and authority.

The Bon Hommes were literate and held learning in great reverence. When the Church sent Dominican Friars to educate them regarding their errors and bring them back into the fold, the prelates found that they had more than met their match, and complained afterwards to the pope that the Cathars knew more about theology than the Dominicans themselves did. The Good Men believed the Church was to be found in the lives of the faithful and not in buildings or fine robes, and they argued that this was the true vision Jesus had demonstrated by his own simple life. Their only prayer was the Paternoster, and they refused to be bound by any oath, regarding oath taking as being contrary to free will. They believed that if an action was worthy it did not need an oath to enforce its implementation, and if the only reason one did something was because of having taken an oath to do so, then it was not worthy of doing. Their beliefs were simple and faultless, and presented no threat to society whatsoever, other than that they challenged the Christian status quo.

Had Catharism been a small, insignificant sect that kept itself to itself it might not have been seen as such a threat to the authority of the Church; but it was no small sect. It had been openly embraced by both peasants and nobility alike, and offered an alternative to the hegemony of Roman Catholicism. In short it had come to a position of significance in the area to the south of the Frankish kingdom and felt confident enough not to cower away in the hills and forest glades. Many lived openly Cathar lives and it was a situation the Church could not allow to continue. The denial of Jesus as the true Son of God was the most heretical of their beliefs in the eyes of the Catholic Church, but perhaps even more dangerous was their dismissal of the priesthood as unnecessary. This was a notion that undermined not only faith in general, but threatened the privileged position the hierarchy of the Church enjoyed. Over the years prior to this there had been a steady growth of the heresy, which, if allowed to continue unchecked might have spilt over into other regions. The Pope officially damned them as heretics at the Third Lateran Council in 1179 and declared anyone who harboured them to be excommunicated. This in effect isolated the Good Men, and laid those who supported them open to confiscation of lands, imprisonment or even execution; for it was by methods such as these that the medieval Church maintained the purity of its doctrine.

The Bon Hommes were celibate, vegetarian and peace-loving, and cared nothing for the comforts of life, an attitude that earned them the nickname '*Parfait*' or Perfect Ones from their enemies - a sarcastic jibe that was aimed at their aspiration to righteousness. This self-denial was a deliberate attempt to rid the body of the craving for material satisfaction and free the mind from earthly distraction. As examples to the common peasants the Good Men were nothing less than true paragons of virtue who, by their example, highlighted the excesses of the established priesthood. They were hard working and were often craftsmen and artisans, in many instances linked to the craft of the weavers and the fur traders who crossed into Europe from the Balkans and beyond.

The situation between the Cathars and the Catholic Church started to deteriorate during the closing years of the 12th century and in 1208 the Pope moved openly to eradicate the threat they posed to Christendom. He called a holy war against them that was to become known as the Albigensian Crusade after the town of Albi, a particular stronghold of the heresy. From the book 'God's Heretics' by Aubrey Burl we learn that the pope excommunicated Raymond VI, Count of Toulouse for being what he described as a 'protector of heretics'; and further urged that 'he who dispossesses you will be accounted virtuous, he who strikes you dead will earn a blessing'. The pope further railed against the Cathar heresy which he said '...gives birth continually to a monstrous brood, by means of which its corruption is vigorously renewed, after that offspring has passed on to others the canker of its own madness and a detestable succession of criminals emerges'. He went further, urging the king of France, Philippe Auguste, to go to war against them, to 'eliminate such filth' and let the 'misery of war bring them back to the truth'.

To those who took up arms in the name of Christ he offered the same indulgences that had been offered to those who fought the Saracens in the Holy Land. These were absolution from the sins of the past, present and future, all debts being put in abeyance except for debts to Jews which were completely cancelled. With the chance of booty and land up for grabs, the call to arms was not short of volunteers, for it is not difficult to find men who will work for God when their reward is land and riches, and when they can kill and maim without troubling their consciences because they can claim they are doing His bidding. In the summer of 1209 a large contingent of soldiers under the command of their Frankish nobles from the north wound its way through the verdant valleys and out on to the lush, fertile coastal plains of the south, and descended on the town of Beziers.

Thirty-five years of slaughter was about to begin.

Bloodshed in the name of Christ

Pledged to non-violence the Cathars offered no resistance, their only strategy being to hide themselves among the ordinary Christians. It is testimony to how well the Cathars were thought of that the local barons and peasantry alike defended them to the end, often perishing themselves in the protection of a group that never amounted to more than a fifth of the population of any area. In all 20,000 people are thought to have been killed in Beziers alone - Cathar and Christian alike. Unable to compel the ordinary Christian townspeople to give up the Cathars in their midst, the besieging forces were presented with a problem in that they did not know whom to kill and whom to spare. The Pope's senior prelate in the area, Arnold Amaury, was an arrogant bully and had been scorned and ridiculed some years earlier when trying to preach the Christian message in the area. He had a long memory, and no doubt saw the chance to ruin Beziers as settling an old score. With shocking sang-froid he ordered that they all be killed. 'But what about the Christians?' he was asked, before giving the famously chilling reply, 'Kill them all, God will know his own.' When contemplating the enormity of this ghastly statement from a man of God, it is difficult not to think of the Ikhwan el Safa and their tolerance of all faiths. We also begin to see why ordinary people may have wondered if such measures were truly the design of God, or were the works of Man dressed up in divine clothing.

If the Church had reached its nadir in the East with the bloody sacking of Jerusalem, then its blackest moment in the West must surely be the slaughter of every man woman and child, whether Cathar or faithful Christian, in Beziers that bright sunny day in July 1209. Not satisfied with having merely killed both the heretics and those who gave them shelter, Amaury then instructed that the fields around the town be sown with salt to render them infertile for generations to come, and in a chilling postscript wrote of the slaughter in a letter to the Pope... 'The workings of divine vengeance have been wondrous'.

The soldier in overall command of the crusading army was Simon de Montfort. Created Earl of Leicester by marriage, he was shortly thereafter dispossessed of all his English lands and was left with only a small estate north of Paris. Having made a name for himself as a military tactician crusading in the Levant, he saw an opportunity for re-establishing his fortunes and offered his sword to the Pope. The pickings were rich indeed, with wide flat plains of excellent soil, a thriving economy, and many lucrative trading ports on the Mediterranean coast the prize for success. On taking the city of Beziers he declared himself Viscount thereof, and when Carcassonne followed shortly thereafter, he added that to his titles too. He was an accomplished warrior, though one more used to fighting battle-hardened Saracens on the field of war than in hunting simple, unarmed and unresisting peasants in the fields and villages of a Christian country.

Cathar ethos forbade fighting, so their only option was placing themselves where their enemies could not reach them. A visit to the countryside of the Languedoc reveals many fortresses like Queribus here on previous page, built on incredibly high pinnacles of rock. Puilaurens, Peyrepertuse, Lastours, Cabaret, and many other lesser fortresses - all share one thing in common - their precarious locations, and all prompt the same thought; why did anyone build castles only eagles could reach with ease? The answer lies in the Cathars' refusal to take up arms against their enemies, for they considered fighting too worldly for their spiritual sensitivities. So they built their castles among the clouds so that they would not have to fight, but could hide, secure in the knowledge that few enemies would have the fortitude to scale the sheer cliffs below the castle walls. Sadly for the Cathar heretics the Church of Rome was no ordinary enemy, and nothing could withstand the onslaught it unleashed against them.

As one pitiful example of how de Montfort succeeded at his appointed task he sliced off the lips and noses and gouged out the eyes of the people of the walled town of Bram, save one man who was left with one eye, to lead the others in a bedraggled procession to the next town to spread terror among its inhabitants, that they would perhaps think twice before sheltering the heretics in their midst. Horrors like this were perpetrated all across Occitania, against people who were guilty of nothing except believing something other than what they were told they must. De Montfort was finally killed besieging Toulouse, when a stone fired from a catapult within the walls caught him squarely in the face and killed him outright. Whilst the Church sang his praises for his tireless efforts in the name of Christ and erected a monument in his honour in the Cathedral of St. Nazarius in Carcassonne, those whose loved ones he had butchered and whose lives he had ruined thought otherwise of him, perhaps best summed up by the *Song of the Cathar Wars* translated into English by Janet Shirley in 1996. Composed whilst the atrocities were still ongoing, it refers to the above-mentioned monument, and pulls no punches in telling what the people thought not only of him, but those who sanctioned him to destroy their lives in the name of Christ.

'The epitaph says, for those who can read it,
That he is a saint and martyr who shall breathe again
And shall in wondrous joy inherit and flourish
And wear a crown and sit on a heavenly throne.
And I have heard it said that this must be so -
If by killing men and spilling blood,
By ruining souls, and preaching murder,
By following evil counsels, and raising fires,
By ruining noblemen and besmirching honour,
By pillaging the country, and by exalting Pride,
By stoking up wickedness and stifling good,
By massacring women and their infants,
A man can win Jesus in this world,
Then Simon surely wears a crown, resplendent in heaven'.

The final major act of the crusade took place over the winter of 1243 - 1244 when the last substantial group of Cathars was trapped within the walls of the precipitous mountaintop fortress of Montsegur. It was thought impregnable, and indeed it was – from armed assault – but in the end even majestic Montsegur fell, its lofty heights no protection from hunger and thirst. Starved out, the Cathars could do nothing but surrender; and surrender for them meant death.

The 200 Cathars who had survived the ten-month siege of Montsegur were offered a stark choice on surrender; renounce their heretical ways and live, or carry their beliefs with them into the purifying flames of eternal damnation. They chose the latter and were thrown, indeed some reports say they threw themselves, willingly, on to hastily built bonfires on a saddleback ridge below the crag on which their castle stood. A small cairn topped with a simple stone memorial marks the spot to this day, and even in the summer of 2005, seven and a half centuries later, spray-painted graffiti on a nearby rock proclaims 'Vive l'Occitania', showing that feelings about the massacre still run high in the region.

Standing atop the fortress of Montsegur today, gazing out over the diminishing ripples of tree-clad hills that fade into the hazy distance, the world seems remote indeed. Looking down, cars on the road a thousand feet below seem like ants on a branch, and one does indeed feel unassailable in that eyrie of stone. And as one labours back down the tortuous path over the hard, unforgiving rocks below the castle in the wake of those gentle Bon-Hommes who passed that way twenty-five generations ago, one cannot fail to sense the overpowering sadness that wells from the rock underfoot, every step of the way down from that lonely pinnacle.

The thirty-five years of savagery that the peace-loving Cathars and their supporters were subjected to were unrivalled in Europe until the extermination programme of the Nazis during the Second World War. The Cathars were a quiet, honourable, peaceful people who were no match for any army. They regarded their own plight as similar to that of the first Christians who had been persecuted mercilessly under the Romans. The Cathars, like the early Christians before them, gladly embraced death rather than submit to a doctrine that they did not believe in, but where the Christians of Rome had initially been the oppressed, they had now become, in one of the great ironies of history, the oppressors.

The massacre at Montsegur broke the back of the heresy, but it was not completely finished. Though the armies withdrew, their work done, the persecution of the last few Cathars continued under the ministration of a new organisation set up specifically to root out any whiff of their heresy. That institution was the Holy Inquisition, the brainchild of the fanatical Spaniard, Dominic Guzman, and is arguably the most iniquitous body of men ever to have blighted mankind. Having earlier founded the Dominican order, Guzman extended his fanaticism for the Gospels by founding the Holy Inquisition in 1233, specifically to identify and eradicate the Cathars and their heretical ideas.

By 1412 the last vestige of this heresy was gone from Europe, but the Inquisition had found its forte. Having proved itself as a useful tool in the Languedoc, the Inquisition then went on to investigate other deviations from official doctrine, among any groups or individuals anywhere in Christendom. Right up until the Reformation and even beyond, the Holy Inquisition travelled the length and breadth of Europe, striking fear and terror wherever they went. Their inquisitorial procedure was deliberately designed to instil in its unfortunate victims such bleak despair and abandoned hopelessness that their reputation for cruelty preceded them wherever it went. The intent was to stifle heresy before it began, and force those contemplating such a path to think again. Europe was caught in an atmosphere of dread and terror, where even the slightest of deviant opinions, if voiced publicly, could be passed to the inquisitors if the wrong person overheard. With unimaginable methods of torture at their disposal, and the final handing to the secular arm for burning, they were spectacularly successful in their endeavour. Had a new version of the pagan mystery schools existed at that time as I suggest it did, then it would have had to survive in that climate of fear.

Though I have not drawn a direct link between the heresy of the Cathars and the mystery school that I suggest had been instituted during the Crusades, there are several reasons for their inclusion here. In the first instance the Cathars are proof that heretical notions such as the denial of a divine Christ not only existed in Medieval France, but that they were popular and flourished.   The region where the Gnostic Manichaeism/Bogomilism took root is also close to the cultural homelands of the nine men who founded the Knights Templar. Heretical ideas had existed for many years prior to the public flowering of the heresy in the middle of the 12th century, and those nine men could well have harboured notions about the allegorical nature of the Jesus narrative long before they presented themselves at the court of King Baldwin II of Jerusalem and sought quarters in his palace. As opposed to them becoming heretics as a result of discovering something in the Holy Land, the seeding of their attitude towards the Christian narrative may well have been present before they went.

In the second instance, the treatment of the Cathars demonstrated plainly that to openly display heresy spelt certain annihilation. Could there be a more pointed lesson for those who would follow a heretical path, that to try to do so openly would be the road to oblivion? If the followers of the Mystery of Christ needed a reminder that the way of the Druze and their use of taquia to mask their true beliefs was a good idea, then the annihilation of the Cathars would forever be that reminder. After such atrocities carried out against peace-loving Europeans who wanted nothing but to live quietly and follow the faith their conscience told them was the true path, the need for utter secrecy among the followers of the mystery would have been self-evident. It is little wonder, then, that a system of complex initiations and secret words and handgrips was developed, using symbols, the meaning of which could be passed off as Christian, yet have other hidden meanings to the initiated.

Another important element in the crusade against the Cathars is that whether by good fortune or design, and history tends to favour the latter, the French king greatly consolidated his domain by adding to it the many southern fiefdoms seized from the Cathars' sympathetic overlords. Not long after the end of hostilities the French King acquired the lands de Montfort seized, and in doing so left himself in control of the entire land-mass between the Alps and the Pyrenees; all that is, except for the massive tracts of land which the Templars owned within the borders of his kingdom. Over those he had no control whatsoever, neither judicial nor fiscal, and that was to be a major factor in the chain of events in the early 14th century that would ultimately spell the end for the order.

Like so many actions of the Middle Ages there was often an ulterior motive that usually involved gain of some form that stood quietly in the shadows behind deeds that were ostensibly religious in nature, and the Albigensian Crusade was a case in point. Would it have happened at all if the control of the land was not a factor and vast wealth available to any who would take up the sword and do God's work?

In 17th century England, Matthew Hopkins, self-styled witch-finder general, travelled far and wide 'discovering' witches in towns and villages throughout the land. The town burghers paid well for the service, relieved to be rid of the devils in their midst. When attitudes matured however, and voices were raised against the mediaeval superstitions that led to the deaths of so many innocents, payments for the services of the likes of Hopkins dried up. The money gone, the witch craze was over - instantly - and normality returned once more to the quiet, leafy villages of rural England. Again and again we see men use piety to fuel their own ambition, and I believe the motivation behind the Albigensian Crusade was a case in point.

The thirty-five-year crusade against the Cathars begs the question as to how much influence the French king, who was the ultimate winner, brought to bear on the Pope's decision to call the Crusade in the first place. The entire episode was to be replayed during the following century when another French king, Philippe IV, would again use religion for his personal gain, and achieve a result almost identical to the end of the Cathars, only this time it would be upon the Templars that his attention would fall.

The Cathar faithful had been structured into two groups; the Good Men who held the doctrine, and the commoners or credentes, who comprised the rest. Where the Bon Hommes travelled through the countryside, living an ascetic life of self-imposed hardship, and literally were of no fixed abode, the credentes lived their lives like anyone else. Whereas the Good Men were learned and understood their theology, the credentes took little or no interest in the deeper message of their faith. In this, Catharism functioned very much like the pagan mysteries, where a few devout individuals possessed the inner knowledge, whilst the masses satisfied themselves with the outer, less complicated, aspect. We know that the credentes knew little of the deeper side of their faith because during questioning their inquisitors often recorded that it was difficult to prove that their doctrine was incompatible with Christianity because they had such little knowledge of what it was they believed. Though for many of them their only error was to revere the Good Men and follow their lessons, the inability to prove heresy did not necessarily stay the torturer's hand.

When reading treatises on the Cathars, the word *Texerant* or 'Weaver' is often used in its place because they were so often weavers that it became interchangeable with the word Cathar. It appears that many of them worked in that trade as a cover for their other, less obvious business, because as weavers and textile traders they would have been able to move freely around the countryside, preaching as and when the opportunity arose. It also gave them a legitimate purpose if accosted by a prelate or other agent of the Inquisition. In trading furs they often journeyed eastwards into the Balkans and beyond; travel which offered an opportunity to maintain links with the Bogomils who still existed there. In following a trade as a cover for their clandestine meetings we see a precursor for the link I suggest later existed between the Templars and the stonemasons, for as we will see in later chapters, the lodges of stonemasons would provide an eminently suitable cover for the continuation of the mystery once the Templars had fallen and were no longer able to promote it themselves.

As an addendum to the Cathars' use of commerce as a cover, there exists a record of one of the last Cathar Bon Hommes in Europe, Pierre Autier, who carried and traded a bunch of Parma knives as a cover for his preaching, so it seems that promoting an alternative spiritual path whilst participating in a more mundane trade was not unheard of in medieval Europe.

I had mentioned earlier that one of the strictures of the Cathar faith was that they refused to be bound by any kind of oath, believing that oath taking stood against the free will that was all-important to them. Initially that was a major difference between them and the followers of the Mystery of Christ, because the proponents of the mystery were so reliant on oaths that even in more enlightened times they still remained as an important though symbolic part of the ritual. However, when the Cathar heresy was all but spent, a group of them was discovered high in the Alps in 1387, almost a century and a half after the fall of Montsegur. What is particularly interesting is that where oath taking had been frowned upon in the past, those latter-day followers of the faith met in secret, at night, took strict oaths of secrecy, and knew each other by secret signs and handgrips, exactly as Masons do to this day. They had obviously learned the lesson of the past, and had chosen to keep their faith in secret rather than tilt at the windmill of an all-powerful opponent. So in this cell of Cathars then, we have all the ingredients; heresy, secrecy, oaths and clandestine recognition signs, that the mystery would have required for survival in the hostile religious landscape of Medieval Europe.

It also has to be remembered that almost all the information we have about the Cathars is from those who tried, tortured, condemned, and executed them, and that is like looking to the Nazis for information on the Jews. We have already seen that the credentes, who made up by far the biggest portion of the believers, were uneducated in matters of doctrine, so the information extracted from them under examination would shed little light on the inner tenets of the faith. The Good Men on the other hand were very knowledgeable about their faith but were far too deeply committed to reveal their innermost beliefs to those they considered their enemies. If the Inquisitors were fanatical in their devotion to eradicating heresy, the Bon Hommes were equally fanatical in their devotion to their own ways. It would have taken a particular mindset indeed to condemn oneself to a life totally devoid of pleasure, or indeed to walk calmly into the flames, so it is unlikely that they gave out under duress that which they did not want to.

In conclusion, we have looked at the Cathar heresy of the 12th and 13th Centuries and found that its influence covered a huge swathe of Europe from Italy to Spain and its main heartland was the Languedoc region of southern France. The area in which the heresy flourished was relatively close, in a pan-European sense, to where the founding Templar knights originated, and it had been fermenting there for hundreds of years before making its presence felt. It is quite possible therefore, that some of the beliefs of Catharism could have influenced the founders of the new knighthood, even before they ventured to the Holy Land. We have also seen how the Cathars, in publicly professing their faith, were brutally suppressed for having the temerity to challenge the Roman Catholic Church. The suppression of their heresy was one of the bloodiest and most cruel chapters in European history, deliberately so, to send out the message that the hierarchy of the Church would not tolerate any challenge to its authority, or permit another spiritual path to co-exist beside it.

The Holy Inquisition was instituted specifically to root out the heresy of the Cathars but lasted long after the last of them perished in the flames, casting a shadow of fear across the continent for hundreds of years hence. The way the Church dealt with the heretics, and the birth of the Holy Inquisition, would have had dire ramifications for those who would institute and follow a new, mediaeval version of the old mysteries. We have seen that Cathar beliefs included the denial of Jesus as a corporeal entity who died on the Cross, and that their belief that salvation was to be found through personal spiritual union with God rendering the priesthood superfluous was a sentiment with which the followers of the Mystery of Christ would have readily identified. Those who promoted the mystery would also have seen exactly what was entailed in openly challenging the Roman Catholic Church for the hearts and minds of the people, and perhaps decided that secrecy and obscure symbolism was the only feasible way for them to proceed.

We have also seen how the Cathar preachers used the weaving trade as a cover for their other activities to allow them the freedom to travel from town to town without arousing suspicion. This is precisely how I suggest the mediaeval mystery was carried forward by stonemasons after the suppression of the Templars - a possibility that we will look at in the following chapters. We have also seen how individual cells of Cathars, having learned the error of openly confronting the Catholic Church, turned their back on their earlier openness and kept their faith alive in total secrecy. They achieved this by holding their meetings at night behind closed doors, using secret handgrips to identify each other and swearing oaths to protect the identity of their brothers, oaths which were not merely symbolic but quite literally a matter of life or death. This is precisely how I suggest the followers of the Mystery of Christ would have preserved themselves in the hostile environment created by the Holy Inquisition.

So what of the Templars themselves? What became of them, and are there any indicators from within their order that they may indeed have been the promoters of the Mystery of Christ? Much is made about the suddenness with which the Templars were destroyed, because in popular imagination the Templars were caught off guard and were utterly destroyed when the mighty fist of the king of France descended on them out of the blue at dawn on Friday 13th of October 1307. Certainly their seizure in France was sudden, but was it truly out of the blue? Or is it possible that the mystery's controlling hierarchy could have foreseen the approaching demise of the order and made other arrangements for the tradition to continue? If there had been a secret tradition carried at the centre of the order, is it possible that those who promoted it had warning that the end was coming, and were they therefore able to find an alternative vehicle to carry it?

CHAPTER 10

IN ANSWER TO the question of whether or not the Templar hierarchy could have foreseen the suppression of their order, it is quite plain that although they may not have realised how cataclysmic the end would be, they would certainly have known that trouble was coming. They would therefore have been able to develop a survival strategy for their mystery. The move against them in France was undoubtedly swift, but the suppression of the knights in other countries was either haphazard, belated, or in some instances completely non-existent. It is the Scottish Templars that particularly interest us here, and it was fully two years before a trial took place in Edinburgh. There were also quite a few portents of their upcoming fate, not least the untimely deaths of two popes and the relocation of the papacy from Rome to Avignon in the heart of the French countryside, but to examine the situation fully we must back-track to see where the Templars' troubles first started.

The beginning of the end for them could be said to have started more than a century before their eventual demise, with the virtual annihilation of their forces by Salah al-Din, known to the West as Saladin, in a battle at the Horns of Hattin just north-west of Lake Tiberias in July 1187. That decisive victory by the Muslims shattered the aura of invincibility that surrounded the Templars, and was the turning point in the Arabs' fight for their territory. Jerusalem was lost within a year, followed by region after region in a gradual haemorrhaging of land over the next hundred years. After the initial success of the First Crusade that ushered in eighty years of European supremacy, the situation in the East had been in steady decline.

The Europeans were very much in the minority, far from home, and their tenuous toe-hold was only possible as long as the Arabs were divided. When Saladin united the disparate groupings under one banner the result was the victory at Hattin and this spelt a change of fortune for the Europeans in the Levant. As the years progressed, the enthusiasm for crusading among the European nations lessened in inverse proportion to the determination of the Arabs to remove the invaders from their land, so the end was inevitable. There were to be eight crusades in all but none came anywhere near the success of the first. Militarily the Templars had one setback after another, fostering a growing certainty that the European presence in the Levant was drawing to an end. The final death rattle for the Crusader ideal to keep the Holy Land under European control came in 1291 when the Arabs finally pushed the Templars into the sea at Acre, the last Christian city to fall. Although at that point the Templars had widespread interests in every European state, were involved at the very heart of European diplomacy and culture and were massively wealthy, their main reason to exist as an order had vanished overnight. In disarray, they regrouped on Cyprus, which became their new Eastern headquarters, from where they contemplated their uncertain future.

But the loss of the Holy Land was only part of their problems.

By the time the Holy Land was finally lost, the Templars were already grossly unpopular. Although individually pledged to poverty, the institution they belonged to was wealthier than any kingdom, and a certain cavalier attitude had grown in their ranks. They had virtual monopolies in certain industries, amounting to the world's first business conglomerate, which impinged on local barons' and merchants' abilities to trade, and whilst such a situation had been tolerated while they toiled against the Moslems, that was no longer the case after Acre. *What did the Templars need such vast revenue for*, asked their critics, *if they did not use it in the service of God?* It had been almost two hundred years since the order had been sanctioned and given its privileges, and the world had changed much during that time. Not only had commoners come to regard the Templars as haughty and arrogant, but both clergy and the nobility had grown to loathe the privileged position the knights enjoyed. Princes and kings, always in need of money for the maintenance of their own domains, saw vast revenues just beyond their grasp, and in short, they were jealous.

The Templars did themselves no favours either with the secrecy with which they cloaked their affairs. Although their dealings with the outside world were quite open, their chapter meetings from which the lower level initiates were excluded were rigorously protected from eavesdroppers. History does not record what took place behind the closed doors of their meetings but the opportunity was certainly there for them to have promoted a mystery school in such circumstances. In guarding their meetings from outsiders and sealing them against eavesdroppers, they behaved exactly as we would expect them to if they were followers of a mystery tradition they had picked up in the East. They even persuaded the pope to create confessional priests within their own order, so even on that level they would not have to interact with the outside world, and could more easily maintain their secrets among themselves. Unfortunately their pre-occupation with secrecy was to be a gift to the king of France when he set about orchestrating their downfall, for in the absence of any good reason for their obsessive secrecy he was able to level all manner of charges of heresy against them.

As well as the Templars' financial privileges chafing those they dwelt amongst, they were also not answerable legally to anyone in the world but the pope. This made any territory they owned a safe haven for anyone in conflict with outside agencies, and indeed many sought sanctuary within the walls of their Commanderies, as people do nowadays with their embassies in foreign countries. The Templar holdings were vast, spread across the entire continent, and often placed too close to seats of power for comfort. Nowhere was this better demonstrated than in France, where in return for loans to the French King Louis VII during the Second Crusade in 1147, they had been given lands on the outskirts of Paris. These lands became their headquarters in the west and were virtually an autonomous state in the heart of France over which the king had no jurisdiction whatsoever. By the end of the 13th century Paris had grown considerably bigger, surrounding the Templar lands, and leaving the order with ownership of almost a third of the French capital. In essence those Templars' Paris holdings were like Monaco or the Vatican City today, being a self contained state, and were right on the doorstep of the French king yet tantalisingly beyond his grasp. And Philippe IV, who was to become the architect of the Templar's downfall, had quite a grasp. He stood at the head of a long and distinguished family that had ruled the Franks since the year 987, and was well aware of his powerful position and the trust placed in him to maintain his family's supremacy.

The very uncertainty surrounding the future of the knights of the Temple provided an added incentive for Philippe to rid himself completely of the Templars within his borders. By 1306 their new eastern headquarters in Cyprus was under threat and there was much speculation as to where they would move. Having supported an unsuccessful coup against the king of Cyprus, the Templars were becoming increasingly unwelcome on the island, and rumours abounded that they were considering pulling back to the west, intending to make the Paris Temple their overall headquarters. Whether this was ever given serious consideration or was perhaps just a rumour that suited the purposes of the French king, he used the possibility to plot against them. Had it happened, it would have placed a foreign regime that was above all secular laws right in the heart of his kingdom, and was a threat to his sovereignty that he was not prepared to allow.

One of the strongest rulers the West has ever seen, Philippe maintained his position through the strength of his will, and would stop at nothing to get his way. Always short of money to finance his lavish lifestyle and his war-mongering with the English to the north and Flanders to the north-east, he had opportunity to see the wealth of the Templars at first hand when he had once been given sanctuary in the Paris Temple. Fleeing from a mob, angry at yet another devaluation of their currency, he had been glad to accept the Templars' protection. In doing so, they unwittingly sealed their own fate, for whilst he was in their headquarters he saw the vast wealth held in their treasury which put his own finances to shame, and it was probably during that visit that he hatched his plan to rid his kingdom of the Templars once and for all. In doing so he could at a single stroke rid himself of the potential threat the Templars posed to his rule, cancel his debts to them, and if he played his cards right, possibly even get his hands on their massive wealth as well.

The Templars had been at the very heart of diplomacy in Europe for almost two hundred years. They, more than any other organisation, knew and understood the machinations of politics, and would have been well aware of the growing predicament they were in since the fall of Acre. From their heyday when all of Europe had sung their praises for keeping the Holy Land Christian, they now found themselves at the other end of the spectrum; vilified for the loss of the Christian states in the Levant, and despised for their wealth and status. In short their day was over and they knew it. The Knights Hospitallers had re-invented themselves, fighting the Turks on Rhodes and building up a fleet to combat the pirates who infested the eastern Mediterranean, whilst the Teutonic Knights busied themselves in the cold northern lands of the Baltic States. But the Templars were singularly without employment or the likelihood of any in the near future. Their only hope was another crusade, but even a casual observer would have known that that wouldn't happen. If this was not bad enough they also had Philippe of France to contend with, and with their knowledge of his power-lust and the parlous state of his finances, they would have been all too cognisant of the threat he posed to their continued existence. The

Templars were wealthy and vulnerable, and the French king possessed a voracious appetite for money.

In 1302 he caused uproar when he did the unthinkable and taxed the French clergy to reduce his deficit, provoking Pope Boniface VIII to issue a Bull, or papal edict, to thwart him by forbidding the French clergy to pay money out of church funds without papal permission. Philippe responded by prohibiting the export of gold and silver from France, which stopped the pope getting his percentage of monies raised from the faithful within the kingdom. In retaliation Philippe also seized the property and lands of any clergy who sought to uphold the pope's edicts, and publicly accused the eighty-four year old pope of sexual licentiousness, a charge not entirely without foundation. Outraged, Boniface excommunicated the French king, although Philippe's henchmen intercepted the document before it could be proclaimed. The pope then deposed him, claiming the authority of the Donation of Constantine. This document had been purportedly written by the Roman Emperor when he elevated the Church to the official state religion in the 4th century, in which he acknowledged the pope's authority over all secular rulers, and 'gave' his empire to the pope. In return, Constantine was granted the right to rule his own empire - with the pope's blessing. This document which was used to great effect by medieval popes in their disputes with temporal rulers was only in more modern times proved to be a forgery. Having thus proclaimed Philippe deposed by the authority of a forged document, the pope then invited the Emperor of Austria to take the crown of France for himself. Such was the nature of mediaeval politics.

Philippe became tired of these shenanigans, and brought matters to a head by sending his chief advisor William de Nogaret and three hundred soldiers across the border into Italy to kidnap and threaten the pontiff. Forcing their way into the papal apartments, they held and terrorised the ageing pope for three days before he was eventually freed by an angry mob. He was not a young man and the rough treatment he received during his captivity affected him adversely, and whether as a result of this or more direct means, he was dead within a few weeks.

Having rid himself of this problem Philippe hoped for more favourable treatment from the next pontiff, but although his adversary's successor, Benedict XI, removed the sentence of excommunication against the French king, he re-ignited the financial war that his predecessor had started. Philippe in his usual forthright manner had no intention of rejoining that particular battle, and had the new pontiff poisoned instead. With the church in disarray, Philippe took a hand in the election of the next pope and succeeded in having one of his own creatures, Bertrand de Gotte, Archbishop of Bordeaux, enthroned in the chair of St. Peter. As part of the deal hatched between them the seat of the papacy was to be permanently removed to France, and so on the 17th December 1305, two years before the Templars' seizure, the new pope was crowned at Lyon, taking the name of Clement V. Philippe now effectively had the Church in his employ, and intended to use that to his advantage. One of Clement's first actions was to create twelve new cardinals from among the ranks of Philippe's cronies, which gave not only himself but also the French king a greater circle of influence in the Church.

In one of the most notable pointers of the fate that was soon to befall the Templars, one of the new pope's first proclamations was to give Philippe his blessing to dispossess all French Jews of their property and banish them from his kingdom. This was an obvious favour in return for Philippe's support of Clement's elevation to the chair of St. Peter, and lowered the proclamations of the papacy to the level of those of mere politics. It also did nothing to repudiate the general belief in the Middle Ages that the papacy was as worldly and corrupt as any secular power, and increases the likelihood that some sought a spiritual path that did not involve the Vicars of Christ.

The Knights of the Temple, on seeing that the Church could so easily be manipulated into such a move against the Jews, would surely have seen the writing on the wall for their own order. If the pope could be coerced into authorising the French king to dispossess an entire section of society for nothing other than that monarch's own financial gain, then it would be a small step for him to similarly permit the ruination of the by then redundant order of warrior monks. This fact more than any other would have left the upper echelons of the Templar order aware that as 1305 drew to a close, the storm-clouds that spelt the end of their brotherhood loomed darkly on the horizon. They were rich, they owned vast tracts of land that the king wanted for himself, and they were grossly unpopular both within the Church and outside it. They had outlived their usefulness and were vulnerable in their own homeland, and they well knew it. They also knew they were totally powerless to resist the fate that rumbled towards them with inexorable certainty, and when the end came, as they knew it would, it was sudden and brutal.

Philippe's move had to be all or nothing. The Templars were too powerful for him to attack piecemeal on his own. He needed the pope's backing and he also had to besmirch the Templar's reputation by blackening them with accusations of heresy and immorality that would leave them unlikely to receive assistance from anyone.

The charges Philippe's advisors came up with were not particularly inventive and were largely the standard heresy charges of the day, wheeled out to suppress any group or individual those in power sought to remove. A recent document unearthed in the Vatican Archive by the Italian scholar Dr. Barbara Frale, and referred to as the *Chinon Parchment*, shows that the pope carried out his own appraisal of the charges against the Templars without the knowledge of the French King, and found them to have no substance whatsoever. This proves that even at the time the pope did not believe the charges laid against the Knight's of the Temple, but nevertheless left them to their fate. Until the Chinon Parchment was found in 2001 we were totally ignorant of this fact, demonstrating well the capricious nature of recorded history and reinforcing the notion that we simply do not know everything that happened in the past.

As mentioned earlier, it is tempting to pick out a few of the charges as bolstering the premise of this book that the Templars were indeed heretics, but to do so would be disingenuous, because while specific charges may hit the mark, unless the bulk of the charges were proved, we must lay those that 'fit' at the door of coincidence. That the charges were 'proved' by the confessions extracted under torture means nothing, for even the fear of torture will extract what the inquisitor wants to hear rather than the truth. It is difficult for us in the 21st century with an impartial justice system, or the newspapers to fight on our behalf, to envisage the despair and sense of desolation that anyone accused by the Inquisition must have endured. It may be patently obvious to us in the 21st century that words were put into the Templars' mouths by their inquisitors, but in the medieval mind it was considered acceptable to rip and burn their victims until they either confessed their crimes or died in the process.

From their seizure in 1307 until their official disbandment in 1312, the French king kept the pressure on the pope and other secular rulers to suppress the order throughout Christendom. Whereas his own strike against the Templars in France had been completely successful, the Brotherhood was not crushed elsewhere to anywhere near the same degree. This mattered little to Philippe other than that he wished to ensure that they did not regroup beyond his borders and come back to bite him. In terms of settling his own internal affairs he had succeeded in his aim, and the charges of spitting on the cross, sodomy, and denying Christ had the desired effect of branding them as pariahs, leaving them 'untouchable' and therefore beyond assistance. Within months of their seizure, Clement issued a Bull saying that as a result of the inquisitorial process the charges against the Templars had been proved. This, perhaps more than any other factor, sealed the Templars' fates in the eyes of the mediaeval world. The fact remains though that despite the brotherhood being officially smashed, the overwhelming majority of those who comprised the order survived.

If we for a moment consider that they were indeed the propagators of the new mystery, then it is unlikely that it would have ceased with their suppression. Only a percentage of the Templars in

France were apprehended, and when considered as a whole, the number of those who were actually incarcerated has been estimated to be around twenty percent of the entire order. I do not claim, as others seek to do, that the knights elsewhere were rallied by those who escaped Philippe's clutches, and between them hatched a plan for the continuation of their brotherhood. Nor do I suggest that their incarcerated Grand Master called a clandestine meeting at which he passed authority to another and that a succession of Grand Masters exists from that day until this. The Templar order ceased to exist in 1312 with its official dissolution by the pope, but it is a simple fact that had the knights who had been initiated to the higher levels followed a medieval version of the old mysteries, then in no way would that mystery have died with the order.

Assumptions abound that the Templars, because of their brutal destruction, sought to avenge their fallen brothers against the Church that had abandoned them to their fate at the hands of the king of France. Another theory suggests that they had become accustomed to living high on the hog and did not want to give up that status. Yet another popular premise has them protecting the bloodline of Jesus, the Rex Deus kings of Europe. Or perhaps they simply wished to live on to keep their vast treasure out of the hands of either king or pope, but the hoarding of treasure for monetary gain is transitory and only brings out the baser side of human nature. Revenge may well have brought to fruition the Grand Master's plea as he died burning at the stake in 1314 that both the pope and King Philip appear before God within the year to answer for their actions, for whether by hand of man or coincidence, both were dead within twelve months. But would such base endeavours as treasure or revenge inspire men over such a long time, or leave such a legacy as would have become the foundation for Freemasonry four hundred years later?

What we see today looking back is only the exoteric aspect of the order. The mystery tradition was not all there was to the brotherhood, and was simply something that was held within. The destruction of the Templars was not the end of the mystery then, merely a change of direction. On the official sanctioning of the order in 1128 the brotherhood developed into the band of warrior monks that history has recorded, leaving the mystery to operate quietly behind the scenes. It was the outward, exoteric aspect that was shattered in 1307, not the esoteric, because the esoteric was intangible and could not be destroyed. If the followers of the mystery needed a lesson in why their endeavour was worth preserving, the brutal suppression of their own order would have been a spur to their flanks. Surely they would have seen that any institution which needed the torturers of the Holy Inquisition to enforce its doctrine had lost touch with the true meaning of religious faith, and would have been doubly convinced that they must preserve their own way at all costs.

In functioning as a modern mystery school not every member would have been party to the arcane secrets at the core. The lower level initiates would have believed in the literal Jesus, exactly as they would had they not followed the tradition, and He would have been venerated as in any other order. They would have considered themselves faithful servants of Christ, in the way that the followers of the outer mysteries of Dionysus believed in the literal reality of that God. Only those brethren who sought it out would have been initiated into the levels that would have given them the deeper knowledge. History records that the knights had three levels of initiation, but those would have been only the exoteric side of the order, perhaps equating with the outer mystery. There is no telling how many secret degrees of knowledge were contained within the esoteric side of the inner mystery. Even today we do not know the true structure of the hierarchy of the Druze sect, and had the Templars been the same, there is no way we could know what additional levels of teachings they preserved within the hidden side of their closed chapter meetings.

When we look back we find that the complex philosophical ethos and esoteric knowledge of groupings like the Druze, the Alawites and the Ikhwan el Safa is closely aligned to that contained in modern Freemasonry. Prior to the emergence of the Craft in the 17th Century we find semi-literate stonemasons carrying that arcana. If they did not devise it themselves then it must have been put there by others, and the Knights Templar were eminently suitable for the job. They were geographically in the right place at the right time in history, and would have had the wherewithal to embed the new tradition within their own order. There would have been no better place to hold the mystery than within an autonomous organisation which had been placed above all laws, both secular and ecclesiastical, and which answered to no-one but the pope himself through its own Grand Masters.

Since the mystery would have been such a heretical idea and was born into such a hostile environment as existed during and after the Cathar suppression and the formation of the Holy Inquisition, secrecy would have had to be absolute. In a time when the power of the Church was ever-present, like the all-seeing Eye of Sauron in Tolkien's trilogy of Middle Earth, it would never have been an option to follow the mystery in public for it would have been persecuted out of existence as the Cathars had been.

By embedding the teachings allegorically within rituals that would have seemed innocuous to those on the outside, those rituals would not have appeared unorthodox. This served two functions. In the first instance it allowed the lower level initiates, those not interested in the inner truths, to participate without specific knowledge of the tradition. In the second instance, the hidden, dualistic nature of the teachings meant that the ceremonies and rituals would survive, even if the meeting had been infiltrated by spies, or *'cowans,'* as Freemasons term them nowadays. The rituals, then, because they had exoteric meanings and relevance, could stand on their own as simple, if somewhat curious rites. Their esoteric meaning would not be directly referred to in the ceremonies and thus could be denied completely if the need arose. Even if a meeting were infiltrated by an agent of the Inquisition, the rituals would have seemed quirky, but not in contravention of accepted Christian doctrine. Today, Masonic ritual is similarly obtuse, and whilst outwardly appearing to have one meaning, the true purpose of the metaphors is to allude to an unseen body of knowledge that underpins the very essence of the Craft.

The advantage of the duality of the rites in the earlier mystery was that the rank and file would not even have known of its existence. Those who had been accepted for the higher levels would have been true to their vows of secrecy and would have guarded the knowledge from everyone, even the lower-level members. The truth would never have been spoken of, other than inside the walls of a properly convened Chapter meeting. The Cathar Bon Hommes were so committed to their ideas that they went willingly into the flames, and it is reasonable to assume that those who promoted the mediaeval mystery would have been similarly disposed.

The brethren of the mystery would have guaranteed the privacy of their meetings against outsiders by guarding the doors and carefully blocking up every crack and opening against eavesdroppers. This is exactly what history has recorded of the Knights Templar. Likewise the lodges of operative stonemasons too were obsessive about the privacy of their meetings, and barred all but the initiated from taking part. With their initiations, passwords and means of recognition, the stonemasons structured their ceremonies around the guardianship of their arcane knowledge, and the Craft inherited that system. Freemasonry today preserves those methods of exclusion as an inherent part of its culture. We cannot see the secrets looking back, just the ceremonies used to secure the lodges, but that ritual security is itself evidence of a continuity of something over the centuries.

What we will discover in the next part of the book gives form to the metaphors of the lodge room, and lays bare the truly ancient nature of its allegories. When I reveal the real meanings of those metaphors, it will become clear why both the stonemasons and the Templars that went before them were obsessive about the privacy of their meetings.

The choice of the Templars as the proposed bridge between the teachings of the Ikhwan and the lodges of stonemasons in this thesis was not arbitrary, because at the outset of this quest we had seen how the knights are regarded by many as playing a part in the origin of Freemasonry. I have shown that the Templars were ideally positioned to have absorbed the ethos of the Ikhwan, and indeed have suggested that the bloody sacking of Jerusalem would have encouraged its adoption. Also if there was a transfer of ideas from the Holy Land to Europe, some organisation that had a presence in both places must have been responsible for it. We had noted earlier that the stonemasons themselves were semi-literate and therefore unlikely to have had the capacity to imbue their rituals with esoteric notions. If the Scottish Templars had become stonemasons on the destruction of their order, and had taken their mystery tradition with them, then the problem of how stonemasons' lodges carried abstruse notions is resolved.

The difficulty for modern researchers is that both these groups, Templars and stonemasons alike, were living, breathing organisations in their own right. Outwardly the Templars were exactly what has been recorded of them, and the lodges of stonemasons were exactly what we, looking back, see. But that does not preclude there being a hidden side to their existence that was not visible to the outside world then, and so is not visible now.

Though I have portrayed the Templars as secretly carrying a heretical doctrine, I have not as yet offered evidence that they did. We have not yet looked deeply enough at the symbols employed by the mediaeval mystery tradition and latterly by Freemasonry to fully understand their nature, but when we do, we will return to Templar symbolism, to show that it carries exactly the very same allusions. For now, however, we will speculate on how the mystery tradition could have survived the fall of the Templars, and made its way into the lodges of stonemasons in Britain and Ireland.

CHAPTER 11

IF THE KNIGHTS of the Temple had indeed formed a new version of the mystery as outlined above and promoted it whilst they were in a position to do so, then their downfall in 1307 would have removed that ability and forced a re-evaluation of their *modus operandi*. They would have been forced to find another home for their rituals if those rites were to survive, and where better to take them than into the lodges of operative masons with whom they had been in close contact for almost two centuries? It is very likely that some of those stonemasons already comprised part of the group that followed the mystery, so the move to their lodges could have been planned long before the order fell.

The Templars were a body of men whose previous lives had been turned upside down with the suppression of their order in 1307 and who had to invent new lives for themselves. Though they had been noble and mighty warriors at the height of the Crusades, on the destruction of their order they were knights no more, and their options would have been somewhat limited. Had they become working stonemasons and used the closed lodge environment to continue their labours, the mobility of the industry would have enabled them to travel between sites and spread the mystery anywhere masons worked.

For several hundred years the craft of the stonemason continued to flourish, well able to promote the mystery, but there came a time when stone-working faded, replaced by cheaply produced and more easily handled clay brick, reducing those lodges to mere shadows of their former selves. They would still however have been driven from within by their esoteric component, and in such circumstances it is easy to see why they would have invited non-operatives into their midst - a fact which is not otherwise easy to explain. Perhaps the very simplicity of the stonemasons' attitudes to the world, and their Spartan lives, contributed to the survival of the tradition intact, because had they been more educated they would undoubtedly have found the need to analyse and improve on it, as was to happen later in the 18th century, almost to the loss of the ancient meanings.

It would have taken quite a feat of memory for simple working men to remember complex rituals with deep esoteric meanings, and this brings us to mnemonics, or the Art of Memory, which was an intrinsic part of the early Craft. Mnemonics was a method from Classical Antiquity for improving memory, and involved, in the case of Freemasonry, the association of things to be remembered with the layout and structural details of a building. Associations of that which was to be remembered were made primarily with the rooms, then on a more detailed level with the architectural details, objects within the room, and finishes. By mentally wandering through the building and remembering what had been associated with each object, minute details could be recalled from the depths of the mind.

The Art of Memory was re-established in the Renaissance, and was closely associated with Hermeticism. It also carried overtones of the divine, and of striving for perfection. Professor James Stevens Curl, in his book *The Art and Architecture of Freemasonry* has this to say about it… 'In Scotland, Fellow Crafts were not admitted to the Freemasons' Lodge without "pruife of memorie and art of craft". Thus proficiency in mnemonic technique was regarded as an essential part of the Freemason's skills… Esoteric knowledge, too, was not safe in the hands of the ignorant or the profane, so it was safer for initiates to remember such material, possibly using emblems as aids, rather than to commit secrets to the page.'

This technique is perfectly suited to teaching complex rituals that contained esoteric knowledge, and that it was so closely associated with Freemasonry in Scotland in its earliest days is fascinating in considering the thesis presented here. If it was necessary for Masons to remember convoluted and abstruse rites in such a way, it hints that those who used the technique may have been ignorant of the deeper allusions in their rituals. But ignorant or not, by utilising the Art of Memory, the rites would survive regardless.

There are various admonitions given to the candidate throughout the three degrees of Craft Masonry that are in my opinion rather heavy-handed and perhaps even unnecessary for mere workers in stone. Articles like having to warn brethren of impending danger, needing to use complex signals to vouch their status to others, charging them not to take advantage of the female relatives of those they lodged with, and exempting them from attending their lodge meeting if imprisonment prohibited them from doing so.

Though stonemasons had more freedom to move around than most others in the feudal system, many of the projects they worked on lasted for their entire working life. Travel was not that common, though to listen to the Masonic admonitions, you would think stonemasons spent their lives like virtual nomads. The exemption from attending lodge meetings if imprisoned is particularly odd; both for mediaeval stonemasons and more modern Freemasons, but it we look at it from the viewpoint of the teachers of the secret mystery moving around the land, we start to see a reason for such an indulgence.

The work of building in stone took the lodges around the country, and would have provided a number of 'safe' environments in cities and towns, similar to the Commanderies and chapter houses the Templars had possessed whilst still an order. Those teachers of the mystery, who possibly did not even work in stone themselves, would have travelled from town to town, needing a system of vouching to enable them to be received among men who had never met them before and who were ever-fearful of infiltration by the Inquisition. They would also have needed accommodation, food and money to help them onwards to the next lodge in the next town or city, and would also have had to be trusted not to abuse the hospitality of those they lodged with, particularly in the matter of sexual intimacy with family members. They would also have been expected to warn their brethren of impending danger in the form of the Inquisition, when as ordinary stonemasons, the most danger they should expect is falling masonry, badly erected scaffolding or an ill-tempered overseer. All these points are covered explicitly in Masonic obligations, and whilst the charges seem excessive in terms of mere workers in stone going about their business, they are perfectly tailored for the itinerant promoters of the secret mystery tradition outlined above.

Whilst in the early days of the Craft it was rigidly enforced that brethren must attend their lodge meetings, and indeed they were fined heavily for not doing so, one of the reasons accepted for non-attendance was imprisonment, and this is even specified in the wording of the admonition to the candidate. Whereas a prison sentence would today bring shame and disgrace and the likely withdrawal or expulsion from the Order, if seen in the context of apprehension by the Inquisition, it would be quite the opposite. The possibility of seizure was part and parcel of following the secret tradition and it is easy to see why such an exception in relation to imprisonment would be made, and also that no stigma would have been attached to it.

In such conditions as I have outlined here, the mystery could have maintained itself indefinitely until the 17th century, when it remained as an assortment of ancient stonemasons' lodges dotted over the British Isles, some of them still quite active, others less so. As we will see in later chapters, whilst the Templars survived elsewhere, the dynamic that drove the Mystery of Christ lay in the British Isles, providing the basis that gave rise to the Craft.

Perhaps rather than there being a sudden influx of non-operative outsiders within the time frame of the 17th century, it was the gradual fading of the operative element that caused the lodges to become purely speculative. I suggest that both operatives and speculatives had been there all along and that over time the operative element simply faded, to a greater or lesser degree, depending on the state of the stone working industry in each area. This scenario certainly goes further than more traditional theories in explaining the disparate and conflicting early reports of the state of the Craft in the years prior to 1717 when the so called transition from operative to speculative is believed to have occurred. It explains why lodges were spread evenly over the entire British Isles, and why some of those lodges seem to be exclusively speculative at an early date whilst others are demonstrably operative, and are only seen to be admitting non-operatives relatively late.

So why did the secretive mystery change in the 17th century? Why do we start to see evidence of its existence? I would suggest that the change was in the world outside and not something that happened within the Craft at all, and was a gradual process that had begun some time previously. After the Reformation had lessened the threat of heresy charges, the lodges simply became less guarded about their labours, and those who were initiated felt more relaxed about recording their membership. This would explain the gradual references we start to see, where for the first time, people like Elias Ashmole recorded their initiations in their diaries and elsewhere. The Reformation had greatly reduced the power of the Church, and offered the Craft a much less restrictive environment in which to follow its path, and so it in turn started to allow knowledge of its own existence to filter out for the first time. In addition, few were literate in the earlier years and it may only have been as literacy improved and the Enlightenment started to give intelligent men the confidence to change the world that knowledge of what had previously been a closely guarded secret gradually started to seep out. An example of this is the gradual emergence of the '*Mason's Word.*'

From the 1630s onwards we find the Mason's Word mentioned in Scotland or in connection with Scotland, and it is usually attached to esoteric notions like 'second sight'. The *Muses Threnodie* of 1638, a poem by Henry Adamson of Perth, contains the words...

'For we be the brethren of the Rosie Cross,
We have the Mason Word and second sight,
Things for to come we can foretell aright.'

The Mason's Word was a peculiarly Scottish notion at the time - yet more evidence for the origin of the Craft there - and during the next quarter century was mentioned with increasing regularity. It is testimony to the seriousness with which those entrusted with the 'word' took their oath to keep it secret that though outsiders knew of its existence, they did not know what the word was or what it meant, specifically. It is also worth noting that among those who held the word, which can only refer to those initiated into the esoteric secrets of the speculative Craft, we find many Christian ministers. This suggests that the esoteric tenets of the Craft were not only quasi-religious, but were not considered beyond the pale, in terms of heresy, by those who knew their nature. It was only outsiders who projected sinister overtones on to possession of the word.

Professor David Stevenson, in his excellent book *The Origins of Freemasonry*, relates that a young minister, James Ainslie, put himself forward for the post of minister in Minto, Roxburghshire in 1652. The presbytery, on checking his credentials, noted that he was in possession of the Mason's Word. Several presbyters voiced concern over the matter, and extensive enquiries were made. The findings are interesting, for it was found that 'ther is neither sinne nor scandale in that word because in the purest of tymes of this kirk, maisons having that word have been and daylie are elders in our sessions...'

So what became of the earlier mystery? How and why did it fade to the point that it had to be 'rediscovered' in the 17th Century?

As the work of the stonemasons dried up the active promotion of the mystery would have ground to a halt with the advent of brick becoming a major construction method. The tradition would have continued, then, in separate cells, that were isolated from one another. Consequently it would have been inevitable that discrepancies would have crept into the rituals of the various pockets of the tradition, no longer having a mobile teaching base to keep them fresh. Perhaps over the years interest in the mystery waned, and it could have been during this time that the original, secret meanings of the rites were lost. Nothing lasts forever, and understanding of the archaic origin could have simply faded away, leaving only the rites themselves to stand against the march of time.

We all remember rhymes teachers dinned into us to help us remember, but learning by rote does not guarantee understanding of what has been learnt. The rhyme remains but the understanding fades, and so it could have been with the mystery, which lost track of its past because the industry to which it attached itself fell into decline, causing its active promotion to grind to a halt. As the Middle Ages wore on the original meanings of the rituals were simply forgotten as the train ran out of steam. Each ancient lodge would have been true to the precepts and ethos of the general mystery, but the more esoteric meanings may have fallen by the wayside, until the revival of the mystery that occurred in the 17th century, when the newcomers extracted whatever meaning they could from what they found.

The foregoing lays out a possible path of the mystery from an origin in the Holy Land during the Crusades, and its transference to Scotland by the Templars. A large point in favour of it being the Templars rather than another group is that with them the mystery would have lost its host in 1307 when the order was crushed, and this gives us a perfectly reasonable explanation of how the esoterica came to be present in the stonemasons' lodges. The lodges the redundant knights would have joined are also in exactly the same region where the Craft emerged from four hundred years later. It also explains the presence in the rituals of those stonemasons' lodges of the deeply mysterious notions that historians generally cannot attribute to those simple working men.

The above offers an explanation of how the structure and esoteric teachings of the pagan mysteries of the ancient world could have found their way back to Europe, into stonemasonry, and on through to Freemasonry. What we haven't looked at yet is why this tradition came to Scotland, for the question of why the Craft emerged there is undoubtedly the biggest question in all of Masonic history. Chapter two identified the sun as being the focus of the rituals of the modern lodge room – so it seems reasonable to take the sun as a starting point in our search for a reason.

At the outset of the book I showed that the sun's rising and setting points on the solstices form a true square, or perhaps more pertinently a true cross, in southern Scotland. As we move into the next part of the book we will look at the importance of the sun to ancient Man, and seek indicators that the true cross of the sun was indeed known to those who went before us.

In the course of that exploration we will also examine the development of Christianity in Ireland and Scotland. Since those lands remained outside Roman influence, largely not having succumbed to Rome's legions, old customs may have persisted there as Christianity came to the west. Where the Roman influence had perhaps predisposed England towards acceptance of the Pauline Christianity that emanated from Rome, the ancient ways appear to have lingered in the Celtic lands, and we will see in the next part of the book that the Christianity that flourished there was liberally sprinkled with pagan observances.

Those earlier peoples venerated the sun as the ultimate deity. If crusaders brought a tradition to western Europe that regarded aspects of Christianity as allegory, the natural home for that tradition would perhaps be in those lands where the light of the ancient pagan ways had not entirely gone out. If those initiated into the mystery of Christ had come to regard the true cross of Jesus as an allegory that was based on the cross formed by the sun everywhere on earth, they would perhaps have been drawn towards the place where the sun forms its own true cross on the landscape.

In part two of the book we will examine the ancient's understanding of the sun's cross in general, and then focus on the place where it forms a true cross - Scotland. By doing so we will discover why the Mystery of Christ that was born in the East was drawn to make its base in the Scottish countryside around Edinburgh.

THE CRAFT AND THE CROSS

PART TWO

THE SUN'S TRUE CROSS

THE CRAFT AND THE CROSS

CHAPTER 12

THE SUN WAS all-important in the lives of the people who inhabited these islands in antiquity. It warmed the ground, enabling plants to be grown in a rhythmic cycle of death and re-birth which was repeated year after year.

Today, we are well aware of the laws of nature that govern our world. We know that the sun, one of over a hundred billion stars in our own galaxy alone, is about half way through its life cycle, and will burn for around another five billion years, driven by the complex engine of nuclear fusion.

Our ancient forbears had no such certainties.

The sun's annual rhythm saw it rise high in the summer, giving long, bright, warm days, and sink low in the winter, giving shorter, colder days. The visual manifestation of this rhythm for the ancient peoples was the movement of the sunrises and sunsets across the horizon from high summer to mid-winter. We are no longer dependent on the changes of the seasons, nor constrained to rise with the sun and go to bed when it sets as they were in times past. When it gets dark early we simply put on a light, and when we get cold, we turn up the heating a few degrees. The seasons are now barely noticed as they pass, but it was not so for the ancients who occupied this land before us.

The four main points of the sun's movements through the year, the solstices and the equinoxes, coincided with events in the cycle of growth and death of vegetation which were vitally important in people's lives. The winter solstice marked the sun's nadir, when it triumphed over the darkness and once more started its slow ascent of the heavens. For the early peoples this time would have been full of fear and doubt, and of course hope that the sun would indeed triumph and be reborn. It is understandable, therefore, that they would have made offerings and said prayers to assist the sun-disc in its battle with the forces of darkness at this time. Their spiritual lives revolved around the various stages of the sun's year, and their celebrations took place when the sun reached certain points on the horizon. The massive stones and mounds they erected in honour of the sun are a measure of the awe in which they held its burning orb.

Newgrange, on a bend of the river Boyne in the Republic of Ireland, encapsulates perfectly the ancients' awe of the sun. Built around 3200BCE it predates the Pyramids of the Giza Plateau by some seven hundred years, and has its entrance and passage to the inner chamber perfectly aligned to the rising point of the winter solstice sun. It appears in older books as a passage grave, but is more recently understood as being conceived to honour the sun at the moment of its triumph over the cold darkness of winter.

Ruinous and overgrown for four thousand years, it was rediscovered in 1699 when a landowner sent a work-team to gather stone for a new road. Clearing nettles and bracken from what was then a tree clad hill, the work stopped when massive boulders with ancient runic designs of spirals and diamonds were found. By good fortune, an archaeologist was touring Ireland at that time. He was summoned, and when he opened the passageway and crawled into the inner chamber, he was its first human visitor in four thousand years. It was he who classified it as a grave, and even today the label sticks. It would be in the 1960s, when the site was further cleared for restoration of the monument, that the true meaning of the structure would be revealed. Above the entrance was a lintel, and above that was an oblong opening that was there to allow the sun to penetrate to the very deepest recesses of the inner chamber at dawn on the winter solstice. So rather than the mound's purpose being about death as a tomb, it was instead about life, and as Man penetrates Woman in the act of procreation, the sun penetrated Mother Earth through this opening. The symbolism appears to be that as the union of male and female produced a child, the union of the sun and the earth initiated the new year and brought the possibility of new life to the fields, a new crop, and the continuation of life.

The sun-window at Newgrange was unique when it was built by the people of the Boyne Valley, and was invented without recourse to anything in existence before. When today one clambers into that sacred place built two hundred generations ago by people about whom we otherwise know nothing, one can only wonder at their ingenuity and dedication to the task of building a two-hundred-thousand-ton mound

around their special place. They worshipped the sun from that ridge for a thousand years, but around 2200BCE they disappeared completely from the historical record. It is intriguing that during the time of its occupancy those greatest achievements of Ancient Man, the great pyramids on the Giza plateau which are also wrongly regarded as tombs, were also built. Is there a possibility that those who worshipped the sun in these cold, cloudy lands went south; in search of somewhere the sun shone all the time?

Although Newgrange itself is aligned to the winter solstice, other ancient mounds on the same bend in the river Boyne were laid out to honour the sun at different times of the year; those other times being important in peoples' lives too. The Mound of Knowth with its east-west alignment honours the equinoxes, and the rising and setting of the sun on those days. The spring equinox on the 21st of March was around the time when new shoots first nosed their way above the hard, cold ground, initiating the new growing cycle. So the spring equinox has therefore been associated with birth and re-birth since before history was recorded - not only of plants, but of the gods who were associated with the growth cycle as well.

A quarter year later, Midsummer's Day marked the pinnacle of the cycle of the sun, and was honoured by the lighting of Baal-fires that brought the brightness and warmth of the sun to the night skies. High summer was also a time for contemplation of the turning of the days, the ripening of crops, and the hard, backbreaking work that went with it. The autumn equinox coincided with the end of the growing season, and marked the harvest celebrations when thanks were given for the bounty of Mother Earth. After months of hard toil in the fields the harvest was safely stowed away, weighed and apportioned out to last through the upcoming winter. The measuring of the harvest was equated with the scales that were used for that measurement, the scales also being representative of the balancing of the two halves of the year that happened at that time. The autumnal equinox, which occurred during the harvest, marked the balance point between the light half of the year that had just passed and the dark half that was just starting, so it is no coincidence that Libra, the Scales, signifying that balance of nature, was associated with the equinox itself.

Confronted with the death and decay of vegetation all around there was a sadness for the year passed, but counterbalanced with a joy that it was merely a part of the process of death and rebirth. Many of the stories of the gods of ancient times had them dying at the September equinox with the death of the light half of the year, and passing for a time into the Underworld before being reborn half a year later in the spring. Death and later rebirth has therefore been associated with the equinoxes since pre-history, and this fact will become hugely important later, when we look at the Masonic 3rd Degree.

The quarters of the year and the celebrations they heralded linked the lives of men with the seasons and the movements of the sun in a very tangible and deeply felt way. The celebrations were not obscure rituals plucked out of the ether, carried out on arbitrary days that had no relevance; rather they were at the very centre of life for the common people and therefore made perfect sense to them. At every notable point of the sun's year the people held ceremonies that gave thanks and encouragement to the sun as it passed from one season to the next.

Services of thanksgiving in which they thanked Mother Earth for her bounty would have taken many forms. In some cultures special veneration was reserved for the last stalks of corn to be hewn from the fields, which were woven into the figure of a man, dressed in fine clothes and given pride of place at the harvest celebrations. At festival's end, the mannequin was returned to the fields and ritually burned with the stubble, providing enrichment of the soil for the following year's growing season, and closing the book on that part of the cycle of life.

If plants died only to be reborn later, surely then mankind would be reborn also, so the notion of the continuation of the soul was formed from the observation of nature and its ability to replenish itself. A woodland burned down, and in its burning enriched the ground for new

 wood to grow all the quicker in its place. The skeletal head of the Green Man found peeking from the stonework of many early Christian churches with leaves curling from mouth and eye sockets was a human manifestation of this same re-generation, where the body rots and dissolves into the earth that receives it on death. It isn't hard to observe, even to-day that the patch of ground where an animal dies and decays into the soil will become rich and verdant for years to come. In merely observing this, without needing to understand the chemistry involved, the ancients could see that on death the body replenishes Mother Earth with nutrients that assist her fecundity in the future. The new tendrils growing from the eyes-sockets and mouth of the Green Man perfectly demonstrate this re-birth that is a natural part of the process that is death.

It is a fact that the Green Man is not actually an ancient pagan symbol, for its first appearance outside Classical Antiquity is in Christian churches. But as we noted above it refers to a pagan concept that has nothing to do with Christianity, so why therefore is it found in its churches? The answer to that goes to the very heart of the thesis presented here, for it would have been used to draw into the fold those of a pagan mindset whose previous spirituality was focussed on the yearly death and rebirth of the world around them.

So the pagan peoples who were our forbears had an affinity with the earth and the seasons, and gave thanks in celebrations that were drawn directly from the interaction of nature on their lives, and so those festivals had real significance for them.

Then came Christianity.

When the story of Jesus and his sacrifice for the redemption of man came to the British Isles it was devoid of sacred days and observances. Where the paganism it sought to supplant had a long-established calendar of holy days that were dedicated to a plethora of gods and goddesses, Christianity had nothing – not even a date for its saviour's birth and death. The new faith solved this by gradually taking over the sacred days and sites of the pagans, and giving them Christian connotations that were irrelevant to the earlier faith. There had been a time in the very early days of Christianity when the appropriation of pagan dates was frowned upon by the Church Fathers. The scholar Origen around the beginning of the 3rd century preached that it was wrong to honour Jesus in the same way that Pharaoh and Herod had been honoured, because birthdays were for pagan gods. Within a hundred and fifty years, however, Jesus' birth had become firmly linked to the winter solstice festival, prompting the comment, attributed by many to St Augustine of Hippo, 'we hold this day holy, not like the pagans because it is the birth of the sun, but because of him who made it'.

The pagan world had been full to bursting with a plethora of gods and observances that appealed to the populace on many levels, whereas Christianity in its purest form was austere in comparison. The only way the Christian Church could hope to win peoples' hearts was to give them a Christianised version of what they already had, and so pagan sites and festivals were syncretised into the emerging Christian faith. At the start this was claimed to be solely on the grounds that it was necessary to consecrate the sites that had previously seen the idolatrous worship of false gods, but this was no more than a deliberate obfuscation of the real reason, which was the inability of Christianity to wean the people from such ingrained traditions.

St. Justus, who died in 627, was one of the companions of Archbishop Augustine of Canterbury who was so instrumental in the conversion of the Britons from paganism, and having written to the

Pope St. Gregory the Great for advice on how to best achieve this, he received a reply that said the following. 'When you are with our brother Augustine, tell him that after long consideration and careful examination of the English question, I judged that you should not destroy the pagan temples, but only the idols in them. You should purify them with holy water, take the idols from the altar, and put relics of Saints there. For if these temples are well built, let them pass from the worship of the Devil to the service of the true God. If the people see that the places to which they are accustomed are conserved, they will go to them more readily. And since they are used to sacrificing bulls to the Devil there, some solemn ceremony related to the martyrs whose relics are there should replace this. You should raise tents around the temples transformed into churches and celebrate the feast there with meals. Instead of sacrificing animals to the Devil, you should kill them for the people to eat and give thanks to God, Who gave them the food. This way, apart from the sensible manifestations of joy, they can more easily be introduced to the spiritual joys [of the Faith]. For it is impossible to detach all the customs at once from hardened spirits. By moving slowly, one goes far.' Quote from R. Morris, *Churches in the Landscape*, 1989

And this was from the very pen of the Vicar of Christ himself. I would particularly draw attention to the words 'some solemn ceremony related to the martyrs whose relics are there should replace this,' for there is no better evidence of the arbitrary nature of the Christian ceremonies which replaced the old pagan ones than these few words. It did not matter what ritual was put in place of the bull sacrifice, as long as it could be seen to be demonstrably Christian.

Ancient symbols, too, were retained as part of the new faith. Again and again, existing pagan icons and observances were reassigned Christian meanings that varied only slightly from the originals. Sacred pools and springs that had been governed by Celtic gods were transformed into holy wells and dedicated to obscure Christian mystics who shared many similarities with the original Celtic gods they sought to replace. Although people still continued to bring gifts to the spirit of the waters that magically welled from the ground, those gifts were now received in the name of the Christian saint. Monasteries were built near or in many cases directly on top of the sites where the sun had been venerated for thousands of years, and saints with names similar to the local pagan deities were credited with founding those sites. In allowing the names of the deities and the dates upon which they were worshipped to remain virtually unchanged, the transition to Christianity was effected with little disruption and gradually gained acceptance. Not only were pagan gods reborn in the Christian world as saints, but the days upon which the new saints were worshipped remained practically identical to the days the old pagan gods had been venerated for millennia.

A particularly good example of this process is the transformation of the Celtic goddess Brigit into a Christian saint. Known in Ireland as Brigit or Brid, as Brigantia in Roman Britain, Bride in Scotland and Briganda in Brittany, the goddess was venerated by the lighting of fires to mark her feast day on the 1st of February. When Christianity was introduced she became St Brigid, a miracle-working abbess who became second only to St. Patrick in the hierarchy of the Celtic Christian Church. Legend has it that her consecration was so charged with holiness that the bishop who ordained her became 'intoxicated with the grace of God' and ordained her Ireland's only female bishop. Unremarkably, her festival in the Christian calendar was also fixed as the 1st of February, the same day upon which the Celtic Goddess who preceded her had been honoured for thousands of years.

The Celtic goddess had traditionally been honoured at a shrine with a perpetual flame at Kildare, which was attended by virgin priestesses. When Christianised, the shrine became a convent and the virgin priestesses became nuns, but the perpetual flame was allowed to burn for another five hundred years until the local bishop deemed it too pagan and extinguished its ancient light around the end of the 12th Century. The 12th Century was a time of enormous religious change in Britain and Ireland, and will be referred to often throughout the rest of the book.

Few stories better demonstrate how the Christianising process in Europe gradually weaned pagans from their ancient ways than the above tale of St. Brigid. In allowing the flame to burn for over five hundred years, the Church permitted the old ways to continue within the Christian church, allowing the people to identify the now Christian shrine with its pagan past, and forcing no great shift in belief. When the time was right however, when the original meaning was finally forgotten, the flame was extinguished, and in doing so the last vestige of the pagan origin of the religious observance was removed. Now, eight hundred years later, nothing remains but the Christian aspect.

As with many of the early saints, no contemporary evidence of St. Brigid exists, simply tales of her miracles and wonderful works, written centuries later by those who adored her. Like other instances of the Christianisation of pagan ideas, then, we can see St. Brigid as a construct - a Christian version of what the people already had in the Celtic world. Whether a person existed in reality around whom the myth grew is of no importance, for the real person's life would have been so altered and embellished by legend as to render the donor completely superfluous.

Symbols carry different meanings for different people, and this fact was instrumental in the success of Christianity over the pagan beliefs that preceded it. What one person sees when he or she looks at a symbol may be completely different from what the person standing beside them sees. The Swastika can be found on early Christian crosses in Ireland, and has been a deeply sacred symbol to Hindus and others for five thousand years. It invokes altogether different feelings, however, in those who suffered under Nazism in the 20th century.

Many modern popular television programmes have reached cult status because they appeal to different audiences. Shows like *The Simpsons* make the youngest children laugh, and yet the appeal of the show does not stop with the slapstick that amuses the young. Teenagers 'get' the more adult references which pass straight over the heads of their younger siblings, whilst beyond that, adults find subtle references to the icons of their youth that teenagers are unaware of. Likewise the humour itself is multi-layered, with obvious jokes which are understood by even the dullest people sitting cheek-by-jowl with subtle puns which take a little more thought. In such a way the humour is designed to appeal to many audiences and so is successful and enduring.

It was precisely the same duality of meaning which enabled the symbols of both paganism and Christianity to blend into one, and in doing so eased the conversion of the masses from their pagan ways. When the people of Britain who had worshipped Brigit as a Celtic goddess for many centuries were offered St. Brigid instead, and found she possessed many of the same attributes and characteristics as the Celtic goddess, it was not such a wrench as it would have been had the worship of the goddess simply been outlawed.

The most enduring symbol of St. Brigid is the St. Brigid's Cross also known as a Corn Dolly. It is thought to have been woven from last straw of the season to protect the homestead 'til the following spring, hundreds if not thousands of years before the saint is supposed to have lived. It is therefore demonstrably not Christian. Like the swastika and many other variants, the four points allude to the sun on the solstices, and the cross they form to the crossing of the sun on the equinox. The sun-gods of old died on the same crossing of the seasons with the vegetation at that time of the year, so we can see why it was an ancient practice that was easily converted to a Christian emblem.

The design also incorporates a square at the centre of the cross, a fact that will become more relevant to our quest as we continue. It was fully seven hundred years later that this pagan cross took on Christian connotations because of the crucifixion, and the Celtic goddess after whom it was named was lost into the Christian pantheon of saints. Memory fades with time, as surely as old family photographs become pictures of strangers when parents pass away, and time was one thing

the Church had plenty of. For many years, many lifetimes even, the faithful would still have seen their old Celtic goddess in the references to St. Brigid that adorned the newly Christianised religious sites, and the Corn Dolly would have retained its ancient meaning for centuries before it inexorably became the Christian cross. Over countless generations the original goddess slowly faded from memory, and eventually the Christian saint was all that was left.

Whatever deep-seated spiritual nourishment had been derived from the adoration of the Celtic goddess was now drawn from St. Brigid, so the people still had their icon, and the dictates of the Christian Church had been satisfied. Those who wished to see her as Christian could do so, whilst those for whom she was pagan were satisfied too. This 'engineering' of perception was repeated over and over again with other observances, and was how the continent of Europe was weaned from paganism to Christianity. The same absorption of the past is visible in many other ostensibly Christian observances.

The spring equinox and its celebration of re-birth became Easter in the Christian calendar, with the pagan festival of Oestre even giving its name to the Christian version of the celebration. The date of the festival varies from year to year, with the date falling on the first Sunday after the first full moon after the spring equinox. No satisfactory explanation exists for this oddball way of determining the most important festival in the Christian calendar - the death and resurrection of Jesus - other than that its link to the equinox proves its pagan origin in the veneration of the sun. The celebration is, of course, based on the Jewish feast of Passover, but that too is linked to the equinox.

We have Easter Eggs and Good Friday's hot cross buns that are thoroughly pagan too; the cross on the buns originally referring to the cross of the sun. The Easter Egg is now far removed from a religious custom, but it once was very much a religious observance. In ancient times, in almost all cultures across the world, the egg was a symbol of the universe, and was venerated as a sign of spring's regeneration of the earth. In bygone times a hard-boiled egg was the first 'fat or fleshy nourishment' taken after the abstinence of Lent. Eggs were taken to the church by the head of the family to be blessed and have the sign of the cross made over them before being taken home and eaten.

Easter coincided with the crossing point of the year, when the sun passed from the southern hemisphere into the northern. Making the sign of the cross over the eggs at Easter, given the egg's association with rebirth, is therefore a clear reference to regeneration of life that was the pagan veneration of the sun.

Croagh Patrick in Co. Mayo in the west of Ireland is a strikingly conical peak that dominates the south of the county, and is the most famous pilgrimage site on the whole island. The mountain is held in reverence to this day, and can be seen as the Irish equivalent of the Jewish Mt. Sinai or the Greeks' Mt. Olympus.

Traditionally St. Patrick lived on the mountain, exposed to the elements, for forty days and nights, battling and eventually overcoming the demons that were there. More prosaically he was making a public demonstration of the power of Christianity over the pagan gods of old, a fact which inadvertently reveals that the site was indeed sacred since earlier times. The peak is climbed on Garland Sunday, the last Sunday in July. The date gives us the true significance of the observance; for it is the Sunday closest to the Celtic festival of Lughnasadh on August 1st. Lugh was the greatest of Irish sun-gods, so the purpose of the veneration of the mountain becomes clear.

At the summit is a modern Catholic oratory, a focus for today's pilgrims, some of whom make the arduous, 2000 foot climb barefoot, or if feeling particularly penitent, on their knees. The peak was excavated in the mid 1990s, and the remains of a Christian oratory were discovered dating from the earliest days of Patrick's Christian mission. Even older, was found the remains of a Celtic enclosure from pre-Christian times encircling the summit.

It is thought that the veneration of the mountain is very old indeed. Proof of this came to light in the 1990s when a very interesting alignment between the sun, the mountain, and an ancient standing stone was discovered by amateur historian and archaeologist, Gerry Bracken, whose discovery was covered in the journal of the Westport Historical Society, Cathair na Mart, 1993.

SETTING SUN ROLLS DOWN CROAGH PATRICK

18TH APRIL & 24TH AUGUST

Mr. Bracken lived locally, and though it took many years to find, he noticed that when viewed from a particular place to the east of the mountain, the setting sun first stands momentarily at the very top of the peak, then 'rolls' right down the mountain's north side. The position of the sun in the sky changes daily, and there are only two days a year that the 'rolling' happens - the 18th of April and the 24th of August. What is interesting is that these two dates, when combined with the winter solstice, divide the year roughly into thirds. The date in August is particularly interesting, for it was traditionally the start of the Irish harvest. This last fact is probably why ancient man was drawn to where the phenomenon occurs, for in the days before calendars, Man depended on solar or astral occurrences to know when to plant his grain and when to harvest.

What is even more interesting is that the position one must stand at to view this phenomenon is an ancient megalith known as the Boheh Stone. Regarded as one of the most decorated Bronze Age stones in the British Isles, there are over a hundred cup and ring marks over the various facets of the huge stone. Since it is from this stone that the phenomenon of the sun rolling down Croagh Patrick's flank is visible, the Bronze Age markings on it

show how old the veneration of the sun is in relation to the mountain. The stone was not erected as were many other decorated stones in Ireland, but is an outcrop of living rock. It was therefore just a coincidence that the solar phenomenon was visible from there, but did ancient Man perhaps see what he perceived as the hand of God in it's being there. And did the appearance of the sun at the very apex of the mountain on the day they started to reap the summer's harvest cause them to climb the peak in ritual veneration? Was it from that time that the mountain became the object of the pilgrimage that survives to this day?

Interest in the Boheh Stone deepens when we learn that it is part of the St. Patrick's pilgrimage route that starts at Ballintubber Abbey to the east of it and ends with the pinnacle of Croagh Patrick to its west. Why would mediaeval pilgrims include in their pilgrimage trail a pagan stone that is now known to be associated with the veneration of the sun if it was not the continuation into the Christian era of something that was thousands of years older? If true, then whilst totally unaware of the fact, those who today toil up Croagh Patrick in honour of the Christian saint are, like those who follow so many other observances, keeping alive the veneration of the sun.

We earlier noted the Masonic veneration of the two Saints John and their link with the two solstices. St. John the Evangelist is also linked to the symbol of an eagle, and it is telling that Croagh Patrick's old name, before the saint Christianised it, was Cruachán Aigle - Eagle Mountain. And the ancient Baal fires which had been lit on mountain tops since pre-history became known, in Ireland at least, as St. John's Fires – an obvious Christianising of the past but one which nevertheless hints again at the central role of the saint we have encountered so often before.

Another manifestation of sun-veneration that became Christianised and forgot its past can be found in the magnificent brass Bible-stand in the shape of an eagle that adorns many of the more prosperous churches. The eagle, which even in Christian lore refers to St. John the Evangelist, would originally have alluded to the summer solstice. That the lectern is brass further alludes to the shining sun, so on a second  count this pivotal piece of church furniture relates to the sun. A third interesting detail is that the eagle stands atop a globe. In Freemasonry, the globe of the sun sits atop a pillar that alludes to the solstice. Here in this symbolism from the heart of the Christian church we find the eagle of St. John standing on a globe that can only be the sun.

The list of pagan gods and goddesses reborn in the Christian world as saints is almost endless, with few dates or saints in the Christian calendar whose origin cannot be traced to an earlier pagan observance,

In Mediterranean lands the festival of Bacchus, the Greek god of wine and revelry was venerated at the completion of the grape harvest around the first quarter of October. The pagan festival of Bacchus became the Christian feast of St. Baccus, whose festival was fixed in the Catholic calendar as the 6th of October.

Around the middle of February was the celebration of Lupercalia, a pagan fertility festival, when all and sundry entered into an erotic celebration of sensual pleasure. It was traditional for tickets with boys and girls names to be exchanged for a similar purpose as car-keys being placed in a fruit-bowl at a 70s swingers' party. This was deemed unacceptable among Christians so was outlawed by Pope Gelasius at the end of the 5th century. A Christian celebration then developed, associated with the martyred Bishop Valentine. He was chosen as the patron saint of the Christianised festival because of a tradition that he fell in love with his gaoler's daughter and wrote her a note before his execution, which he signed 'from your Valentine'. Across Europe various alternatives to the wanton lovemaking were offered, including one which substituted the names of the boys and girls names on the tickets with the names of saints, with the suggestion that those saints' lives be contemplated and emulated instead of sex. Hmmmm! It is little wonder this didn't catch on, but gradually the ancient celebration took on a more acceptable and Christian face. That lovers still exchange cards one and a half thousand years later demonstrates how the old ways still remain with us, and that our pagan past is still buried deep and influences us today.

Paganism is a vague, general term, applied to all non-Christian beliefs across the world. The pre-Christian beliefs referred to above have ostensibly been gone for one and a half thousand years, but even today retain a grip on our collective subconscious. Although the feast-days of the saints have largely fallen by the wayside for the average person the flurry of activity that is Christmas still holds an incredibly powerful draw for people. Many complain that the celebration has lost its original meaning, but in that they are only partly right. For the average man or woman in the street the celebration of the birth of the Saviour has indeed gone, but the original pagan celebration is still there, virtually intact. The feasting, the giving of gifts, the singing of special songs, the Yule log, mistletoe, holly and ivy, evergreen trees brought indoors and adorned with lights - all were the trappings of the various old winter solstice celebrations. Carols, which are now so indicative of the season, had originally been '*caroles,*' or bawdy tavern songs. The *Holly and the Ivy*, one of the better-known Christmas carols, is actually an old pagan song that was popular long before becoming regarded as a Christmas carol.

Christmas in the Christian calendar had traditionally been a time of fasting and quiet contemplation, but over the years the unbridled feasting which was the Roman festival of Saturnalia became infused with it, turning Christmas into the over-indulgent holiday we love to hate. The giving of gifts at the close of the year also has its origin in this and other ancient festivals.

Santa Claus is a modern figure derived ostensibly from the Christian Saint Nicholas, martyred bishop of Myrna in Turkey. But when we learn that the Dutch had a pagan, seasonal visitor called Sinterclaas who landed on rooftops bearing gifts, we have to question if Santa Claus was indeed derived from the name of Saint Nicholas, or perhaps conclude that the saint's name was simply invoked to give a pre-existing pagan observance some semblance of a Christian meaning?

The Magi, if they existed in reality at all, would have been Babylonian Astrologers, probably Zoroastrians, who came to venerate the newborn Jesus - not because of a miraculous star which defied the laws of physics and appeared out of nowhere to hang over Bethlehem - but because their star charts indicated the arrival of a new astrological age. It was around that time that the precession of the equinoxes was moving the sun out of Aries and into Pisces, causing a flurry of expectation that a new religious leader was about to appear. The wheel of the zodiac and the position of the constellations within it were important to the priests who recorded the movements of the heavens, and it happens that the sign opposite Pisces is Virgo the Virgin, which led to a widespread belief that the new religious leader would be born of a virgin. Isaiah 7:14 says 'Therefore the Lord himself shall give you a sign; Behold, a virgin shall conceive, and bear a son, and shall call his name Immanuel.' When we look at the other dying and resurrecting god-men of the ancient world, they were almost all born of a virgin. The Sign of the Fish, which is still a popular Christian motif, was rooted in the sign of Pisces, the new astrological age that was about to start.

So here again we see two of the most potent of all Christian symbols - the Star of Bethlehem and the Virgin birth, as being yet more concepts that originated in Pre-Christian pagan astrology. Taking all these together, then, Christmas has not lost its original meaning at all, but has simply undergone a shedding of its later Christian accretions, and yet again shows the hold that ancient observances have over us all.

One final example of ancient traditions surviving into the present is St. Patrick's Purgatory, a Catholic island-retreat on Lough Derg in Co. Donegal. This age-old institution is fascinating because it is a microcosm of the early Christian story in Ireland and well shows the development of primitive observances into the modern day. Today's pilgrims attend the three-day retreat on the island, the focus of which is a night-long vigil in the basilica. The history of that vigil is truly fascinating, for it has its origin in the pagan past. I am indebted to Joseph McGuinness and his excellent book, *Lough Derg*, for the following information.

Lough Derg is in the west of Co. Donegal. The name Derg is the anglicised Derc, which means pit or cave, and it was an island on the lough that was the focus of the early religious belief. The island in question is today called Saint's Island and on it was a cavern or pit. The lough was a holy site for years beyond count before St. Patrick came to it in the 5th Century. Its waters were home to an ancient deity which became a monster in the Christian way of demonising earlier beliefs. The 'monster' was called 'Caoránach', pronounced *keeronagh*, the mother of demons and devils. St. Patrick banished Caoránach from the lough, but it took up refuge in the pit on the island, and thereafter its dark dank corners were supposed to hold all manner of evils.

Purgatory is a curious place, not being true Hell, but on the very threshold of it. Those who did not attain true piety in life go to purgatory on death, and if their kin pray hard enough, or do good works for the church, the soul of the departed could be released and go to Heaven. Purgatory was therefore a second chance at salvation, but it was no mere way-station. The souls unfortunate enough to go there were subjected to all manner of torture and endless pain and suffering. Through that torment their imperfect souls could be cleansed, and they would eventually make their way to Heaven. The cave on Lough Derg, because of the legend of the beast Caoránach, became a mediaeval purgatory in the physical world, and time spent in it whilst alive would mean one would bypass purgatory on death and go straight to Heaven.

There is no evidence that St. Patrick ever visited the lough but as with so much early Christian folklore it was the Middle Ages before the myths about it developed and were recorded. It is presumed that pilgrims have been coming to the site since Christianity came to Ireland, and likely a long time before that too, but it was the arrival of the Canons Regular that brought it to the world's attention.

In the 1140s the Celtic clergy that controlled the site were replaced by Augustinians as part of the drive to eradicate the older traditions that still held sway in the more remote parts of Christendom. In the following decade a story emerged of the Knight Owein, a nobleman who visited the island to undertake the rigours of the pit. After fifteen days in preliminary devotions he was locked in the pitch black of the cave as the setting sun dipped below the horizon in the west. Groping his way down the passages he eventually came to a glimmering light. An underground world emerged before him, where fifteen servants of God in white mantles warned him that he would be shortly be set upon by devils. 'Those devils would try to make him turn back', he was told, but he must 'remain steadfast against them and remain faithful to Jesus'. He then heard a 'grete dynn' and was immediately set upon by a multitude of dreadful demons…

> 'Then come ther develes on every syde,
> Wykked gostes, I wote, fro Helle,
> So mony that no tonge mygte telle:
> They fylled the hows yn two rowes;
> Some grenned on hym and some mad mowes.'
> From *St Patrick's Purgatory*, S. Wright

He saw souls nailed to the ground with red hot nails, gnawed by flaming reptiles, others roasted on spits or sitting up to their necks in pits of molten metal. The knight was himself seized and dragged backwards through fire by hooks inserted in his flesh. By calling Jesus' name the fires were quenched. Ten times he was set-upon, and each time calling Jesus' name freed him from the torment. In the last he was pushed into one of the molten pits, but calling on his saviour one last time to deliver him, he was released. He then found himself at the mouth of the pit as the sun rose.

He had survived the night.

The story emerged at the same time as the Grail Romances, and in some ways is similar to them. It captured the imagination of the Christian world and pilgrims came from far and wide to experience the Underworld for themselves. The mediaeval mind was fascinated by what happened after death, and the tale of Owein gave them answers, in a tangible, physical manner. It let them sample, in their imagination at least, the iniquities of Hell in advance, and so rumour of its horrors grew in the mediaeval mind.

We will never know what the cavern on the island meant to the pre-Christians, because it was Christians who wrote the history of the island, but it is plain that it had some connection to the Afterworld. It is also interesting that the penitent was lowered into the pit at sundown and released at sunrise. The tale of the knight Owein is from the same stable as many of the other examples of the Christianisation of the pagan past that we have encountered to date, and emerged at that same time in history – the 12th Century. The experience was very far from Christian, for it took the penitent away from the world of light and let him sample life on the other side. The torments of Hell were Christian enough, but the manner in which one accessed those horrors was thoroughly pagan. Like the Celts of old for whom the ancient barrows and underground passages of an unknown past were portals to the Underworld, to the Sidhe, we have an identical allusion in this tale that goes to the heart of the early Christian faith in Ireland, and is an unmistakeable link between the two.

As the years wore on the purgatory was visited by many people, where they, though they didn't understand it as such, hallucinated in the dark and gave way to their own fears. Each of them then took away their tales of the night spent battling the demons of the Sidhe. Through time however the intellect grew, and the Church became less enamoured with the quite ludicrous claim that by spending the night in a pit the penitent could physically visit the Afterworld, and absolve themselves of having to enter the spiritual purgatory on death. By the end of the 15th Century the physical purgatory's day was done, and matters came to a head in the 1490s when a Dutch monk did not feel he had received the torment he had travelled to experience. The fact that he had no money to pay the prior for the privilege was perhaps why his experience was less than he expected. On leaving he wrote a letter to the pope, who took advantage of the complaint and ordered that the whole place be closed down.

The people were undeterred, however, and the pilgrimages continued. Ironically, even a member of the senior clergy, the Papal Nuncio to King Henry VIII, visited in 1517. By then, however, the fantastic visions visited upon earlier pilgrims had disappeared, and the purely penitential notion of a night of contemplation and inner reflection in the dark without food or water had begun to dominate. The pit, or cave, passed out of use, and Saint's Island, with its dubious past, was abandoned in favour of nearby Station Island which became the new focus of pilgrimage. The pit was replaced with a narrow, man-made underground chamber with a barrel-vaulted roof, not tall enough to stand up in. This was a sanitised version of the cave of old, with a sturdy door behind which the penitents were locked in for the night by the abbot.

By the 1630s the Reformation had changed the religious landscape, and the Plantation of Ireland by the British placed the lough in English hands. Seen as a particularly grotesque instance of superstitious Catholicism by the Protestant authorities, it was destroyed in 1632 and the monks driven from the island. The people were not to be deterred however, and in the absence of their usual site they simply came to the lough-shore and prayed. Within a few years the sanctuary was up and running again though in a quiet way and by 1736 a permanent residence was again established. By 1763 the first church was built, then another, larger one in 1780. The year 1870 saw the building of the present basilica, with its plain, austere interior that was designed to mimic the pit of old.

What had started as a descent to the very gates of Hell itself in the pit on Saint's Island, metamorphosed into a nights' fasting and prayer in a manmade souterrain on Station Island, and today the memory of that is maintained in the all-night vigil which is the focus of the modern visitor's three day pilgrimage to the island.

Lough Derg is still a popular destination for those in search of inner peace, and whilst those who make the three day pilgrimage today regard what they do as the epitome of Christian observance, it traces back by a well documented path to the distant past, beyond the arrival of Christianity, and into the misty haze of Celtic Ireland.

We have looked in this chapter at a few examples of the continuation of pagan practices into Christianity. The above vigil on Lough Derg is perhaps one of the more obvious examples, but is by no means alone for similar can be found everywhere. The process happened because those observances were so deeply embedded in the collective psyche that people quite simply refused to be parted from them. The dogma may have changed, but the old ways continued unabated. We have already noted that veneration for the solstices and equinoxes survived the introduction of the new faith, and in the next chapters we will reinforce that notion by discovering that some aspects of the veneration of the sun were so ingrained that they remained right up to the modern age.

I earlier suggested that the mediaeval mystery regarded the true cross of Christianity as an allegory. I had also suggested that because the sun formed a true cross in Scotland that the mystery would have based itself there for that reason. We will now look more closely at how the sun's cross manifested itself in ancient times.

CHAPTER 13

MANY IN BRITAIN will question that the cross could have any other sacred meaning than as the cross of Jesus, but the object in this picture will serve to prove that the cross was venerated for many thousands of years before the Christian era. The artefact is a golden sun-disc, one of a pair unearthed in the village of Tydavnet in Co. Monaghan, Ireland. It is dated to 2000BCE or thereabouts, and is interesting to the thesis on several levels.

The first observation is that it is both circular and gold in honour of the sun. The second is the x shaped cross in the centre of the circle, which indicates the rising and setting points of the sun. It is also interesting that this artefact is of such extreme age, predating the arrival of Christianity by over two

thousand years, for it proves that the cross, in its equal-armed variant is a truly ancient symbol and has nothing to do with Christianity. Perhaps most interesting of all is that it was found at a location that became a notable Christian site in the 5th century in the aftermath of St. Patrick's mission to spread the faith.

One may ask why the early Christians picked the spot for one of their religious houses, but it is a rhetorical question for which the answer is obvious. The words of Pope Gregory we quoted earlier come once again to mind '…you should not destroy the pagan temples, but only the idols in them. You should purify them with holy water, take the idols from the altar, and put relics of Saints there. For if these temples are well built, let them pass from the worship of the Devil to the service of the true God. If the people see that the places to which they are accustomed are conserved, they will go to them more readily…'

Another manifestation of the veneration of the sun in early times was the crossing of the arms in death. Doing this in honour of the sun has long been a death practice among mankind. This is the mummy of Rameses II from around 1200BCE. Though in that period restricted to male pharaohs, by the 3rd Century BCE the practice was common right across ancient Egypt. Exactly the same posture also existed among the early Christians when arranging their dead.

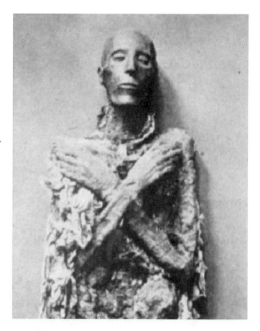

In a British context, the crossing of the arms was invariably associated with the bodies being laid with their feet towards the east. These two gestures are generally claimed to be Christian, with the crossed arms signifying the Cross of Calvary and the orientation being so that on judgement day, when they resurrect, it will be towards Jerusalem. This argument cannot be put forward for the pharaohs of Egypt, however, and nor should it for Europeans, because there is another reason for the gestures, and as before, it relates to the sun.

As we noted in chapter two, the east is where the sun rises on the two days of the equinoxes. The equinoxes themselves were the days on which the dying and resurrecting gods of old passed into, and emerged from, the Underworld. The equinox was therefore a sacred time, when the sun 'crossed' from the dark half of the sky into the light half, and when it did so it rose precisely due east. The association between the east, the orientation of the body, and the crossing of the

arms is therefore obvious, and is rein-forced by the figure in the picture below

The carving in question is on Boa Island on Lough Erne, in County Fermanagh, Ireland, and pre-dates the Christian era by several centuries. It is known as the 'Janus' sculpture because, like the Roman god, it has two faces, back to back, looking in opposite directions. Each of the faces has its arms crossed over its breast -

in a gesture that refers to the x-shaped cross formed by the sun. It also faces due east and west, towards the sunrises and sunsets on the days of the equinoxes. This shows that the ancient veneration of the sun's cross that is present in the Tydavnet sun discs and the mummy of Rameses II, was still in existence in the pre-Christian paganism that existed until the arrival of the Christian era.

In having two faces it looks both forward to the light half of the year that starts on the spring equinox, and backwards to the dark half of the year that has just finished. Perhaps the beliefs about the afterlife of those who erected this stone provided for some sort of symbolic raising with the sun on the equinox, and gives a spiritual basis for the orientation of later Christian burials towards the east.

Perhaps a brief look at the Roman god Janus itself would help to illustrate the likely meaning of the symbolism employed in the Boa Island figure. I quote from a research paper by the Scottish Masonic historian Trevor Stewart entitled *Some thoughts about the Roman god Janus*. 'The god was most often associated with doorways or gateways, and the entering and departing that takes place through them. In one myth Janus was the son of Apollo, the sun-god. He also came to be associated with beginnings, and indeed gave his name to the month that starts the year – January. When conflated with the sun-god Sol, he became Sol-Janus and opened the gates of heaven every morning with the rising sun, and closed them with the setting sun in the evening.' We can perhaps see here a correlation with the coping of the deacon's wands in Masonic ritual at the opening and closing of the lodge. Through time the Sol aspect was lost and became simply Janus. Hymns have him referred to as the beginning of all things.

Tellingly for us he faced both east and west, a fact borne out by his connection with the great ceremonial gateway between the two halves of Rome, built between the Palatine Hill of the Romans, and the Quirinal Hill of the Sabines. He was also associated with time, and represented both the past and the future. As such, he closely corresponds to the Boa Island figure that looks both to the coming season of growth, and the past season of the death and decay of the natural world.

One aspect of Janus is so closely aligned with the thesis presented here that I will quote directly from Stewart's paper '...In the Classical era, Janus was commonly shown as carrying two keys, one of gold and the other of silver, to open and lock each of the two solstitial gates, the Janua Coeli and the Janua Inferni, corresponding respectively to the Winter and Summer solstices. Janus, as Master of Time, was the Janitor who opened and closed this cycle. On the other hand, he was also the god of initiation into the Greater and Lesser "Mysteries".'

Perhaps even more important for our study he was honoured by the ancient world's equivalent of the mediaeval guilds of stonemasons, as Stewart again confirms '...His solstitial festivals were commemorated by the "Collegium Fabrorum" (the guild of artisans) whom some would regard as the Classical forerunners of the Medieval stonemasons. These solstitial feasts of Janus became eventually, in the Christian dispensation, the festival of the Saints John and the medieval operative stonemasons had both Saints John as their patrons. Furthermore, in the very early days of speculative Freemasonry, lodges were known as "St. John" lodges. Remember also that according to Cicero at least, the name Janus has the same root as the verb "to initiate".'

If we consider the two-faced Roman god Janus in respect of the symbolism that I suggest is contained in the pagan carving on Boa Island, the similarities are simply overwhelming. He governed beginnings, and therefore is eminently suitable for the veneration of the sun rising due east on the spring equinox, when the growing season started and the decay of winter was banished. That Janus was also associated with initiation adds considerably to the thesis that the symbolism he embodies was carried into the later Craft. The fact that in Classical times he was depicted facing each of the solstices that stand at either end of the year - the light and the dark halves of the year – places him on the equinox that is the meeting point of those halves, and at the very heart of the symbolism we are examining throughout.

I suggested earlier that the deacons in a modern Masonic lodge room, with the wands they carry, symbolise the two saints John, or the two solstices. I then developed this notion, and suggested that in coping the wands over the altar they symbolised the meeting of the solstice markers on the equinoxes. A very powerful correlation of this same

imagery came to light in the last few years, when another piece of the Boa Island statue was found overgrown with brambles in the corner of the graveyard. At some time in the past the fallen statue, minus its lower half, was resurrected and placed on a cement base. When the rediscovered bottom half is replaced where it should be, we can see that the crossed arms extend down into hands, and the long bony fingers, that were unknown for perhaps a thousand years, reach around to almost make contact with the back aspect of the figure. Was this the twin gods of the year reaching around to make contact on the equinox in a similar fashion to the touching of the deacon's wands?

The Boa Island figure is pre-Christian, and demonstrates a veneration of the sun rising in the east on the equinoxes. The thesis of this book is that such practices survived into Christianity and became embedded in the symbolism of the new faith. The original meaning, however, was later dropped by Christianity once the symbol had made the transition to the new faith. We actually have evidence of this transition in Ireland, because we have another stone figure, almost e exactly the same as that of the Boa Island carving, only this time it is from the Christian era.

This is one of three stones in the town of Carndonagh, Co. Donegal. The middle stone is an east facing high cross, about eight feet tall – one of the oldest in existence and thought to date from the 7th Century. Flanking it are two smaller stones with figures. The figure on the cross's right is this one, and as can be plainly seen, the arms are crossed over the front in exactly the same manner as the Boa Island figure. What is important about this figure is that though the symbolism in the Boa Island figure is pre-Christian, the existence of the same symbolism in a Christian setting in the 7th Century is surely proof that whatever the intention behind the figure in pagan times, it remained well into the period of the new faith. What we have, therefore, is a clear transition from the past into Christianity, of a symbol that had deep spiritual meaning to those who venerated the cross of the sun.

There would be few better ways of venerating the equinoctial sun in death than by arranging the body as the early Christians did, other than perhaps crossing the legs, but that gesture will be examined in detail later. There is no way of knowing for sure what was in the mind of the people who arranged their dead in such a way, but the only reason we accept the argument that it is because Calvary is in the east is because we are ourselves a Christian society and tend to look at things through Christian eyes. When we see a cross we see Christ's sacrifice on Golgotha, but the cross is a more far-reaching emblem than that, and the proof of that lies in these ancient stones.

In the early Christian era we find another symbol that has been altered to suit the Celtic mindset - The Celtic Cross. In the Celtic lands the cross of Jesus was altered by the addition of a circle to the crossing point of the arms of the cross. This circle represents the sun, and is very strong proof of the continuation of the veneration of the sun into the Christian era.

When St. Patrick spread Christianity throughout Ireland he had enormous success. His spiritual competitors were the druids, an ascetic priesthood who worshipped the sun. The cross of the seasons would therefore already have been a sacred symbol for them, so Patrick's introduction of a belief that offered a new meaning for that cross was no great shift in belief for them. Celtic crosses have stood proudly in the landscape for one and a half thousand years, and are perfect metaphors for the marriage of the pagan veneration of the sun and the Christian cross of Jesus.

It is now generally believed that Patrick achieved the success he did because rather than try to usurp the druids; he simply absorbed them into his new faith.

Patrick was a lone man on an island of druids, all of whom belonged to a powerful, hereditary elite. They would not readily have given up that power to a single man with a new religious mission, but by becoming monks in the new faith, they did not need to relinquish that power. Since they had revered the sun for centuries this change was not exactly a tectonic shift in observance. We must ask, however, if they would have abandoned their previous beliefs completely when becoming Christian, or would they have carried their previous understanding with them into their new faith?

It must also be remembered that although St. Patrick is credited with founding Christianity in Ireland in 432CE, the faith was already there in some form. It is not known when the faith came to the island, but there are records of four saints active on the island at least thirty years beforehand. Rather than introduce Christianity then, Patrick was simply a powerful evangelist who elevated the faith to dominate the island.

We must also consider what Christianity actually was in those early days, for there is nothing in history to suggest conflict with the pre-Christian druids. Whilst elsewhere in Europe pagan shrines were destroyed in the name of the new faith and the battle for supremacy led to death and martyrdom, there are few records of Celtic shrines in Ireland being destroyed and no Irish Christian martyrs. This is surely indicative that there was a gradual transition from one faith to the other, and that there was simply absorption of one by the other.

The faith Patrick founded was not as we know Roman Catholicism to be today, but was based on an older form of Christianity than that which centred itself on Rome in the years after the council of Nicea.

There was an original 'pulse' of Christianity that rippled across Europe in the first couple of centuries of the Christian era. That first wave left a variety of Christian groups peppered across the continent that held widely differing beliefs about Jesus. When Constantine and his agent Eusebius drew all the many, separate strands of the Christian faith together in the year 325 at the Council of Nicea, and wove a single set of beliefs from those strands, he facilitated the emergence of a singular version of the faith where there had previously been many.

The faith that emerged after the Council of Nicea was largely based on St. Paul's visions, and so became known as Pauline Christianity. In mainland Europe those other beliefs, such as Aryanism, Nestorianism, Manichaeism and Bogomilism to name but a few, were actively hounded off the landscape for they were geographically mingled with the mainstream faith. Ireland however was at the very edge of the world and remote from Europe. The Christianity that Patrick inherited in Ireland was from that first pulse, and would have been a hybrid mixture of early Christianity and the druidic sun-veneration that went before.

The reader may wonder why Ireland figures so often in a book that seeks to prove Scotland as the birthplace of Freemasonry, and why St. Patrick is central to its importance. As will, I hope, become obvious by the end of the book, the particular strain of Christianity that Patrick presided over was the link between the sun-veneration of the past and the mediaeval period that saw the birth of the mystery tradition in the west.

Patrick was not Irish, but was from the British mainland, and though he tried to set up a church on the British model with a hierarchy of bishops that answered to Rome, he failed. The druidic influence had been too strong, and after his forceful personality was gone, his religious houses lost touch with the rest of Europe. That is not to say Christianity faded, for it did not. A hundred years later another giant of the religious stage emerged in Ireland – St. Columba – and he took over where Patrick had left off. Under his ministration Christianity once more flourished, but there was one major difference – there were no bishops, and no link to Rome. Irish, and indeed Scottish Christianity developed on its own from then on, completely isolated from the rest of Europe. Though remnants of the mainstream church St. Patrick sought to found still existed, such as St. Ninian's religious establishment of Candida Casa at Whithorn in south west Scotland, through time that earlier endeavour was absorbed into the Celtic Church.

Celtic Christianity was, for seven hundred years, an autonomous enclave within the regular church, and was carried to Scotland - where the sun forms a true cross - by St. Columba in the 6th Century. It survived there until the 12th Century, by which time it was known as the Culdee Church, from the Gaelic, 'Ceili De', servants of god. In all that time, between the 6th and 12th Centuries, it held itself in isolation away from the hierarchical Church of Rome, until it was finally subsumed into the mainstream Christian fold.

The path of Celtic Christianity from Ireland to Scotland is of enormous importance to our quest, and will be examined more fully in a later chapter, but as the trail of the Culdee Church starts in Ireland, we are justified in looking there for evidence of the sun-veneration within Christianity.

We earlier mentioned the Janus sculpture on Boa Island, because it is an expression of belief that refers to the equinoxes. Although it is pre-Christian, the basis of spirituality upon which it is based appears to have survived right up to the modern day, in one of our best known symbols of mortality - the skull & crossbones.

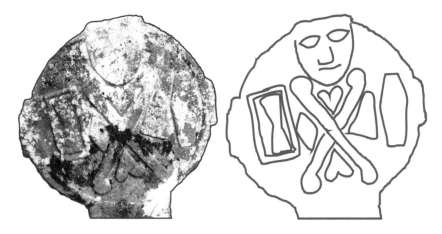

Few symbols remain from the early Christian period. It was not until the graves of ordinary people started being marked with headstones that carried 'memento mori' in the 17th Century that we see the establishment of the symbolism of death. Many of these ancient graveyards have grave markers that have very rudimentary versions of the skull & crossbones, and are closer to the features of the Boa Island figure than they are to more recent versions of the symbol. By the high-Victorian era the symbol was very well developed and quite artistically stylised, but from the mid 17th century we can find precursors of the design. I include on the previous page a highlighted picture of one of many similar examples, and as can be clearly seen, whilst there is a striking resemblance to the Janus figure on Boa Island, we also have a rudimentary skull and crossbones.

Charles Darwin's *On the Origin of Species* demonstrated the concept of evolution by identifying animals at various transition stages between one type of creature and another. By examining symbols on headstones that show a similar transition between one motif and another, we can perhaps demonstrate a similar 'evolution' of a symbol. The picture above is one such example, from a 17th Century graveyard beside the aforementioned Carndonagh Cross in Co. Donegal. Here the crossed bones are separated from the skull, and placed inside a separate circle. We could fill the chapter with examples, each a little different from the others, that all point towards the same thing. If we give the crossed leg bones the same significance as those of Mithras'

Torchbearers and the arms of the carved stone on the Boa Island figure, they would allude to the sun's crossing of the equinoxes. The skull being almost perfectly round is reminiscent of the sphere of the sun, so would well represent that celestial body on the days it crosses from one hemisphere to the other on the equinox. The skull in the example even resembles the setting sun, a motif that is particularly pertinent to death.

I don't suggest that the symbol of the skull over crossed bones was anything other than Christian in the Middle Ages of course - simply that it is a vestige of an older veneration of the sun that became Christianised over the previous thousand years. Standard reference works simply refer to the skull and crossbones as a Christian symbol of mortality, but I would ask from whence that symbol was derived?

To say that early Christians invented the symbol out of nothing, to refer to the Cross of Calvary shows, I believe, a certain naiveté. To accept this is to say that there was nothing that went before that could have a bearing on it, and we have seen time and time again that the crossing of the equinoxes lies at the heart of ancient Man's spirituality as the passage into the afterlife. The skull and crossbones means exactly the same for us in the modern era, so is there not therefore a link? The Boa Island figure shows that the sun rising in the east on the equinox was still relevant just before Christianity appears, so can we really think the skull and crossbones, which is a close pictorial depiction of that, is a purely Christian symbol?

I use an example from Ireland simply because in the carving used the transition between the old and the new can clearly be seen, but the symbol was not specifically Irish. If anywhere, Scotland is likely to be the place where the late mediaeval symbol of the skull and crossbones grew to prominence, for the symbol is more commonly found there than anywhere else. There are actually very few graveyards in Ireland that can boast more than a few such symbols, and all can be traced to Scottish stonemasons in the employ of Scottish landowners who came to Ireland as part of the 'Plantation of Ireland' in the 17th Century. Yet again, then, we have a Scottish connection.

The skull and crossbones is an immensely common symbol in Freemasonry, and if veneration of the sun was the original meaning of the device, then its use in the Craft becomes obvious. When we look at the earliest catechisms of Freemasonry, that are thought to be derived from the rituals of the operative lodges that predated the speculative Craft, we find an obtuse reference to the secrets of the lodge being contained in the skull.

When asked… 'Where lys the key ?' the candidate answers… 'In the bone box.' The bone-box is thought to refer to the skull, and the most obvious meaning of this is that the Mason keeps the secrets of the Craft in his head. If the origin of the skull and crossbones symbol is indeed the sun on the equinoxes, and if the sun lies behind the secrets of the Craft, then, like so many other aspects of ritual, the above answer has two facets – the obvious, or exoteric meaning, and the esoteric, or hidden one. And again, where Christianity can be said to have lost touch with the original meaning, Freemasonry has not, and uses it in its original form.

We have not yet looked at why the equinoxes are central to the rituals of the Craft, but as will be shown later, the symbolic death of the candidate in the 3rd Degree does indeed refer to the passing of the sun from one half of the year into the other one, and as such refers directly to the sun on the equinoxes. It is only when considering all together, however, that the true importance of the skull and crossbones becomes clear.

We have looked so far in this chapter at how the veneration of the sun was relevant to the changing spiritual beliefs of the pre-Christians, but what of the more recent Christians? Can we find evidence that that same veneration of the sun remained for them?

Many will raise their eyebrows at the suggestion that Christian symbols could have a pagan provenance, but as we are discovering, not only do many Christian icons have a pagan pedigree, but it was this duality which allowed Christianity to gain acceptance in the first place. Throughout the Christian world we will see Jesus with a halo. That halo is nothing other than the sun behind his head, and symbolises the light of the faith emanating from him. We sometimes even see a more obvious reference to this in that the halo will be formed from rays of the sun. We will also see the cross with rays of sunlight emanating from it, which is exactly the same as the ring

of the sun on the Celtic crosses of the past. I would even suggest that the Elevation of the Host in a Catholic mass, which involves the priest holding aloft a disc shaped wafer in both his hands, has its origins in the veneration of the disc of the sun.

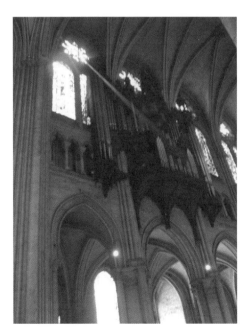

An excellent example of this fusion is to be found in Chartres Cathedral, which rises majestically above the endless, flat, yellow cornfields of north-western France. The quirky detail that deserves mention is the clerestory window dedicated to St. Apollinaire, high up on the south side of the nave. The central panel of the window contains a metal insert with a hole at its centre, and as the sun passes to the south of the cathedral at midday, its light shines through the hole, illuminating the dim interior with a vivid shaft of light. Where the beam strikes the floor it creates a perfect image of the sun, roughly a foot across, on the amber coloured stone flags. As morning passes into afternoon the spot traverses the floor in an arc that is said to strike a brass pin at a particular time each year.

We have no way of knowing exactly what the designers had in mind when laying out this feature of the cathedral, but it certainly hints at the veneration of the sun. Perhaps a clue is to be found in the saint the window is dedicated to, as St. Apollinaire is the  Christianised persona of the Roman sun-god Apollo, so was the intention to reinforce the veneration of that pagan God with the feature deliberately built into the window?

Critics of the attribution of this and other aspects of the cathedral to heresies say, rightly, that ancient buildings like this have undergone many alterations over the years, and that what we see today is not necessarily what was originally there. This is particularly true of this building, for there has been a fulsome series of well-documented alterations and additions to Chartres. The window that allows the sun into this hallowed space may well therefore have been a product of 15th or 16th Century modernisation. Considering that we are looking for sun-veneration persisting into the Christian era, however, the possibility that the above feature was only introduced in the later mediaeval period is an even more interesting prospect than if it were original.

It is important to re-iterate here that this was not heresy, it was simply the process of metamorphosis of beliefs that had been part of all religions for thousands of years. Christianity arose in these islands in the 5th Century, and, as we will see from evidence presented later in the book, it wasn't until the 13th Century that paganism was ostensibly gone. We therefore have a period of eight hundred years during which the process of change was under way. In the beginning that process involved the embracing of earlier ideas and practices and giving them Christian connotations. For a period after the commencement of that conversion process the old co-existed with the new in a hybrid belief system that pleased all, but this was only part of the overall strategy of winning over the populace however, because having embraced those motifs to gain acceptance, the church then sought to distance itself from the true origin of those symbols once conversion had been achieved.

In this endeavour time itself was the church's greatest ally, for as the generations passed, the older meanings simply faded into our subconscious until the pagan elements had disappeared from memory. It is only in more enlightened times that historians can dissociate themselves from dogma and look back dispassionately and piece together the original meanings of the symbols that adorn our earliest churches.

If the cross of the sun does indeed lie behind Christian symbols like the skull and crossbones, then these motifs must have been very important to our forbears, and been part of mankind's thinking for a very long time indeed.

The thesis presented here suggests that as part of the veneration of ancient ways Freemasonry retains understanding of the square of the sun at the latitude of southern Scotland. So far we have looked at examples of this veneration chiefly from Ireland, but if we are to establish a connection with Freemasonry we must now look to Scotland for evidence that veneration of the sun continued there in such a way as to have been available to those who set up the mystery of Christ in the 12th Century.

CHAPTER 14

IN THE LAST chapter we were introduced to the idea that veneration of the sun's solstice cross survived the introduction of Christianity in the British Isles. When we think of the Christian cross in relation to Scotland, one thing immediately springs to mind – the Saltire that is the national flag. The Saltire is ostensibly a Christian symbol, derived from the x-shaped cross that St. Andrew was crucified upon, but when scrutinised from the point of view of the thesis contained in this book, that origin will be proved to be wrong.

In chapter two we had noted, in a general sense, that in southern Scotland the points the sun marks on the horizon on the solstices form a square or true cross. At that early place in the quest I had not attached overly much importance to this point, but when the thesis developed and I became convinced that Scotland was the birthplace of the Craft because of the sun's interaction with the earth there, I was persuaded to look a little closer at the phenomenon.

My reason for doing this was that when the new faith arrived with its veneration of the true cross of Jesus, the true cross of the sun would suddenly have become very relevant. When this thought occurred to me I went looking for the exact place where the true cross of the sun occurs, and when I found it, it told an interesting tale indeed.

I used a simple computer astronomy programme to find where the solstice points were exactly 90 degrees apart. At first I had no success because it turned out that there was no single place on earth where a truly 'true' cross is found. This baffled me because as we mentioned earlier the separation of sunrises on the solstices is roughly 54 degrees at Cairo and 101 at Stockholm. It is a simple fact that somewhere between those two points must lie the place where the summer solstice sunrise and sunset is a precise 90 degrees apart.

When I set the computer programme for the date of the summer solstice, I found the sun to give a perfect 90 degree angle at the latitude of Belfast. The problem was that when I looked at the winter solstice points for that same latitude they were a couple of degrees off a right-angle. This caused me not a little consternation, because it meant that not only was there not a place where a true cross was formed by the sun, but Belfast, where the summer solstice was correct is considerably south of Edinburgh where the Craft developed.

This, I eventually found was because the earth is not a perfect sphere, but is an oblate spheroid or slightly squashed ball, and is caused by the spinning of the earth pushing the equator out a little. After a little head-scratching about the problem it occurred to me that if the winter solstice did not give a true cross at Belfast, there must be another place that did. A few trials and errors on the computer programme gave me the latitude of Aberdeen as having an exact right-angle on the winter solstice, and like Belfast, the summer solstice was a couple of degrees off. This gave a northern and southern boundary to the sun's square, and I have termed the region between the two

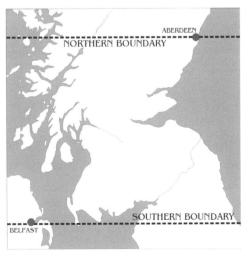

lines the *Land of the Solstice Square*. Though the inconsistency of there being no single line that gave a true square troubled me at first, it was when I plotted both latitudes on a map of Scotland that the true picture emerged, for Edinburgh lies precisely between the two lines of latitude.

It also occurred to me that whereas I was looking at the precision of this on a computer screen, the ancients for whom the phenomenon would have meant something had no such precision. They did not even have a map of Scotland to base their observations on. Where I had discovered the northern and southern boundary of the phenomenon and that the closer to the centre one stood the closer the alignment would be, that is only true in an academic sense. For the ancients who lived in an uneven landscape, and measured the sun's position with wooden shadow-poles, the latitude at the centre of the region would indeed have given a true cross.

This meant that Edinburgh was indeed at the centre of where the true cross or square is formed by the sun. That was by no means the end of the matter however, for when I turned to the origin of the Scottish flag, I was to make a truly startling discovery.

The Saltire

A Saltire is simply an x-shaped cross. Its association with Scotland is from a Dark-Age battle though it was first written down several hundred years after the event in the 12th Century by the monks of St. Andrews. St. Andrew was one of the disciples of Jesus, and was said to have been crucified on an x-shaped cross at Patras in Greece. Legend tells us that in the 4th Century his remains were to be taken to Constantinople, but were removed instead by their guardian, a monk called St. Regulus who was told in a dream by St. Andrew himself to

remove them, and take them to the 'ends of the earth' for safe keeping. The monk removed a tooth, an arm bone, a kneecap, and a few finger bones. These he put in a boat and headed west, where he was eventually shipwrecked near a Pictish settlement on the east coast of Fife known as Kilrimont, later re-named St. Andrews. A chapel was built to house the relics, and later, in 1160, the magnificent St. Andrew's Cathedral was built to give such important tokens of Jesus' time on earth a fitting repository.

The oldest reference to the x-shaped cross of St. Andrew being used as an emblem is on a seal from St. Andrews dating from around 1180. It remained a purely religious emblem for around a hundred years before taking the steps to becoming the definitive symbol of Scottish nationality by being integrated into the seal of the Guardians of Scotland in 1286. It then appears on soldiers' uniforms in the 14th century with a square or circular background, and it wasn't until 1801 that the flag assumed the form we recognise today from the Union Flag of the United Kingdom - oblong, with a dark blue background.

The symbol of the Saltire was said to have originated when the Scots were about to confront the Saxons of Northumbria in battle. Like much of what happened in the Dark Ages the scant sources vary on the exact date of the battle, which could have been anywhere between 747 and 832. For simplicity we will refer to it as being the 8th Century, when their king called upon St. Andrew to help them on the field. The following morning the Scottish army, to a man apparently, saw a white, x-shaped cross of clouds against the blue sky, and, aware of the Saint's death on such a cross, took that as a sign that God would help them win against the Saxons that day. The battle took place near a village called Athelstaneford, so called because Athelstan, leader of the Saxons, fell there at a fording point of a stream.

The story is remarkably similar to Constantine's vision before the battle of Milvian Bridge, and was, I thought, likely to be rooted in the same pagan astrology as the Chi Rho sign that has since been taken to be the Christian Cross. Since I had first identified the fact that the sun gave a true cross in northern Britain I had a vague notion that the four corners of the sun's square might have played a part in the origin of the Saltire, but hadn't initially thought the fact would have any relevance to my quest. I was wrong.

The map shows the area inside which the sun can be regarded as forming a perfect square on the solstices. Legend tells us that the 8th century Scottish king prayed to St. Andrew for deliverance the night before the battle of Athelstaneford. It was not until I looked for the site of the battle on the map, however, that I was to see how undoubtedly astrological the true relevance of the legend of the x seen in the sky on the morning of the battle actually was. Athelstaneford is precisely due east from Edinburgh, and is right on the line where the sun forms a true cross on the solstices.

We have no way of knowing if Christianity had fully taken root in that part of Scotland at that remote time. The thesis presented here suggests not, for we have a tale of the appearance of an x-shaped cross in the sky, exactly on a sacred line where the sun forms a perfect x-shape with its rising and setting on the solstices. If what I offer in this book is right, then the movements of the sun at that exact location were known about for possibly thousands of years, so I would throw a cat among the historical pigeons here and suggest that it is more likely that at this early date the significance of the

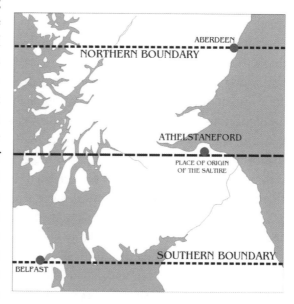

188

cross in the sky would have been due to the sun marking the diagonal corners of a cross on the ground in the area.

The tale therefore has its origin in the existing veneration of the sun, and only later became attached to St. Andrew as part of the Christianising of pre-existing pagan motifs as outlined elsewhere in the book. Documentation from the Dark Ages is thin on the ground, so we only have the 12th century Christian scribe's word for it that the inhabitants of Scotland in the 8th century saw the cross as referring to St. Andrew. Those writers were in possession of what were claimed to be relics of St. Andrew, so is it not likely that they simply invoked the Christian saint who was associated with an x-shaped cross in the Bible, and married the two together when they came to write down their tale, in the normal process of overlaying pagan motifs with Christian themes?

The argument could be taken further, and the origin of the saint's relics in the 4th Century themselves could be called into question, for the subject of medieval relics is a shady business indeed. The provenance of the physical objects was never good, and the brisk trade in them at that time, and the prestige and revenue to be generated by their ownership suggests that many if not all were counterfeit. Relics were an early mediaeval phenomenon, demanded by a credulous population that longed for some physical link with the wondrous tales of those who walked the earth with Jesus. They were an incredible draw for the common man or woman, and a church having possession of even the slightest piece of a saint would ensure that seats were filled and that the collecting plates would sing with the rattle of coins. Even such insignificant and unverifiable items as a fingernail clipping, a lock of hair or a drop of blood would bring the credulous flocking; and where there's a demand, there'll surely be a supply.

It wasn't until Constantine elevated Christianity to Rome's state religion three hundred years after the events in the Holy Land that it became desirable to identify the sites where those events took place, and a search was started under the auspices of the Emperor's pious mother, the Empress Helena. By that late stage it is unlikely if any original tombs could still be found, but a market for relics grew, and soon bits of anyone even remotely connected with the story of Jesus started to appear in churches. In the ensuing centuries many relics surfaced purporting to be the bones of this or that saint, but which of any of them was real is a question that will never be answered, because in the British Isles at least, the zealots of the Reformation destroyed all such idolatrous objects as heathen.

Is it not stretching credibility to think that the legend of the arrival of the bones of St. Andrew on the shores of Scotland within the bounds of the solstice square could be true? Is it possible that a Greek monk in the 4th Century, motivated by events in Turkey and beyond, sailed west with the bones of a disciple who had been crucified on an x-shaped cross, and just happened to be shipwrecked at a location where the x-shaped cross had been a sacred symbol prior to that? The westward passage from Greece by boat would have brought the bones into the Atlantic through the Straits of Gibraltar, not only a considerable distance from the coast of Fife, but to the west of Portugal, Spain, Ireland and France. All of these are further west than Fife, and would have had to be bypassed as the boat doubled back on itself and made its way eastwards along the English Channel and through the North Sea and up along the east coast of England. It seems improbable that one seeking the ends of the earth would choose to take this route.

The legend of the arrival of the bones during Constantine's time therefore associates St. Andrews with the saint from the earliest days of Christianity in Britain, Was this an early attempt to convert the pagan veneration of the sun and to place it in a Christian framework? Was the later tale at Athelstaneford, where the Christian saint was allegedly called upon to assist the Scots in battle, simply another incidence of placing this pagan concept in a Christian setting?

Is it not more likely that the area was already sacred for the reason outlined above, and that the Christian monks of the 12th century brought the pagan tale of the cross of the sun into the Christian fold by attaching to it the story of the martyred St. Andrew, and that bones were procured to Christianise that story? Acca, the Bishop of nearby Hexham possessed a voracious appetite for collecting relics, and bought many bones throughout his life in the 8th century, indeed his abbey in Hexham was dedicated to St. Andrew. He was banished from Hexham in the year 732, and spent his remaining years, with his collection, in what is referred to as 'Pictland', of which St. Andrews was the focus.

It is a fact that Acca lived around the same time as, or shortly before, the supposed battle with the Northumbrians, so perhaps at that time his depositing of some of his collection in St. Andrews was a deliberate attempt to strengthen Christianity against paganism, and put a Christian veneer on the pagan past.

The bones of a Christian saint associated with an x-shaped cross would have been a powerful draw towards Christianity for people that had previously venerated the x-shaped cross of the sun. The arrival of the bones in the 4th Century and the battle with the Northumbrians in the 8th are evidence of two attempts at Christianising the pagan past, and the recording of that battle in the 12th century is simply a third instance of that process.

We have several times already mentioned the Celtic, or Culdee Church. This particular strain of Christianity grew from the druidic past, and is particularly interesting to us because it was carried from Ireland to Scotland in the 6th Century. In the following chapter we will look a little deeper into this enigmatic religious movement that though it had its roots in Ireland, is now equally associated with Scotland.

CHAPTER 15

THE CELTIC CHURCH was the result of the union of the first Christians in Ireland and the druidic traditions of the past. The Christianity that found its way into the doctrine of the Celtic Church had been laid down in the Middle East long before the Council of Nicea had settled the fledgling church firmly in the heart of the Roman Empire, and once combined with the druidic veneration of the sun, presented a dogma that was not entirely compatible with Pauline Christianity. It must be remembered that if the thrust of the thesis presented here about the origin of Freemasonry is correct, then some conduit must exist down which the veneration of the sun passed. The Celtic church is exactly the type of movement that would have carried the ancient knowledge of the sun forward into the Christian era, being a blending of Christianity and earlier druidic teaching. Though it would be several centuries before the name Culdee was attached to the Celtic Church, there is no known point in history where one became the other; rather they are one entity with two names. As such, the name Culdee can be applied to the Celtic Church in any era.

In his book, *The Complete Guide to Celtic Mythology*, Dr. Bob Curran says of the Culdees '… Naturally, with their austere, withdrawn regime and their inward-looking, mystical qualities, the Culdee movement was later considered the repository of ancient wisdoms handed down from previous eras – perhaps even from the druids.'

Dr. Curran further comments that they '… became connected with another element of early Christian lore. This was the 'bachall' or staff of a saint or holy-man. The bachall occupied a central position in Celtic religious folklore. Just as the staff had been the mark of a druid, so it was the sign of an early saint or holy-man with supernatural powers. There were those who said that the bachall was the actual source of those powers. In any event, the bachall was something held in common by the pagan and Christian worlds.'

Considering the importance of the deacons of a modern lodge room and the pivotal role their wands play in the ritual as portrayed in this book, the above quote is powerful evidence indeed for the continuation of ancient rituals into Christianity by these enigmatic monks. If their power lay in the bachall they carried, and was, as Masonic deacons' wands are today in a symbolic sense, for recording the sun's movements, then it is obvious that their power lay in measuring the sun's year, and thereby the all-important calendar.

The history of religious belief has always been a series of marriages. When one is passionately attached to one particular dogma, then that dogma becomes the one single truth and by definition all others are false. But when one dissociates oneself from dogma and takes a broad look at the development of faiths throughout history, they can be seen as a series of pathways that meander across landscapes, collide with others, intermingle with them, and move on, altered. Religious ideas can be seen to be born, to adopt and adapt from the beliefs of others, to metamorphose with time and travel, and result in similar but different faith systems the world over.

Rather than any single dogma being 'true' in isolation from others, then, all religious beliefs simply slot somewhere into the one, long meandering path along which mankind has travelled in his search for God. Why, then, would the pagan veneration of the sun that was so demonstrably central to the druids not be carried into early Christianity? This is made considerably more likely when we consider that the Celtic

Church developed in isolation from the wider Christian community, and was left to its own devices for fully seven hundred years before it was finally overwhelmed.

The Culdee Church was also monastic and existed as individual cells, isolated from one another and not beholden to the hierarchy of the Church of Rome. Each Culdee abbey or monastery was in the sole care of an abbot who was answerable to no one but himself. As a result, the Culdees did not have a hierarchy to oversee them, nor to make them accountable to the higher authority of Rome. In the Celtic church, each abbot was in total control.

When Freemasonry emerged it too was based on the same principle; of autonomous lodges quite separate from the others, and though all adhered to a single doctrine, each was without an external hierarchical structure of control. It is also a vital part of Masonic protocol that the lodge is under the total control of the Master, whose word, symbolically at least, cannot be questioned.

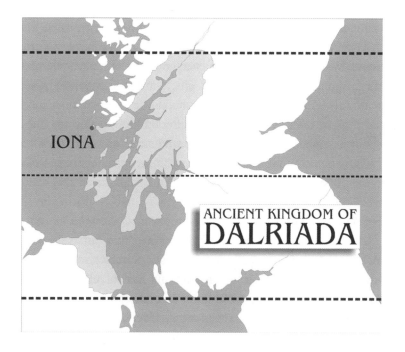

Since St. Columba's time in the middle of the 6th Century the Celtic Church's base had shifted from his original monastery on Iona to Dunkeld, and from there to St. Andrews. From there it had spread throughout Scotland, and by the 12th Century was in possession of thirteen important monastic locations, St. Andrew's itself becoming their main site.

Even the arrival of the Celtic church in Scotland is fascinating to the thesis of this book in that St. Columba brought it with him from the north of Ireland in the 6th century. In those early times one ancient realm spanned both countries - the Kingdom of Dalriada - and led to an intermingling of people and ideas between the two landmasses. The ancient kingdom took in most of Co. Antrim in Ireland, and the Isles and long headlands of Scotland's south-western seaboard. Dalriada, in both its parts, lies completely within the solstice square; indeed it actually spans precisely the entire region between the two locations where the solstice sun forms a square.

The migration of the Celtic Church from Ireland to Scotland is a vital part of the thesis presented here that the veneration of the sun found its way into Christianity, and this will be looked at more fully later in the book. For now, however, we will simply note that St. Columba, the man who carried the Celtic Church to Scotland, was born in Ireland, of royal lineage, inside the boundaries of the solstice square. It is also a fact that his mission to Scotland was entirely his own endeavour as a Celtic Christian, without recourse to the authority of the wider Christian community. This in itself is not surprising, because there was open hostility between the mainstream church and the Culdees.

When St. Columba set up his mission in Scotland he did so on Iona – the most remote place in all Dalriada. That particular isle was sacred long before he arrived, and had been a centre for druidism for many years before. So sacred was the site that a reputed forty-eight Scottish, four Irish and eight Norse kings are buried in and around the area of the old abbey site. As has already been noted, Iona lies well within the solstice square, and whilst following in Columba's footsteps,

I discovered a very pertinent link with the line of latitude where the true cross of the sun is formed, that gives another enigmatic layer to the thesis, and is a fact that had no relevance until now.

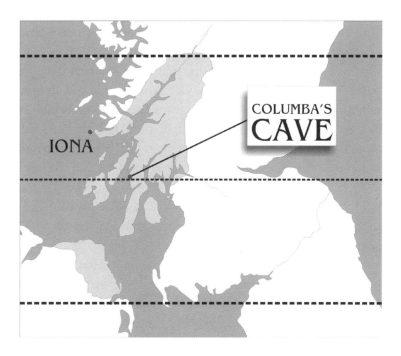

Legend tells us that when St. Columba first arrived in Scotland he spent some time living in a cave whilst he considered his next move. This cave is near Ellary on the northern shore of Loch Caolisport in Knapdale on the Mull of Kintyre. The spot is marked on maps to this day, and is precisely on the same line of latitude as Athelstaneford, where the symbol of the Saltire originated several hundred years later. Does St. Columba's association with the site then indicate that the sun's true cross was important to his particular faith?

When I stood in St Columba's Cave in Knapdale in the summer of 2007 I first considered the possibility that the site's link with him hinted that he was indeed aware of the sun's square. As a result of further research that we will cover later in the book, I can now say with certainty that there is no doubt whatsoever that he was indeed aware of the square of the sun, and that he went to Argyll in search of the sun's true cross.

We will revisit Columba's spirituality later when we have advanced further along the path, but for the rest of this chapter we will examine what happened to the Culdees in the 12th Century, for that was the era that saw the demise of their particular strain of Christianity.

The 12th Century was a time of immense religious change in the British Isles. The Synod of Whitby in the 7th century can be considered the start of the Christian Church's push to Christianise these islands. This was the start of the end of the Dark Age, and was the church first flexing its muscles against the older traditions that it shared the land with. The 12th Century saw another push to Christianise these islands for the Normans had arrived, bringing with them their more religiously orthodox, European ways. At the cutting edge of this was the arrival and promotion of the Canons Regular – the orders of Augustinians, Cistercians, Franciscans, Benedictines *et al* – and a huge building programme of friaries and abbeys.

There was no place for the Culdees in this new religious world.

Not only did the Culdees hold to doctrines that were beyond the Roman pale, but they accepted no authority other than their own and so were outside the dominion of Rome. This was a situation that could not be allowed to continue, and the Church moved against them with vigour. From the early 12th Century onwards the Canons Regular established themselves throughout the British Isles, spreading what we could regard as true Roman Catholicism to the ancient Celtic homelands where many aspects of paganism still remained. Though a religious endeavour, this cannot be divorced from the desire to govern, for it was to establish a hierarchy of bishops ruled ultimately from Rome that the Culdees were subsumed into the wider faith.

Though not at strong as they were in Scotland, the Culdees still had a presence in Ireland at that time of change. As well as politically and militarily stamping their authority, the Norman invaders of Ireland brought with them the regular orders to establish a framework of mainstream religious houses to wean the Irish from their more primitive ways. In one of the better-documented instances of this John De Courcey, Master of Carrickfergus Castle, drove the Culdees whom he regarded as heretics from Down Cathedral in 1183, and established Benedictines in their place.

In Scotland the great push against the Culdees started in St. Andrews, which by then was their main site and had been since the 10th Century. So important was the Culdee community in St. Andrews that in the year 943 the king, Constantine II abdicated the throne to become leader of the monastic community. The town became thereafter the seat of the mainstream Church's power in Scotland as it is to this day, and hints at the strength of the Culdee Church at that time. One by one, the Canons Regular took over Culdee centres, forcing conformity to mainstream doctrine.

The first Culdee monastery to fall into line after St. Andrews was on St. Serf's Island on Lochleven, where the new priesthood of St. Andrews gradually gained control and expunged those elements that were considered undesirable. Succeeding in that task, they then turned their attention to nearby Portmoak on the shores of the same loch and brought that religious house under their control too. Over the next century and a half all thirteen Culdee sites were subjugated to the dictates of the See of St. Andrews, some by peaceful means, some by more stringent measures, and in that short space of time the Culdees, with their unique mixture of Celtic and Christian thought, were no more.

The important point to be drawn from this is that the move to eradicate the Culdees originated in St. Andrews, initiated by the selfsame priests that brought us the story that the x-shaped cross in the sky had been inspired by Jesus' disciple Andrew. The legend of the Saltire being associated with the Christian saint also emerged just after St. Andrews had been wrested from Culdee control and brought into the

Christian fold, indicating that both endeavours sought a common goal. Is it not likely that the Christian monks deliberately absorbed the Culdee veneration of the sun into the Christian story as a way of converting the followers of the Celtic church from their pagan doctrines in the age old way; by offering a similar Christian notion to offset the loss of the pagan one? Thus was born the legend of the Saltire being a Christian symbol, whilst the true origin, like so many other instances noted within these pages, simply faded with the passing years.

The thesis laid out in this book seeks to prove nothing more than that the veneration of the sun survived into Christianity, and that it emerged as Freemasonry in the 18th Century. What I discovered of the origin of the Saltire is proof, surely, that the veneration of the sun was indeed in existence in the 12th Century. The tale of the Sun's true cross is not limited to the origin of the Scottish flag, however, for the true cross of the sun emerges again in Scottish history - as the Holy Rood of Scotland.

CHAPTER 16

SCOTLAND'S KING DAVID I, who ruled from 1124 to 1153, was the man who oversaw the gathering of the Culdees into the fold, and it is him who we next find at the centre, quite literally, of the Saltire line. His involvement in our tale dates to 1128, the very same year that he made the grant of land to the fledgling Templar order for their Scottish headquarters, but his particular involvement in this instance is in relation to the Holy Rood of Scotland.

The Holy Rood, sometimes called the Black Rood, was reputedly a piece of the True Cross of Jesus, and was said to have been brought into the country in the 11th century. The bones of the tale are that the Rood came from Hungary in 1057 in the entourage of Edgar Aetheling and his daughter Margaret. That relic came to Edinburgh as a dowry when Margaret married Malcolm Canmore, King of Scotland. So pious was Margaret that she was later canonised and became St. Margaret. After her death the Holy Rood passed into the care of her son, King David I in 1124, and four years later he founded Holyrood Abbey to house the relic. The tale that surrounds the king's decision to build the Abbey, the date he did so and the location of it, are all of immense interest to our tale.

The story of Holyrood Abbey's founding starts with King David hunting in the wild forest to the east of Edinburgh one day. He thought he had cornered a stag in a clearing, but found to his dismay that it had actually cornered him. Fearing for his life he prayed for help, whereupon he saw a vision of a golden cross descending from the clouds to hover between the stag's antlers, and thus he was delivered. To show his appreciation he founded an abbey on the site of the incident, to house the relic that was in his care. This is how Holyrood Abbey came to be built a mile due east of the crag upon which Edinburgh Castle sits. To this day the long straight road that runs between the two is still called the Royal Mile.

The precious relic rested in its abbey until the war with the English in the closing stages of the 13th century, when along with the Stone of Destiny, the Rood was purloined by King Edward I, nicknamed Longshanks. After various travels it ended up in Durham Cathedral where it remained until the Reformation, during which time it was destroyed as idolatrous.

So that is the legend of the Holy Rood, but what of the truth behind the myth? Again we have exactly the same elements as we have found elsewhere, and I would suggest that the Holy Rood of Scotland is as historically insubstantial as the bones of St. Andrew. As before, it is the geography that is important, for we can see from the map on the right that the incident occurred, yet again, on the same line of latitude as the true cross of the sun. When we see how close to this line the abbey was built, we can surely see the solar origin of the tale.

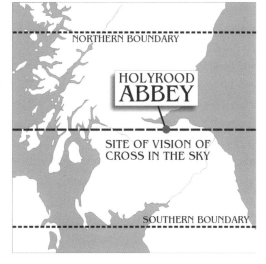

NORTHERN BOUNDARY

HOLYROOD
ABBEY

SITE OF VISION OF
CROSS IN THE SKY

SOUTHERN BOUNDARY

As noted before, the 12th Century was the era of the relic, when a credulous population needed physical objects to venerate. There is no doubt that there existed a piece of wood that people of the day believed was part of the True Cross, but I would suggest that it came from a similar source as the bones of St. Andrew, and that its purpose was to give the people a tangible, physical object of veneration in a time when that was what people needed from their faith.

Another aspect of the tale that is intriguing, and tends to reinforce my suggestion that the Holy Rood as a symbol has its origin in the sun, is the inclusion of a stag in the tale, for the stag has an association with an aspect of ancient mythology that we have yet to look at, but which will become a dominant theme in the rest of the book.

Cerunnos, the Horned God, had many depictions throughout the Celtic world. In the majority of them he was depicted either as a stag or as a man wearing antlers, and sometimes appeared in folklore as the Master of the Wild Hunt. The stag sheds its antlers in autumn and re-grows them in spring, so its link to the cycle of the seasons is obvious. As touched on earlier, the ancient Celts divided their year into two, with the sun ruling the summer and various other gods ruling the winter. Cerunnos was one such god, and if the sun had been previously venerated in the area, then the defeat of the stag under the sign of the cross is a very succinct reference to that fact.

What we have in the tale of the siting of Holyrood Abbey is, I suggest, exactly the same Christianising of the veneration of the sun that we have seen elsewhere. In Celtic myth, the sun defeated the darkness of winter every year, so King David's battling with the stag of Cerunnos is therefore a mythical reference to this. By associating this tale with the true cross of Jesus, the author of the tale is thus Christianising the same pagan notion we have encountered elsewhere.

This happened at exactly the same time in history that the priests of St. Andrews were setting about their subjugation of the Culdee Church, and in the same way as the tale of the Saltire Christianised the sun's cross, David I's building of Holyrood Abbey appears to have served an identical purpose. In the process, he converted the true cross of the sun to the true cross of the Son.

We must also remember that St. Margaret is recorded as having brought the relic to Scotland in the 11th Century, so we can see that as simply another attempt to Christianise the past. The tale is also incredibly similar to the vision associated with the earlier Dark Age battle that gave us the sign of the Saltire, and the village where that happened, Athelstaneford, is only twenty miles to the east of the abbey that was built for the Holy Rood. Are they not therefore likely to be based on the same phenomenon?

The dating of the abbey's building is significant to our story on another level too, because it was founded in 1128 - the very same year the Templars received their Rule from St. Bernard, and the same year that Hughes de Payens, first Grand Master of the new order, visited Scotland seeking donations. That same year the new knighthood was given lands at Ballantrodoch for their Scottish headquarters to the south of the city, also close to the centre of the solstice square as seen by reference to the map on the left.

It was King David I who gave them that land - the same man who possessed the Holy Rood, and had claimed to have seen the cross descend from the sky. This link in geography and time, between the king who built Holyrood Abbey and the Templars who I suggest were the originators of the Mystery of Christ that venerated the cross of the sun, is surely too potent a mixture to ignore.

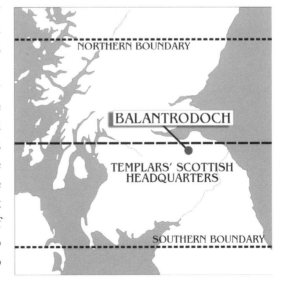

The myth of the Holy Rood has far too much in common with the veneration of the sun we have seen elsewhere for there not to be a connection. And are we really to believe that, like the bones of St. Andrew, part of the True Cross came by chance from Hungary to Scotland, coincidentally brought to the very same area where the sun had a special relationship with the landscape, in a place associated with a golden cross in the sky? I would suggest not, and that the term 'True Cross' inasmuch as Scotland is concerned, is a metaphor for the sun's behaviour, and arose at a time when the Church needed a strong Christian claim on the phenomenon to wean the people from its true meaning.

Even the fact the English placed the seized Rood in Durham Cathedral has significance to our tale, because Durham lies on the same line of latitude as Belfast – the line where the sun gives a true square on the summer solstice. If the sun was venerated at locations where the true square occurred there may well have been a strong veneration for the fact at Durham. Placing a part of the True Cross there would therefore have been yet another incidence of cleansing the paganism of the past with a powerful Christian relic.

The All-seeing Eye. A symbol for God which can be found in many ancient cultures.

The mound of Newgrange, 3200bce.

Celtic High Cross, Drumcliffe, Co. Sligo.

Sun pillar seen just after sunset.

Interior passage, Mound of Knowth. This mound is even older than Newgrange, its east-west passages built in honour of the sun on the equinoxes.

Tydavnet Sun-disc, thought to be around 4000 years old.

Mithras' Torchbearer.

Cross-legged Knight, Temple Church.

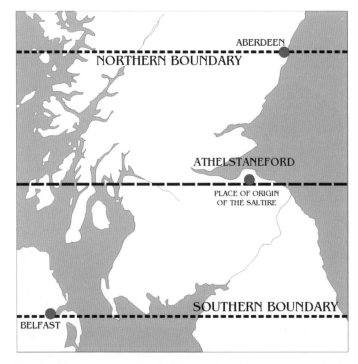

The line of the true cross that gave rise to the Saltire as the symbol of Scotland.

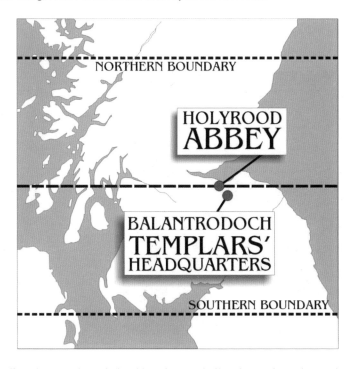

The line also runs through the abbey that was built to house the Holy Rood.

The fortress of Montsegur; last bastion of the beleaguered
Cathars, 1244.

Hiram dying in the west .

555, the latitude of the true cross.

Station 2, Glencolumbcille. It is difficult to see these symbols of squares and right-angles as Christian. If venerating the right-angle of the sun on the summer solstice at this exact latitude however, they make perfect sense.

The summer solstice sun setting on the square of Glen Head.

The setting sun seen the moment it touches the square of Glen Head as viewed from Station 2. Its first moment of contact with the earth as it sets on the summer solstice is right on the point of the square.

CHAPTER 17

IT'S AN OFT-quoted maxim that the ancients worshipped the sun. Whilst this is perhaps true of primitive man, by the time of the Celts, many other gods peopled their religious landscape. By the time the likes of Llew, Nuadha and Maponos came about, the sun had retreated as an object of worship, but nevertheless retained its position as the ultimate power behind the gods. We know this because the tales of those new gods were woven from the movements of the sun.

We earlier mentioned the mystery cults of the east and observed that their figureheads – Dionysus, Thammuz, Mithras et al – were created around a single template. The same can be said of the gods of the Celts, for many of them too are based on a single principle. As mentioned earlier, the Celts divided the year into two halves – a light half and a dark half. The sun ruled all, but for half the year night was longer than day, so during that period the sun was *in absentia*. Who, then, ruled in its absence, over the cold, dark days of winter, when nothing grew and the summer colour withered into the soil? A second deity came to fill that void - the *lord of the winter*. This gave two gods, who between them ruled the year. In essence the two were aspects of the same God, and were a mirror image of each other.

The lives of the fearful and superstitious peoples who lived in these cold northern latitudes long before us were completely dependent on the sun, for when it rose high in the sky in summer the crops grew in abundance, but when it dipped under the horizon during the winter, when night ruled, everything died. The sun ruled the summer, then, a time of life and abundance, but when it departed into the underworld during the winter the second god took over, ruling the cold period of death and decay in the sun's absence. This second god, who was not in any way malevolent, was known by a variety of names such as Cerunnos and King Donn, and all fulfilled the role of the lord of the winter. Rather than being an adversary for the sun, however, the lord of the winter was the sun's complement, and the two worked in harmony to rule the year, for as the sun was absent for half the year, the cycle of the seasons needed the second god to rule that half.

The ancients called the light half of the year *Samos* over which the sun ruled, and the dark half they called *Giamos*. Samos is the time of growth from the equinox in spring to that in autumn, during which nature blossoms into life and light exceeds dark. Giamos starts in autumn, and marks the period of death and decay that is the winter months. If the lord of the winter ruled the dark half of the year and the sun ruled the summer, there had to be a time when they physically changed places with each other, and that changeover took place on the equinox, the day of balance between light and dark, when their powers were equalised. Each of them therefore ruled for six months at a time, in an endless rhythm that is repeated year on year forever. Although the Celts celebrated their main feasts at the cross-quarter days between the solstices and equinoxes, on days which marked the middle of the seasons rather than their starts, the days of equilibrium that are the equinoxes were still the basis of the division.

This juxtaposition of twin deities was one of the most common themes in ancient mythology and can be identified in the legends of peoples right across the world. The similarities between them come from the fact that they all use the same basis for those legends – the relationship between the sun and the lord of the winter. As we will see later, many of them also derived their lords of the winter from one particular common source – a source we will find to be of enormous importance to the mysteries of Freemasonry.

Many myths were created through the ages by various peoples as to the relationship of these two gods, how one usurped the other for a time before being in his turn dispossessed by his alter-ego. The sun took over from the lord of the winter on the spring equinox, reaching the zenith of its power on the summer solstice, whilst the positions were reversed on the autumnal equinox, leading to the sun's nadir and rebirth on Mid-winter's Day. In all this it was the sun that was all-important, and the entire belief system was created to honour the sun's triumph over winter. This happened on the spring equinox, so that day, which has been associated with rebirth since civilisation began, was the most important day in the process.

When I became aware of this fact as I studied and tried to make sense of ancient myth, I was reminded of the pre-eminent position of the equinoxes in the rituals of the Craft. It had started to look to me as if this principle from the ancient past, with its emphasis on the solstices and equinoxes, played a part in the allegories of Freemasonry, but it would be some time before I was to realise how close to the truth I had actually come.

CHAPTER 18

IN THE LAST chapter we saw how the year was divided into two halves, and how each of those halves was ruled over by a separate deity. In this chapter we will look more closely at the interaction between those twin gods, because it is vital for understanding the Masonic 3rd Degree, which I have discovered was structured around the very same principle.

Ancient myths are not generally the stuff of academic research, because they are like sprites that dance through the mist, disappearing from sight one minute only to re-appear somewhere else the next. They do not constitute history as such, and have come down to us in incomplete, fragmentary form, in poetry and song, from when the deeds of men were told and sung of around the bright hall-fires of a long forgotten age. Because of the oral tradition of the Bronze and Iron Age peoples we call the Celts, they did not overly concern themselves with correctness and the faithful recording of detail. Their stories have survived in folk tales, only later recorded by scribes long since dead, on parchment long ago turned to dust. Often now we only have fragmented snippets of quotes, by a few scribes whose work by quirk of fate has somehow survived the ravages of time. Few if any such tales have survived in their entirety, and have had to be reconstructed from their various parts. That is to assume, of course, that there ever was one single myth, because more often than not the legends exist as a patchwork of stories, having little or no relevance or connection to each other. Whilst varied and disjointed, however, the core tales of many gods of old can still be seen to be drawn from the movements of the stars and the interaction of the sun with them.

There were variations in the date of the births and deaths of the gods among the ancient peoples, and it is not always easy to discern precisely how their particular systems worked. In some instances their gods were born or died at the solstices, whilst in others they died or were reborn on the equinoxes but attributed the start of the process to the solstices. So whilst the sun - the lord of the summer - can be said to be born at the winter solstice, that day does not indicate the end of the reign of the lord of the winter, for it would come a quarter year later at the spring equinox when night and day were equal and the two had therefore reached an equilibrium of power.

In Celtic mythology we have a very good depiction of this in one of the stories of the death of Llew, the Welsh god of Light, who can only be killed whilst standing with one foot on the rim of a cauldron and the other on the back of a goat. When he is in this position, Goronwy, Llew's lord of the winter who is hiding nearby, attacks him with a spear. Rather than being killed, however, Llew transforms into an eagle and flies off. The eagle is telling, for in mythology, as indeed in our tale here, it represents the summer solstice. Llew then returns six months later and catches Goronwy balancing as he himself had done, on the rim of the cauldron and a goat's back, attacks him, and resumes his position as ruler of his domain.

The details that underpin this tale are straightforward, and more obvious in this legend than many another, hence its inclusion here. In mythology the cauldron was the summer solstice, represented by the astrological sign of Cancer. The goat is a plain reference to Capricorn, the sign of the winter solstice. In the myth, Llew must be balanced between these two dates to be killed. This day of balance was the autumn equinox, when day and night were equal and darkness can triumph over light. The reverse happens six months later at the spring equinox, when light is poised to exceed darkness. Neither god died however, because in dying to the world of light, they gained the throne in the Otherworld. From this can clearly be seen the division of the year, and that Llew was the sun and that his adversary Goronwy represented the dark half of the year.

The same theme crops up again and again in Celtic mythology. In the tale of Myrddin Wyllt we find the hero fleeing the horror of battle into the dark forest, where, traumatised by what he witnessed on the field of war, he descends into madness. In his absence his wife takes another man into his house, but as Myrddyn languishes in the forest, he befriends the animals, learns from them, and replenishes his life-force – nurtured back to health by Nature herself. Slowly he achieves his former state, and when strong enough, returns to his home and attacks and kills his wife's new lover. In doing so he resumes his rightful position as ruler of his own domain. Like the other myths, then, he can be equated with the sun. His defeat and flight into the forest represents the sun's retreat under the horizon during the dark winter months, and his later defeat of his rival as the sun's triumphant return in spring.

Another ancient myth that reinforces the position of the lord of the winter in myth is the story of Nuadha of the Silver Arm. This picture is of what is known as Tandragee Man, thought to be an effigy of Nuadha holding his silver arm. Found in a garden in Tandragee Co. Armagh Northern Ireland, it is thought to date from around 1000BCE and now rests in St. Patrick's Church of Ireland Cathedral in Armagh. The story of Nuadha is that he was one of the greatest kings of Ireland, and lost his arm in battle against a challenger called Bres. The ancient kings of Ireland had to be bodily perfect in order to rule, so after having his sword-arm smitten off, Nuadha was forced to abdicate in favour of his opponent.

Bres was the sun, and was accredited with building Newgrange, whilst Nuadha is equated with the constellation of Orion. The origin of Nuadha's miraculous arm is believed to come from the fact that Orion stands in the sky beside the silvery ribbon of the Milky Way, his raised arm reaching upwards into it. The river Boyne was regarded as the sacred outpouring of milk from the goddess Boann - the Mistress of the white Cows - and the Milky Way was the heavenly version of the earthly river. By Orion placing his damaged arm in its silvery goodness, he obtained succour and was thus revitalised. Thus was born the legend of Nuadha of the Silver Arm.

In the myth, Nuadha lost his throne to Bres, but while the usurper ruled, Nuadha departed into the Underworld where he existed between life and death in the company of its keeper King Donn. As time passed he had a replacement arm made out of silver, and suitably revitalised, he once more engaged Bres in battle. Defeating his adversary with the power of his mighty new limb, he returned in triumph once more to the rule of the land. On the face of it we have, yet again, the elements of the twin gods, one of whom is at first cast down, only to arise once more and resume his rule. What is particularly interesting in this myth is the inclusion of the constellation Orion, for as we will see in upcoming chapters, that constellation is of the utmost importance to the meaning behind the rituals of Freemasonry.

The underlying principle of the above Celtic stories, and their ultimate point, was the coming to power of the sun after its six-month sojourn below the horizon. I had already discovered that Freemasonry used the sun as a symbol of deity, so was it possible that the myths associated with the Craft's symbolism could carry the same allusion? If so, how better could that be achieved than by structuring the complex rituals of the lodge room around the identification of the moment when the sun triumphs over dark? This suggestion will come as a surprise even to Freemasons, for I am not aware of it ever being made before. Once one looks at Freemasonry from this perspective, however, various aspects of it seem to confirm the possibility.

I had mentioned in chapter two that in the early days of the Craft there were actually two Masters who ruled the lodge for six months each. One was installed to office on the summer solstice, the other on the winter solstice. This would place them as representations of the two gods that ruled the year between them.

When I had advanced the thesis to the point we have now reached, I took a long, hard look at the ceremony for installing a new Master, to see if what I saw confirmed the meaning I now attach to the moment.

During the installation ceremony, both the incoming and outgoing Master take great care not to leave the chair vacant for any time at all. To enable this, the outgoing Master takes the new Master by both hands before he leaves the chair, and as he rises, he guides his successor into the seat as he himself vacates it, in a carefully controlled circular movement that is totally in keeping with the symbolism of the handing over of authority as suggested here. He even refers to vacating to the south so his successor can arrive from the north. Since on the equinox the sun passes from one hemisphere to the other – from north to south and back again six months later, this can surely therefore be seen as an allegorical representation of the changeover of one god to the other on those days?

I also cast my eye over other aspects of ritual, to see if the same symbolism could be found elsewhere. I mentioned in chapter two that I

212

believed that the coping of the deacons' wands over the altar at the opening and closing of the lodge signified the sun's rays shining over the proceedings. This is what I said then, summarised... 'Another time we see this angle is at the moment the Lodge is both opened and closed with the coping of the deacons' wands over the altar..... Whilst obviously not precisely 60 degrees, the coping can nevertheless be seen as symbolic of the sun's rays over the altar,'

Looking closely at that part of the ritual again, and having become more alert to its nuances, I noticed that at each of the two times it occurs the behaviour of the deacons is slightly different, depending on whether the lodge is being opened or closed. The small difference reinforces the veracity of my original supposition that the coping of the wands may indeed indicate not only the exact moments of sunrise and sunset in particular, but encapsulate the two equinoxes as well.

The sunrise

At a given time during the opening ceremony the two deacons assemble at the altar, just before the Master declares the lodge open. They arrive at their given places a few seconds before the Master speaks and stand motionless, facing inwards, their wands vertical, resting on the ground at their feet. They wait until the precise moment the lodge is declared open, before quickly raising the wands overhead and crossing the tips over the centre of the altar. They continue to stand like this until the end of the opening ceremony, when, without verbal instruction, they drop them to their sides again and return to their seats.

The closing ceremony is slightly different in that this time the deacons, though they assemble at the altar as before, cope their wands immediately on reaching the altar without waiting for a verbal indicator to do so. It is only when the Master declares the lodge to be closed that they un-cope them and bring them smartly to their sides. The catalyst this time is to uncope them as the lodge is closed, the exact mirror image of the opening.

The difference may be small, but it means that before the lodge is opened there are no rays over the altar, and that at the very instant the lodge is opened, the metaphorical rays suddenly appear and remain for the duration of the opening ceremony. This can surely be seen to indicate that the sun has arisen and the day has started. Likewise the rays are present until the moment the Master declares the lodge closed, whereupon they disappear, indicating that the sun has set, ending the day. So the instructions enshrined in the ritual are to cope the wands at the precise moment of the lodge's opening, and to uncope them at the precise moment of its closure, indicating that the sun is shining for the duration of the meeting.

To add to the above we also have another action that takes place at this same time. The Senior Warden's position is in the west of the room, in line with the east-west axis. In front of him is a table, and on it sits a small column with a globe atop. This column starts off lying flat, and at the exact moment the lodge is declared open it is raised to the vertical. This, then, signifies the rising of the sun with the raising of the globe. The exact reverse happens as the lodge is closed, with the column being returned to the horizontal, therefore representing the sun setting. When asked his duty in the lodge room, the Senior Warden replies '… as the sun sets in the west to close the glorious day so the Senior Warden stands in the west, to close the lodge…' Taking the lowering of the globe at the same moment as the un-coping of the Deacon's wands, it surely cannot be denied that the setting sun at the end of the day is what is intended in this part of the ceremony.

In studying the ritual even closer, I have come to the conclusion that the coping of the wands at the opening of the lodge also alludes to the spring equinox and the coming to power of the sun, and that the closing refers to the other equinox, when the sun hands back power to the lord of the winter. This, of course, would signify that the sun is in control of the heavens whilst the lodge is at labour.

The equinoxes

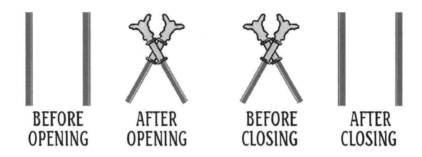

BEFORE   AFTER   BEFORE   AFTER
OPENING   OPENING   CLOSING   CLOSING

Before the lodge is declared open, the deacons keep their two wands vertical by their sides, making two parallel lines, and then cope them over the altar forming an x-shaped cross at the moment it opens. In the symbolism we have seen elsewhere, the two parallel lines formed by the vertical wands can be equated with the two solstices, or the two saints John. The Senior Deacon, standing to the south of the altar therefore represents the winter solstice or St. John the Evangelist, whilst the Junior Deacon in the north becomes the summer or St. John the Baptist. The period before the lodge is opened can therefore be seen as the segment of the year during which one of the solstices occur.

At the exact moment of the opening of the lodge the deacons form an x-shaped cross over the centre of the altar with their wands, displaying the same symbolism as the torchbearers in the Mithraic Tauroctony when they stand with their shins crossed. Those torchbearers encapsulate the equinox in that stance, and I suggest the deacons do likewise. In that movement, then, from holding their wands vertical to crossing them, the deacons signify the change from solstice to equinox.

We could also safely surmise, bearing in mind the Craft's honouring of the summer solstice sun, that the equinox referred to in the opening is the one in spring that heralds the light half of the year and the sun's coming to power.

The closing ceremony is the exact opposite of this and commences with the wands already coped, signifying an equinox at the start of the ceremony. At the exact moment the lodge is closed, the wands resume their vertical stance, again indicative of the solstices. We can see the altering of the wands' stances here from coped to vertical as indicating the passing of the sun into the dark half of the year, and the start of its six-month sojourn under the horizon.

The fact that the tips are crossed rather than merely touching therefore brings another, much deeper layer of esoteric symbolism to the opening of the lodge than simply sunrise and sunset. I mentioned in chapter two that the tips of the wands are brass, to add to the allusion that the sun is intended, but there will be those who say that the deacon's wands in their lodge rooms are tipped with silver or chrome rather than brass, so my reading of the symbolism must therefore be wrong. We must, however, never lose sight of the fact that the relevance of these little details was lost to the Masonic world centuries ago, so tarnished old brass-tipped wands may over the years have been swapped for shiny new silver or chrome ones, without anyone realising that their originally being brass carried symbolic significance.

From the foregoing about the relevance of light and dark to ancient man, we now also have a more precise explanation for the black and white pavement on the floor of the Masonic lodge room. We have seen how the ancient world divided the year into two halves, with the divisions being the equinoxes. These dates were the portal to the Afterlife – the dates on which the gods entered and exited the Underworld – and so presumably man's soul did likewise. Though we have yet to look at the Masonic 3rd Degree, we will see that it is a figurative death and rebirth ritual that involves temporarily entering and exiting the Underworld in a symbolic fashion, similar to the pilgrims on Lough Derg and the candidates for the mysteries in the ancient world.

We will come to the detail of that degree shortly, but for now we will expand on the notion of the black and white referring to passage into the afterlife. If Freemasonry is structured around the symbolic death and spiritual re-birth of the new Master Mason, the attachment of black and white to the Craft is obvious, and deeply meaningful.

As mentioned before, the black and white pavement is also one of the aspects of the order that hints at a link with the Knights Templar. We noted in chapter two that their battle-flag, the Beausant, was black and white. It is usually claimed that the black and white simply refers to good and evil, and of the dark past and pure future of those who joined the order. I have shown throughout, however, that black and white have a deeply esoteric meaning that is truly ancient, so perhaps we can consider that the black and white had a similar meaning in the Beausant?

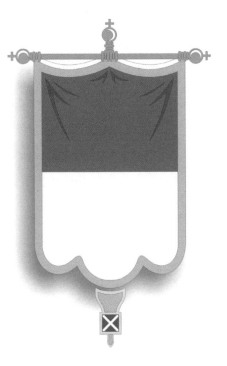

We must also remember that the Beausant was the Templar's battle flag – the emblem they carried with them into battle and to possible death. Considering the relevance I am attaching to the use of black and white as a reference to the threshold to the Afterlife, there could be no better device to have as a battle flag than this.

The word 'beausant' is French for piebald; or simply, black and white. In our modern world the only time we would use the term piebald is in relation to an animal like a horse, or a bird such a magpie. This leads some modern commentators to make the suggestion that the same was true of the Templar's Beausant, and that it simply refers to the piebald horses they rode. To accept this is to accept that the Templars only ever rode piebald horses – a suggestion that is frankly unlikely.

As far as the thesis presented here, the black and white has a very definite esoteric meaning that relates to the division of the year into its light and dark halves, and the portal to the underworld that resides at the boundary between those halves. That is an altogether more substantial purpose for the use of a piebald flag during battle than suggesting that it refers to the markings on the horses some of them rode.

What lends weight to the esoteric notion that black and white was indeed deeply symbolic for them is the fact that they also used it in the most famous of all their buildings – Temple Church in London.

The picture above is of its interior, and as can be plainly seen, they have set black Purbeck marble columns against the stark white of the Caen stone walls. We must consider that this is the most important church they ever built, and as such suggests that the black and white was indeed more important than the colour of their horses.

We must also consider that black and white is a dominant theme in Freemasonry too. Its use there is perfectly consistent with the deeply symbolic division of the year and the symbolic access to the Underworld that those days signify. Or are we to think that the use of the same contrasting colours by both organisations is merely coincidence?

Temple Church is also famous for its effigies of cross-legged knights. Knights presented in such a fashion are found all over the British Isles, but there are more in Temple Church than at any other single location. Of nine effigies in the round church, six are arranged in this peculiar way, linking the practice very definitely with the Knights Templar. So what are we to make of their stance?

One popular theory is that the crossing of the legs simply indicates that the deceased was a Crusader, and that where the legs crossed referred to the number of times the individual went to the Holy Land. Crossing at the shins indicated one trip to the Levant, at the knee meant two times, and the thigh three. The problem with this is that many figures so depicted never went anywhere near the Holy Land, so we must discount that argument. In the absence of this suggestion however, no other reason has ever been offered for the curious posture.

We must also remember that Mithras' Torchbearers crossed their legs in similar fashion, in reference to the sun's crossing of the equinoxes. As we will discover in following chapters the crossing of the legs is also a defining element in Freemasonry, and will be shown to refer, yet again, to the equinoxes. The thesis presented here suggests that the stance of the cross-legged knights was, like the skull and crossbones motif, a direct homage to the division of the year into two halves that lay at the heart of the spiritual tradition they themselves promoted. The crossing of the seasons was the equinox, and it was on that day that the membrane between the worlds of light and dark was thinnest, when the passage between them opened. What better stance could an effigy of a dead knight who followed a tradition that venerated the equinoxes because of that association display, than to have his legs crossed in such a fashion? And in grasping his sword pummel his elbow is also held at a right-angle in many of the carvings, as can be seen in the above picture, so we may also have included that other aspect of ancient spirituality that is still practiced in the Craft today. And surely the presence of so many cross-legged knights in a building that is itself black and white adds considerably to the above suggestion?

There is also the fact that the church is circular, a building style that was particular to the Knights Templar, so could that have been in honour of the sun too? Many commentators before me have suggested this, but by adding the significance of the black and white and its connection with the cross-legged posture of the knights inside the church, the claim is greatly strengthened.

We also have to consider that the Templar's main feast day was that of St. John the Baptist, which is elsewhere throughout this book seen as a reference to the summer solstice. In addition we must also consider the Knights' use of the Agnus Dei, perhaps the most prominent of all their icons, for as mentioned earlier; it is a reference to the spring equinox when the sun is reborn after its winter absence.

When we consider all the Templar iconography we have mentioned, we have black and white, both in their battle flag and Temple Church, that can be attributed to the equinoxes – we have the Agnus Dei, which is specifically the spring equinox – we have the crossing of the legs, which is ripe with the symbolism of the sun's crossing between the light and dark on the equinoxes – and we have Temple Church being built on a round plan in mimicry of the sun. Taken together, there can be little doubt that all fit into one complete spiritual path that is identical with that of Freemasonry.

We have already looked at some of this in our examination of the Craft, and will see more in the course of the next few chapters. The use of these symbols also has a 'back history', in that every element can be traced backwards to an origin in the distant past. The spirituality they point to is not Christian, so proves that the Templars did indeed hold doctrines that were beyond the orthodox pale. An examination of the symbolism they employed, then, does nothing to dissuade us from the proposal that it was indeed they who brought the Mystery of Christ to Britain.

I have tried to demonstrate throughout this book that ancient notions, though their context has changed over the centuries, are still with us. In one last comment on the meaning of black and white, I would suggest another use of it in the modern age that underpins an origin identical to that discussed above. We see black and white in the chequered flag that signifies the end of a race. We have attached the use of those colours in an alternating pattern to the end of life, and in denoting the conclusion of a race the chequered flag also denotes the end. So we have yet another example of the modern use of ancient symbolism that has totally lost its original meaning along the way – but is nevertheless still with us.

We have mentioned the Masonic 3rd Degree often throughout the narrative, and in truth all that has gone before has been structured to bring us to the point where we can look at that degree with an analytical eye. It holds a particularly important place in the Craft – not just because it is the defining moment of a Mason's Masonic career – but because it was not a part of the ancient Craft that was handed down by the stonemasons. It was added around 1728 to the two degrees that were already in existence, and as such is a product of the emergent Craft.

From the point of view of this thesis, the 3rd Degree was always going to be the most important part of all, for in being written during modern times, it is likely to have clearer indicators to the underlying meaning of the Craft than those more obscure, long forgotten rituals of the stonemasons. It is therefore only now, after the revelations in the earlier sections of this book that have set the scene in context, that we are able to appreciate fully what the 3rd Degree actually means.

PART THREE

WRITTEN IN THE STARS

THE CRAFT AND THE CROSS

CHAPTER 19

THE THIRD DEGREE is simply a piece of theatre that tells the story of the building of Solomon's Temple and of the death of its architect, Hiram Abif. In essence it tells the story of the architect of the Temple in Jerusalem and his murder at the hands of three of his employees. In choosing death rather than betray the trust placed in him by refusing to give the secrets of a Master Mason to those who had not earned the right to them, he stands as a shining example of fidelity for all Masons to emulate. What higher aspiration can a man have in life than that he be true to his word? If the concept of fidelity could be conveyed to the candidate through Hiram's sacrifice, then the idea of trustworthiness and dependability will be impressed on him and may trickle down into all aspects of his life, and as a result, society can only be the better for it.

That is the message of the degree, but even a cursory glance at the ritual shows it is overstuffed with quirky detail, that to my mind at least has to allude to something that is not immediately obvious. We will now look in depth at that ritual, and as in the other chapters of this book, I am quoting from the ritual of the Irish Constitution and no other unless specified.

There has been much speculation as to where the story came from, for though there is a Hiram mentioned in the Bible, he was not the architect of the Temple. In fact there are two Hirams mentioned in the Bible. The first is Hiram King of Tyre, who supplied materials and labour to Solomon who had neither the manpower nor the resources to build the temple his father David had been instructed by God to construct. The other Hiram is recorded as an artisan, skilled in working with brass, and was a widow's son from the tribe of Naphtali. Masonry's Hiram seems to be a mixture of both these characters. He had the title Abif appellated to his name in Masonic lore, which is explained as meaning 'Father', denoting that he was a master at his craft. Nowhere outside Masonry is this man referred to as the principal architect of the Temple, but nevertheless, many Masons over the years have believed that he existed as a real historical character.

The Temple of Solomon as recorded in the Bible was an immense structure, which used vast resources and took many years to complete. In the Masonic legend, Solomon sought help from his friend Hiram King of Tyre, and it was this man who appointed Hiram Abif as chief overseer of the project. The three of them formed a triumvirate to co-ordinate the building's construction and organise the labour, which would be under the ultimate supervision of Hiram Abif, then titled Grand Master.

At that time there were three grades of worker; apprentices, journeymen and masters, whose titles are self-explanatory and indicate the rank that each worker had obtained. The masters were virtually architects in their own right, skilled in all areas of building, and were paid in gold. The journeymen were paid partly in gold and partly in kind, whereas the apprentices were paid only in kind - salt, corn, oil etc. Apprentices had a hard life, and spent their days in the quarries hewing the living rock into approximately square blocks known as rough ashlars. They longed for the day that their arduous apprenticeship would be over, when they would be promoted to the next level where they would at least get a wage. Journeymen, or Fellow Crafts as they are called in Freemasonry, were skilled in working with stone and dressed the rough ashlars to the complex shapes required for the building. With a little gold in their pockets they were better off than the apprentices, but they all had their eye on the ultimate level, that of Master Mason. Masters were skilled in all areas of the craft and acted as foremen or overseers. Their position was envied by all, because they got paid handsomely and could afford luxuries that the others could only dream about, and as a result, the elevation to Mastership was a very much sought after prize.

Each grade was given a secret word to denote its level of skill, and when it came time to be paid each week, the secret word was given to the paymaster who then paid out according to the skill of each man. So highly was the position of Master regarded by the triumvirate that they decided that the secret word that identified the Master Masons should only be communicated in the presence of all three of them.

It was the custom at the end of a building project to promote those who had proved their worth, and as the Temple neared completion, the workers waited anxiously to see who would be promoted. As the day drew near when the promotions were to be announced, a group of fifteen Fellow Crafts huddled together to discuss their prospects. Fearful that they would not be elevated to Mastership, they hatched a plan to extract the secrets of a Master Mason from their Grand Master by whatever means necessary.

It was known that the Grand Master remained in the Temple in the middle of the day while the workers were called to refreshment, where, in the quiet cool of the unfinished building, he would take some nourishment himself and offer a prayer at the hour of noon. When the day came for the conspirators to put their plan into operation, twelve of them thought better of it and withdrew, but three were adamant that they would still go through with it. Armed with the working tools of their trade they positioned themselves at each of the three gates of the Temple to lie in wait. The candidate assumes the role of Hiram throughout the ceremony and is symbolically assaulted by each of the three as the story unfolds.

The Grand Master first approached the Southern Gate, where he was accosted by the first conspirator who was armed with a 24-inch rule, and who demanded the secret word of a Master Mason. Hiram remonstrated with him, saying that he could not give him the secret that way, and that if the Fellow Craft only bided his time he would become a Master in the proper fashion. Committed to the course of action, the conspirator raised the rule and struck Hiram a blow across the throat. At this point the Junior Warden, who plays the conspirator, symbolically strikes the candidate across the throat with his rule. Hiram staggered backwards and fled, intent in making his escape through the Western Gate, but was confronted there by the second conspirator wielding a heavy, metal 90-degree square. The same argument ensued at that gate, with the Grand Master still refusing to divulge the secrets to one who was unworthy, whereupon he was struck on the left breast with the heavy square. Similarly the Senior Warden symbolically strikes the candidate on the left breast with the square he has previously armed himself with. Reeling backwards from the blow and slightly dazed, Hiram Abif then stumbled towards the Eastern Gate where he was met by the most ruthless and desperate of the conspirators played by the Master of the Lodge, armed with a heavy setting-maul (mallet).

After an increasingly acrimonious exchange where the Grand Master for the third time refused to reveal the secrets unlawfully, the conspirator raised the heavy maul to strike him. Hiram, realising he was about to be killed, pleaded for mercy. He raised his hands in surrender, and crossed his right leg over his left. This cross-legged stance was mentioned earlier, for it is identical to that of Mithras' torchbearers and Temple Church's cross-legged knights. Whilst the raising of the hands is understandable under the circumstances he found himself in, the crossing of the legs is more obtuse, and is completely unexplained in the ritual.

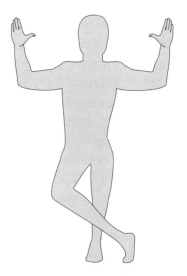

The candidate is then placed in this precise stance, with his legs crossed and arms upraised.

The two wardens, having left aside their weapons, now position themselves on each side of the candidate and grip him by the arms, ensuring he remains precisely in the upright position adopted by Hiram Abif. Unmoved by his Grand Master's plea, the conspirator again demanded the Master Mason's secret word. When Hiram refused for the final time, the Fellow Craft lunged at him, striking him a fatal blow to the head. At this moment in the drama the Master lunges at the candidate, symbolically striking him on the forehead with the maul, whilst at this same instant the conductor pushes him backwards. Assisted by the firm grip the wardens have on his arms, and unable to correct his balance because of his crossed legs, he finds himself on the floor where he realises there is a white sheet spread underneath him. At the exact moment he is struck the lights are turned out, plunging the room into darkness; all except for a faint glimmer of light at the east end of the room.

The three conspirators then buried the body roughly under some debris whilst they decided how they could best extricate themselves from the disastrous situation they found themselves in. Reckoning that their best option was to flee westwards to the coast and perhaps make their escape by ship, they then uncovered the body and re-buried it outside the city walls in a shallow grave. In this part of the drama the second burial is marked by placing a golden square on the candidate's chest to identify him as the Grand Master before wrapping him in the white sheet, covering all but his eyes in symbolic representation of burial. Having thus hidden their crime, the three conspirators, or ruffians as they are also known, then fled west to the coast to make good their escape.

That afternoon Solomon, concerned that Hiram was not in the Temple as he should have been, sent messengers out to enquire where he might be. The twelve who had withdrawn from the treachery, realising that the worst must have happened, went to their king and told him of the three's plan to extract the Master's secrets illegally from the

Grand Master. Solomon, fearful that the secrets of the Master Mason - the word used to elevate the Fellow Craft to the position of Master - had been lost, divided the twelve into groups and sent them out on a two-fold mission. He charged them to discover what they could of the fate of the Grand Master and also to search for the three ruffians in order that they could be brought back for punishment.

Some of them journeyed south, though nothing could be discovered of the conspirators there and the party returned to Jerusalem empty-handed. Another group went west to the coast at Joppa, where they heard voices coming as if from under the ground, and realised that the sound was coming from a cave on the seashore. Crouching near the entrance, they listened to what was being said inside, and realised that it was the three by now penitent conspirators arguing over what they had done, and discussing what the probable outcome of their impetuosity would be. The three discussed what punishments they would be likely to receive if they were found and taken back to face the wrath of Solomon.

The first conspirator reckoned that his throat would be cut across and his tongue torn out at the roots. The second thought that his breast would be ripped open and his heart torn out. The third suggested that his body would be sawn in half at the waist, his bowels removed, burnt to ashes and scattered to the four winds. Having by then heard enough, the search party rushed in, overpowered them, and took them back to Jerusalem, where Solomon decreed that their words should become prophetic, and had them executed in the manner each had described.

These methods of execution became the salutes of the three degrees, with the first salute being the hand drawn across the throat, the second symbolically drawing the heart from the chest, and the third drawing the hand across the abdomen as though cutting it open. What intrigued me when I first started to examine the ritual was that the first two methods of execution follow precisely the wounds inflicted by each of those conspirators on the Grand Master. The first ruffian referred to having his throat cut, and it was he who had struck Hiram across the throat with the 24-inch rule. The second spoke of having his breast torn open and the heart plucked out, and it was this ruffian who had struck the Master on the breast with a heavy square. The third conspirator however, having killed Hiram with a blow to the forehead, then changed the method of execution to being sawn in half. This seemed anomalous at first - a contrivance to identify the salute as being different than the other two – and hinted that it held allegorical import. The importance of this gesture escaped me for some time, but as a result of later discoveries its significance became obvious, and went a good way to proving the entire hypothesis. We will return to it in a later chapter.

The third search party, having travelled east, were disappointed not to have found anything of their Grand Master's whereabouts and sat down dejected by the side of the road to discuss what they would tell Solomon on their return to Jerusalem. On climbing to their feet again, one of the men tried to pull himself upright with the assistance of a bush growing nearby, but to his surprise it pulled out of the ground when he touched it, and he realised that it had already been uprooted and replaced in loose soil. Realising that the disturbed ground may well be a shallow grave, they knew that they had in all probability found the grave of their Grand Master. Dismayed, they placed a sprig of acacia on top of the loose soil to mark the spot and returned to Solomon with their sad news.

The king was devastated and instructed the party to return to the place to recover the body of the dead Grand Master and bring it back to Jerusalem for a fitting burial. As the secrets of the Master Mason were now lost, the King realised that substitute secrets must be found to replace those which were lost, until such time as the real secrets were found once more. He instructed the party to closely observe what happened when the body was raised so that if anything out of the ordinary were to happen, whatever it was could form the basis for what would become the substituted secrets.

Returning to the site, the party started to clear the earth away from the body. First they removed a small amount of soil, represented in the ritual by uncovering only the candidate's face. Realising that they had indeed found a body they then uncovered a little more, causing the stench of rotting flesh to arise, making them recoil in horror. This part is symbolised by the removal of more of the sheet and the party turning away from the grisly sight. Steeling themselves, they cleared away the rest of the earth, exposing the gold square on Hiram's breast, which left them in no doubt that they had indeed found the body of their Grand Master. In the ritual the conductor throws the remainder of the sheet clear of the candidate, indicating that the grave has been excavated.

All that then remained was for the body to be raised from the ground, and so first one of the party, played by the Junior Warden, tries to lift Hiram with the grip of an Entered Apprentice. The rotting flesh pulls from the hand and the arm falls back onto the ground. Next a second workman, acted by the Senior Warden, tries to lift the body with the Fellow Craft's grip, but more flesh is ripped from the bone, and that attempt also fails. Finally a third steps forward, this time acted by the conductor, and using a strong grip known as the Lion's Paw or Eagle's Talon, (digging the fingernails into the sinews of the wrist), successfully raises the body out of its shallow grave. In one fluid movement, the putrefying body is raised from the horizontal to the upright. In being lifted, the candidate is symbolically raised from a dead level to a living upright into the curious position mentioned in chapter two known as the Five Points of Fellowship. It is whilst in that position that the conductor whispers a word in the candidate's ear which is said in the ritual to mean 'the flesh is falling from the bone,' in reference to the fact that Hiram was in an advanced state of decomposition when he was raised.

The whispering of this word is the defining moment of the candidate's Masonic career, and he is now a fully-fledged Master Mason. Since Solomon had asked those present at the exhumation to note anything untoward that happened so that it could form the basis of the substituted secret word, it was this utterance which became the new Master Mason's Word.

So what is this word?

Lest I be accused by my fellow Masons of divulging the innermost secrets of the lodge room, I will quote it from John Robinson's book, Born in Blood, a study of the Knights Templar. On page 228 he says, 'The Scottish 'Mason's word' is Mahabone'. The situation regarding the alleged secrets of Freemasonry is nowhere better illustrated than by the furore this word provokes. Masons perhaps rightly regard the word which is at the centre of the entire Craft as sacrosanct, but the idea that it is in any way secret is nonsense, as it has appeared in countless books about the Craft, even from as long ago as the exposures of the 1730s, and yet Masonry still clings to the notion that it is secret. Like all Masonic secrets, it would perhaps be fair to say that it is not the word at all that is the secret, for it would not be possible to stop knowledge of it escaping from a fraternal society like Freemasonry, rather it is the hidden meaning that lies behind it that is the true secret, even if knowledge of that meaning faded long ago. Clinging to the attitude that it is a secret, however, allows the word to remain part of the ritual, which is vital if it has an esoteric, allegorical meaning, and disallows its removal and replacement with another, which would in any case be divulged also.

The legend played out on the lodge room floor is replete with quirky details, which is exactly what we would expect of an allegory that has a deeper, hidden meaning. Why three gates? Why draw attention to 12 who withdrew from the conspiracy? Why attack at noon? Why 3 assailants? Why attack the Grand Master in three different ways? Why was Hiram buried twice – once under rubbish in the Temple, and again outside the city wall? Why place a gold square on the candidate's chest prior to burial? Why flee westwards after the murder? Why outline methods of execution in advance? Why attempt to raise the candidate three times? And why was the body in an advanced state of putrefaction when it was discovered - so much so that it took the presence of the gold square to enable the Fellow Crafts to identify him?

It seemed to me that the entire legend is so obtuse and contrived that it is obviously laced with allegorical details, structured to facilitate the communication of certain key points. In addition, there are plot inconsistencies that simply do not make sense. In the first place, for instance, we are told that the triumvirate of Hiram King of Tyre, King Solomon, and Hiram Abif each have to be present when the Master Mason's word is communicated. This would indicate that each has knowledge of the word, and yet the death of one of the three renders it lost, indeed lost so utterly that a substitute word has to be invented.

Not only that, but the events that surround the invention of that substitute word also defy rational explanation - Solomon leaving the picking of the new word to the observation of three Fellow Crafts and the chance utterance of one of them. Not being Master Masons, they should not even be in possession of the 'Word,' so how could any word arrived at under such circumstances ever become a closely guarded secret? The predictions by the ruffians of the methods of their execution also become the salutes of the three degrees, but neither the first nor second degree have anything to do with the raising of a Master Mason, so why would those salutes also have to be referred to in the third? It is as if the entire situation was contrived to introduce the substitute word and the salutes to the Craft, and I was to find later that that is precisely the purpose of the degree. But for now, however, we must look at the broader picture, and turn our attention to where the character of Hiram may have come from.

CHAPTER 20

THE VERY FIRST mention of the character Hiram of Masonic lore is in the Cooke Manuscript of c1450, where it says that when Solomon sought to build his Temple, Hiram King of Tyre sent his son, also called Hiram, to be Solomon's Master Mason. The earliest record of there being a 3rd Degree of any description is in the Trinity College (Dublin) Manuscript of 1711, which mentions three classes of Mason - Entered Apprentice, Fellow Craft, and Master Mason - but has no details regarding what the 3rd Degree consisted of. The earliest record of a myth approximating the Hiramic legend is found in the Graham Manuscript of 1726, where the main character, like Hiram the architect, is also killed whilst refusing to divulge secrets, forcing the adoption of substituted secrets. The tale was set historically over a thousand years earlier at the time of the Flood, and the character was, of course, Noah. This is interesting, because it shows that at least one other character was tried out for the myth before the architect of the Temple was adopted, and goes a long way to proving Hiram's mythical origin.

The first appearance of Hiram Abif as architect of the Temple is in Anderson's Constitutions of 1723, though in that first edition there is neither murder nor subsequent raising. It would be the second edition of the Constitutions, published in 1738 before the entire legend is present. It is in Pritchard's Masonry Dissected 1730, one of the first 'exposures' that we mentioned earlier, that we first find the complete myth of the murder, discovery, and raising of Hiram the Architect of the Temple. It seems reasonable to assume, then, that the character was created around that time.

Masonic researchers have suggested many origins for the character over the years, from him being a real person to being a symbolic embodiment of Osiris, the Egyptian lord of the Underworld. I think we can dismiss the possibility of him being a real person on the grounds that nowhere before his sudden appearance around 1730 is there any account of his existence. A further difficulty in seeking the real, flesh and blood architect of the Temple is that it is highly likely that the Temple itself never existed on the scale mentioned in the Bible. No archaeological artefact has ever been found which conclusively proves that there ever was a Solomon's Temple, at least of the magnitude referred to in the Bible records, leaving many current archaeological scholars of the opinion that the history of the Temple grew in the telling while it was orally transmitted, and was further embellished when it came to be written down five hundred years later. So in terms of Hiram, we are left with a fictional character whose story was constructed to convey a moral lesson of fidelity to the candidate undergoing his degree. The question is, can his legend be attributed to anything in particular, or is his tale a random collection of details that don't mean anything beyond the obvious?

There are numerous contenders for the inspiration of the legend's main character ranging from the dim and distant past right up to the era that preceded the first appearance of the myth. In ancient times, mystery religions such as those of Tammuz, Adonis, Attis, Mithras and countless others, all had dying and resurrecting ceremonies similar to that of Hiram, so the possibility exists that those rites were the inspiration. The death and resurrection of Jesus is another possibility, though unlikely considering the de-Christianisation of the Craft around the time the legend was written.

Various mediaeval people and endeavours have also been credited with being the inspiration for Master Hiram, including the murder of Thomas Becket, the persecution of the Templars and the murder of their Grand Master Jacques de Molay, but perhaps the most convincing of them all was the execution of Charles I in 1649. The killing of that king shook the nation to its core, and was in living memory for those first speculative Masons who joined the Craft. In the final months of his reign, right up to his death, the King had impressed many with his quiet dignity, and won himself much sympathy. His brutal execution created a cult of martyrdom, which was encouraged by the publication of the book *Eikon Basilike*, a collection of his personal meditations whilst awaiting execution. Assembled into book form by Dr. John Gaudon after the king's death, it presented the deposed king as the victim of tyranny and a martyr to the cause of the divine right of kings, and was widely read at the time. The king's execution has obvious resonance with the murder of Hiram Abif, who chose death rather than divulge the Master Mason's secret word, especially so, as it took place at the same time that the lodges were becoming dominated by speculative Masons. The king surrendered to the Scottish army in 1646, the same year Elias Ashmole records being made a Mason, and a mere five years after Sir Robert Moray became the first documented initiation of a Mason on English soil.

What sets the older sources ahead of the modern references is that the entire Hiramic legend seems to belong in the tradition of the classic initiation ceremonies of ancient times, where the initiate underwent a figurative death and rebirth, to signify the leaving behind of an old life and the starting of a new. This is reinforced by the inclusion of the sprig of acacia in the Masonic tale, which was used as the marker for the grave of the Grand Master. In antiquity, all the pagan mysteries had an evergreen plant of some sort that was used to denote immortality. Ivy was used in the mysteries of Dionysus, myrtle in those of Ceres, and erica in the cult of Osiris. Being evergreen they do not die in winter and as such can be said to represent immortality. As this fact is even specifically mentioned in the ritual, it can be assumed that Acacia does indeed refer to immortality in the Hiramic legend.

The idea of wiping the slate clean and starting over again is at the core of religious experience, which is why so many faith systems past and present have offered their adherents the chance to leave their past behind and start life anew. Where Christianity offers baptism, the pagan mysteries offered a symbolic ritual based on the death and rebirth of their gods, where the acolyte acted out the role of the God in a drama designed to entertain and impress the lesson upon him or her. Almost all the pagan mysteries mentioned earlier had their initiations where the candidate, after assuming the character of the God, 'died' to the old world before being reborn in the new. On the surface then, this could be seen as relating to the drama in which the candidate for the Masonic 3rd Degree participates, where he is symbolically killed and is then afterwards raised. In assuming the role of Hiram and in dying as him and being raised, could it be said that such a linkage equates the candidate with the acolyte in the pagan mysteries? The Gnostics believed that God was an unknown and remote Supreme Being and that we, as humans contain a divine spark that can only be ignited through attaining gnosis, or knowledge of the divine. This gnosis was imparted through initiations, which must have been broadly similar to the degrees of Masonry. Is it possible, then, that the 3rd Degree ceremony is intended as a symbolic reference to the igniting of the divine spark of gnosis within the candidate?

Of these ancient gods of the mysteries, a brief glance at the opinions of various Masonic historians down the years shows heavy bias towards Osiris as the most likely contender for the inspiration of Hiram Abif, and this is interesting from the point of view of the earlier section of this book which sought to attribute Freemasonry in its earliest form to an adaptation of the pagan mysteries of the ancient world. Osiris was a god of the Ancient Egyptians, and in linking Hiram to him those commentators are therefore attributing to the first Grand Master a certain divinity, if merely figurative. Before continuing with this particular train of thought it would be appropriate to make clear that in no way was Hiram either Osiris or any other pre-Christian God. It will become apparent as we work through the meaning of the ritual that whatever pre-Christian aspects had been woven into the tale of Hiram are purely symbolic, and are used as universal metaphors without specific attachment to any particular dogma.

All those pagan dying and resurrecting god-men of the original mysteries that could be the template from which Hiram was created can be traced backwards to the composite character of Osiris/Dionysus, introduced to the Greek world by Pythagoras, the man credited in Masonic lore with being the father of Masonry. As such it can therefore be argued that Osiris was the father of all the mysteries, and from the point of view of this study of Freemasonry would therefore seem an ideal candidate for the new myth. There is also a second, more compelling reason why he would be eminently suitable for the role, and that is because of the curious interplay between Osiris and his son Horus, who between them formed a composite character upon which the pharaohs based their claimed divinity.

In the Egyptian myth Osiris had been a real flesh and blood King of Egypt from the earlier, idyllic time called Zep Tepi, who was murdered by his wicked brother Seth who wanted the kingdom for himself. Seth dismembered Osiris' body and distributed the parts over the whole country. The reason he did so stemmed from the Egyptian belief that mankind had two constituent parts; physical and spiritual. On death, the physical part was dispensed with, and the spirit continued on its journey into the Underworld. They also believed that if the physical body could be preserved, life might return one day to it. They embalmed their dead and wrapped them in cloth to preserve them until the day when they might conquer death and rise once more. Seth dismembered Osiris' body, then, in a deliberate attempt to ensure his brother could never return to the physical world and reclaim his throne.

Isis, Osiris' wife, was distraught at her loss so she gathered the pieces together and re-made her husband, restoring him to a life of sorts.

He was not restored to full life however, but remained lord of the Underworld, ruling the dark as the twin of the sun that ruled the world of light, sharing between them the two worlds of light and dark. Isis became pregnant by the miraculously rejuvenated and now immortal Osiris and gave birth to a son Horus, who overthrew his wicked uncle and restored the throne to its rightful line. The myth endowed the Pharaohs, who were regarded as being Horus in life and Osiris in death, with a bloodline that was not of mortal man, but had been achieved by miraculous intervention, similar to Mary's immaculate conception of Jesus who was also simultaneously divine and flesh, and perhaps illustrates to us how the Pharaohs, as the God Horus the son, must have been perceived by the Ancient Egyptians.

This myth is particularly interesting from a Masonic perspective, because as Horus was born after his father's murder, his mother Isis was technically a widow. Horus was therefore the son of a widow, and was known as the Widow's Son throughout Ancient Egypt. Not only do Masons regard themselves to this day as 'Sons of the Widow', but Hiram Abif was also said to be a widow's son from the tribe of Naphtali. On an exoteric level, the appellation 'Son of the Widow,' when applied to a Mason could be said to be a simple extraction of the terminology used to describe Hiram in the Bible and therefore did not possess any further significance, but having immersed myself in the obscure symbolism of the Craft over the course of this research, I find it not unreasonable to assume that there is an esoteric meaning also, and that it is the identification of the Master Mason as Horus that is intended. It is the nature of allegory to offer a simple, obvious meaning, whilst at the same time leaving the true import unstated. In identifying the candidate as Horus, then, could this point towards the 3rd degree initiation being intended as a symbolic version of the ceremony each Pharaoh underwent on death during which he became Osiris?

Another small but significant point is that to ascend the throne of Egypt, the Pharaoh's son had ideally to be bodily perfect in every way, to ensure that the bloodline of the Pharaoh would never be compromised. To this day, though not taken literally, a candidate for Masonry should be without maim or defect, a charge that is still enshrined in the wording of the ritual in yet another of those quirks of the Craft which struggles for explanation among the more prosaic origins, but for which an Osirian connection offers a plausible one.

It appears, then, that a cursory examination of the Osiris myth shows there are certainly grounds for looking a little deeper into the attributes of that first dying and resurrecting god-man, to see if he can further be linked to the ceremonies of Freemasonry. So who was Osiris, and what was it about him that would have made him a suitable icon for the new 3rd Degree?

In Ancient Egypt everything was considered the property of the Gods, administered on their behalf by the Pharaohs who ruled temporally, and the priesthood, which kept the religious observances. The Pharaoh was not merely the monarch of his country but was himself considered to be one of the gods. The sun, under a variety of names such as Ra was regarded as the supreme cosmic power, the timeless, unchanging force that governed all. On a lower level there was the trinity of Osiris the father, Isis the mother, and their child Horus, who were deities associated with the death and rebirth cycle of the short growing season that was vital to the very existence of the ancient Egyptian world. Each year around the end of the first week of July the lower Nile flooded the fertile but bone-dry lands which bordered it. This inundation, as it was known, provided the parched earth with water to enable crops to be grown. Careful irrigation spread the water far beyond its natural bounds, and strategically placed dams kept it there for the duration of the growing season. Rainfall was virtually nonexistent, and without the yearly flood the nation would simply not have been able to exist, so it is easy to understand why it was central to their lives. It is perhaps difficult for us in the West to see the Nile inundation as miraculous, because our water supply is so easily linked with our rainfall. For us, rivers flood after a prolonged period of heavier than normal rain, but in Egypt there was no visible reason for the sudden rising of the waters of the Nile. They did not comprehend that the regular flooding on which their economy depended was due to the geography of the Nile Basin, and came from seasonal rain falling on distant mountains far beyond their borders gathering into a flood as it reached its flood-plain, so they regarded the inundation as a miraculous gift from God.

The yearly flooding demonstrated a cycle of birth and death where the river, having brought life to the dry, arid ground then receded, and in its disappearance caused the death of all the vegetation it had previously given life to. The water of the river came to be seen as not only the giver of life, but the life-taker as well, a role normally allocated to God, so it was natural that the river came to be intimately associated with the concept of God. The ground, having been brought to life in July, succumbed to death a few months later, from whence the land remained barren until the following year when the process would be repeated all over again. This vegetative death occurred at harvest-time in September, a time of year that became linked with the death of many if not all of the regenerative vegetation gods. This was not restricted to Egypt, of course, and was one of the standard aspects of deity all across the Middle East and Europe, where the gods died with the vegetation in the autumn, only to return to life with the blossoming of plants in springtime the following year.

In terms of the movement of the sun through the heavens over the year, the autumn equinox occurred during the harvest, and so it became associated with the death of the God, when the sun passed from the light half of the year into the dark half. In ancient Egypt the three different aspects of deity, mother, father and son, were woven into the yearly cycle of the river in the form of three separate, but at the same time interconnected, deities. The earth itself was identified with the female aspect and given the name Isis, the Mother. The rising waters were identified with the male aspect, which introduces into the female the ability to conceive. This aspect was Osiris, the Father. The resultant growth of crops like corn, wheat and barley, which sprung from the union of the father and mother, represented Horus the Son.

As an aside to this, there are two symbols of Freemasonry that can be linked in a very substantial way to this flooding and the life that the rising waters bring to the earth. Moving water and an ear of corn both appear as important Masonic symbols, and are always linked together. Each degree's lesson is illustrated on painted panels called Tracing Boards, and are used in the English and Scottish working to teach the candidate the lessons of the degree. The 2nd Degree tracing board shows a man inside a building descending a winding stair and passing between two large pillars. Beyond those pillars lies the countryside, and plainly visible is a small waterfall or weir, with an ear of corn growing nearby. Indeed the weir can have another more precise allusion to the tale because as a manmade barrier it is for the control of water, and is exactly what the Egyptians utilised to prolong the flooding long enough to ripen their crops. Osiris was linked to the flooding of the Nile, and so can be identified with the moving water of Masonic symbolism, whilst the ear of corn can be identified with Horus, the crop that results from the flooding. In the linking of those two symbols then, we have a direct reference to the Osiris/Horus relationship, which I have already tentatively suggested could be the allusion behind the 3rd degree raising ceremony.

There is another, more obvious explanation in Masonic lore for the presence of the ear of corn on the tracing board, and that has to do with the 2nd degree password. We will examine this because it highlights the difficulty in ascertaining the true meaning of allegories. The password of the 2nd Degree is 'shibboleth,' which in Hebrew means an 'ear of corn'. The word itself is derived from a passage in the Old Testament book of Judges, 12:6 where it says... 'They said unto him, "say now shibboleth:" and he said sibboleth, for he could not frame to pronounce it right. Then they took him, and slew him at the passages of Jordan: and there fell at that time of the Ephraimites forty and two thousand'. Ostensibly this biblical reference is the origin of both the password that means ear of corn, and the moving water represented by the crossing point of the Jordan.

Many Masonic historians are of the opinion that the Craft evolved from a Christian background, and the biblical origin of this password is one of many similar instances in Masonic ritual that would seem to back up that argument. I would turn that idea back to front however, and suggest that the passage was chosen from the Bible because it carried information suitable for establishing an allegorical link to Horus and Osiris as mentioned above. So rather than the word shibboleth being used because it is found in the Bible and its meaning 'ear of corn' being therefore incidental, I would suggest that the passage was chosen from the Bible precisely because the word shibboleth can be linked by the ear of corn to the Egyptian myth of Osiris.

Osiris and Horus both came to be associated with the pharaohs, who were regarded as semi-divine beings. Horus, being youthful, became associated with the pharaoh while he was alive, whilst Osiris, Lord of the Underworld was the aspect he assumed on death. This led to the curious interaction between father and son, who, although two distinct deities, were both halves of the one whole. Between them they governed the world of the flesh and the after-life. Osiris came to life with the rising of the river and died with its recession, but not before germinating the crops, and in doing so facilitating the birth of Horus, who later died when the crop had ripened and was harvested. Yet neither Osiris nor Horus really died at all, because they would both be reborn the following year. So Osiris and Horus were one, standing with one foot in this world and one foot in the next. This was the font from which welled the plethora of dying and resurrecting god-men that we noted in the earlier part of the book, so if Osiris had indeed been chosen as the figurehead of the new incarnation of the mystery in the 1720s, it could be said that the circle was complete; and the very first dying and resurrecting god-man the world had ever seen had been rejuvenated as an allegory, and placed at the head of the newest, symbolic version of the pagan mysteries - Freemasonry.

We now have a developing hypothesis centred around the idea that Hiram was intended as a symbolic version of Osiris, and that in assuming the role of Hiram in the 3rd Degree ceremony the candidate died as him, only to be reborn as his son Horus. The dead Hiram then passed onwards on his spiritual journey into the Underworld as Osiris. In becoming Horus, then, the term Widow's Son, when used to describe a Master Mason, is perfectly in keeping with the thesis.

We could further speculate that in inventing the Hiramic legend a myth pertaining to Osiris was superimposed on to a backdrop of the building of the Temple of Solomon in order to honour both the stonemasons who had carried the mystery and the Templars for whom the Temple was their headquarters. It has to be noted, of course, that the myth of Osiris has not survived as a complete story, rather as a series of snippets from a variety of sources from which a single myth has been reconstructed; but that is true of almost all ancient myths, so it in no way diminishes its relevance. There are also many details in the legend of the murdered Grand Master that have nothing ostensibly to do with Osiris, so we must ask why, if the above thesis is correct, do we not see evidence of the known myths of Osiris embedded within the legend of the murdered architect of Solomon's Temple? In essence, then, I am suggesting that the architects of the legend of Hiram created a new tale, out of more than one character and from more than one source, to tell the story their tradition demanded..

It may seem a strange thing to do today, to construct a new, hybrid character from different sources, but it would have been completely in keeping with the ethos of the mystery schools, whose gods were symbolic allegories anyway. The original Osiris/Dionysus metamorphosed into many versions of the same God, and as such, and bearing in mind that the precedent had already been set by the masters of the pagan mysteries themselves, it seems quite plausible that the first Freemasons could have followed the lead of their spiritual forbears and invented a brand new, allegorical, dying and resurrecting figurehead for themselves and called him Hiram Abif. The Abif appellation is acknowledged in the ritual to mean 'Father,' and is explained to the candidate as implying that he was a master of his craft, but the title also has another obvious, higher connotation, which may well be the intended esoteric meaning of the term. The designation 'Father' could also be a term of address for God. Like the gods of old, Hiram also died a squalid death and was interred in the ground for a time, only to be later raised to eternal life, though that last fact is only implied and not made specific in Irish ritual. In all these points he is identical to many of the gods already mentioned, but there is no suggestion in the ritual that he was resurrected in the afterlife, as Jesus, for instance, had been.

The idea that Hiram could be a symbolic representation of the gods of old seemed to fit the thesis that I had developed, but at that stage I had not yet found the key to the true connection. My research took me away from the legend of Hiram Abif, and I re-examined the evidence for the solstices and equinoxes, trying to make sense of what was then a confusing muddle of tangled paths. What I was sure of, however, was that if any of the above hypothesis was correct, then the minutiae of the legend of the murder and subsequent raising of Hiram Abif would not be mere quirky details without symbolic significance. I felt sure that when understood, the myth would be imbued with references to the solstices, the equinoxes and the movements of the heavens.

In the remaining chapters of the book I will explain how that assumption turned out to be right, and in being so proves beyond doubt that the references to the marking of the sunrises and sunsets during the year, and the ability to determine the important days of the solstices and equinoxes are indeed the esoteric meaning behind the convoluted rituals of Freemasonry - exactly as laid out in the earlier chapters of the book.

How can I say that with such conviction?

Because I found Hiram.

CHAPTER 21

THE SEARCH FOR sense in the thesis had taken me in many directions, and though the identity of Hiram was always on my mind, the trail had gone somewhat cold.

Then serendipity took a hand.

A chance comment by a friend fitted a huge piece of the jigsaw into place. It was early September 2005 and I was preparing to attend my Masonic lodge. It was the first meeting after the summer recess and a friend said… 'it'll not be long now, to we see the big yin again'. By the term Big Yin he meant Orion, the big man of the skies, and the comment brought both the constellation and Freemasonry to mind.

I would describe myself as a star-gazer rather than an astronomer, simply being fond of being out under clear night-skies. Like many sky-gazers, I had a favourite among the constellations and mine was Orion. The three belt stars make him, with the exception perhaps of the Plough, the most easily identifiable and most notable star formation in the whole northern hemisphere, and depending on the time of year, he can be seen arcing his way across the southern sky towards the western horizon. He is a winter constellation, meaning that in the summer months he is not visible in the night sky at all, and that was what my friend meant when he said that it would not be long until we would see him again, because over the months of May and June he cannot be seen at all, only being in the sky during the daylight hours.

As summer gives way to autumn he can be seen very late at night, rising in the east briefly before the sun, which then obliterates him in the lightening sky. His rising gets earlier by two hours every month, so that by September he is aloft seven hours before the sun, and by the middle of the winter he has the night sky to himself, unaffected by the sun throughout his entire transit of the heavens.

The ancients called him 'the Foremost One' and one only has to stand outside on a clear winter night to see why. He is massive, and occupies a huge part of the sky that he seems to have all to himself, leaving him easier to see than any of the signs of the zodiac. I had always wondered why he was not part of the zodiac, but it was not until I started this quest that I came to understand that those twelve signs are the star formations that occupy the particular band of the sky that the sun appears to pass through during its year-long circuit. Orion lies below this band, which is why, despite being among the most notable of all constellations; he is not one of those well-known star-signs. Since the sun's altitude is low in winter and high in summer, the zodiacal belt is similarly positioned, so, through the month of June, when the sun high on the ecliptic edges past Orion, he lies underneath it.

The summer recess during which the lodges do not meet is known as Masonry's dark period. As I entered the hall that night, because of my friend's comment, it occurred to me that this coincided with Orion's time of invisibility. I didn't imagine the two were connected, but the important thing was that I was thinking of both at the same time.

As I pondered, I recollected a few long-forgotten snippets about Orion that had not occurred to me during my present period of research. Many years before, I had noticed that the figure formed by the constellation twists around as it passes from the east to the west. When it rises it is almost horizontal, but becomes more upright as night passes.

My earlier reading about Freemasonry, before I had become a Mason myself, had shown that the symbolism of the Craft was heavily imbued with references to uprightness of character, and at the time I had briefly connected that fact with Orion's becoming upright as he progresses across the sky, before filing it away in one of the dustier corners of my brain.

When the thought came back that night, however, I had become a Mason, and was armed with the knowledge that the defining moment of the 3rd Degree ceremony, indeed the defining moment in all of Freemasonry, involves raising the candidate from the horizontal to the vertical, or as the wording of the ritual has it, 'from a dead level to a living upright'. The behaviour of the constellation, then, could be said to mimic the ultimate moment on a Mason's symbolic path of enlightenment.

I later recollected another vague remembrance from a book on the Pyramids which mentioned that Orion was regarded by the ancient Egyptians as being the heavenly embodiment of Osiris. The constellation in general, and the three belt stars in particular, were seen by the Egyptians as the heavenly pointer to the rising point of another star which was vitally important to the well-being of their country. The belt stars, as they rise, point approximately to a spot on the horizon where Sirius, the heavenly embodiment of Isis and the brightest of all the fixed stars, rises two hours later. Sirius was the key to the ancient Egyptians' calendar, and alerted them to the imminent arrival of the inundation and gave them notice to have the ground prepared. During springtime Sirius is in the same part of the sky as the sun and is only up when the sun is, so is therefore invisible for a time. There comes a day, however, when the sun has moved far enough east of the star for Sirius to rise before the sky lightens, and be seen shimmering above the eastern horizon briefly before sunrise. This first day after its invisibility is known as its helical rising, and at that time in history happened in early July, a short time before the river Nile suddenly rose up and burst its banks.

Orion, being positioned just ahead of Sirius in the sky, and rising ahead of it, came to be seen as the one who leads that important star into vision, and by extension was regarded as the harbinger of the life-giving floods. Orion, then, became associated with the fertility of the land, and it is for this reason that the constellation was associated with Osiris.

These brief recollections had shown that there were certainly links to be explored between Osiris and Orion, and raised interesting questions with regards to the developing hypothesis. I had already noted that the known Osirian myths were absent from the tale of Hiram, so was it possible that the identification of Osiris as Hiram was through his celestial representative, the constellation Orion? My mind raced with possibilities.

Let us suppose the men who decided to add the 3rd Degree to the Masonic fold had looked for something obtuse that would tie the mystery to Osiris that wouldn't immediately identify the degree as pertaining to the Egyptian god. Orion had been regarded as Osiris' heavenly personification, so perhaps an investigation of the constellation would show links to Hiram.

If their focus had indeed fallen on Orion, even a cursory glance heavenwards would have quickly identified the three stars of his belt. Equally spaced in an almost perfectly straight line, those stars would have instantly echoed the 3rd Degree which the Masons sought to illustrate, and the number three was already

all-pervasive in Masonic lore. Orion also dominates the winter skies, reaching its most visible phase around the end of December, the time of the winter solstice, and might therefore have had appeal to an organisation which held that solstice as being one of the two most important days of the year.

So it was towards Orion's link to Osiris that I directed my attention to over the next few months. My knowledge of both astronomy and Egyptian deities was at that time sparse to say the least, so I resolved to learn all I could about both subjects.

CHAPTER 22

OUR TENTATIVE HYPOTHESIS was developing, and to what we already had was added the possibility that the architects of modern Freemasonry in the 18th century had invented a mythical hero based on the original dying and resurrecting God-man Osiris through the person of his heavenly representation in the sky. This was exactly how many of the gods of the mysteries were created, for we must remember that they were myths and their stories were not to be taken literally. To illustrate this point we will once again look at the god Mithras, because the legend that was created for him was constructed in just such a way.

David Ullansey, in his book The Origins of the Mithraic Mysteries explains where the Roman god Mithras came from. He was created around 150 BCE as the outward face of a new mystery, to carry knowledge of the cosmos that had just been discovered. We noted earlier that Hipparchus had brought it to the world's attention that the heavens above are not fixed as had previously been thought, but turn slowly in a vast circle around us. The force that causes this apparent rotation is known as precession, and is the third force that moves the heavens. In discovering this Hipparchus was credited with having uncovered the presence of a hitherto unknown God. This new deity had no historical framework whatsoever, and an entirely new mythology and symbolism had to be created for him. The myth associated with the god was needed to carry knowledge of precession, and was structured around a constellation that was suitable for conveying that knowledge.

The myth of this new God Mithras was based on the figure of the old Greek God Perseus, who, like other gods in the Greek pantheon, had his own constellation in the heavens. It was the position of the constellation Perseus relative to Taurus that made it eminently suitable for the job, because in wishing to demonstrate Mithras' power to move the entire heavenly sphere, this power was demonstrated by having him kill the Bull of Taurus. Precession had caused the sun on the spring equinox to drift away from Taurus and into the next sign on the ecliptic, which was Aries the Ram. It was therefore fitting to illustrate this new God in the act of killing a bull, which is precisely what the Tauroctony shows. In the heavens, Perseus hovered menacingly over the constellation Taurus, and that became the basis for the image of the Tauroctony in which Mithras kneels on a bull's back, plunging a blade into its neck. By inventing the new God, the architects of Mithraism had borrowed the constellation of a pre-existing deity, and reworked it to suit a new story that they wished to tell.

This weaving of a tale around a constellation is vitally important for the thesis presented here, for as we advance through the next few chapters we will discover that those who wrote the legend of Hiram in the 18th Century did exactly the same. Let us imagine that the architects of Freemasonry wanted to write a legend for a fictional character whose story was ostensibly based around the building of Solomon's Temple, but which also carried hidden details pertinent to Osiris, the father of the mysteries. Hiram, the builder of the Temple became the exoteric part, and being anchored in the Bible, paid homage to the tradition's origin in Jerusalem. Osiris then became the esoteric part that linked Hiram to the mystery.

We must remember that the Hiram myth came into the Masonic fold just as the Craft was becoming a more accessible organisation, and what had been a totally secret tradition until then had had to be re-modelled and made suitable for another audience altogether. Freemasonry was a different animal from the original mystery and with the blossoming of the Craft there were sure to be many who would offer themselves for candidacy, but who would not remain as long-term members. What had previously been hidden and only shown to a few dedicated adepts was now shown to all – though only as allegory. For this strategy to work, the esoteric aspect would have had to be incredibly deeply buried, and be so obscure that the details from which the myth was woven would not be visible in any way. In this way, Hiram Abif, the architect of the temple, would never be linked directly with Osiris and through him to the secrets of the universe that had previously formed the core of the mystery school.

To be doubly sure that the link would never be discovered they did not use any details taken from the known myth of Osiris, rather they looked for other ways to represent the Egyptian God, and as will be shown in the next chapter, they used the attributes and movements of the constellation Orion to represent him instead. By doing this, there was therefore nothing in the ritual that ostensibly linked Hiram to the Egyptian god of the Underworld. The identification of Hiram as Osiris, because it was hidden, could therefore be completely denied, as had been the case with the esoteric side of the original mystery in earlier times.

The use of the word 'denied' perhaps implies a certain unwholesomeness to those who do not appreciate the purpose of allegory, but to adopt this viewpoint is to miss the purpose of the exercise. What I suggest is that an ancient tradition had existed in the preceding centuries that carried within its innermost levels of initiation the understanding of the workings of the cosmos. In the past this knowledge was sacred and led the acolyte to gnosis, but by the time the Craft emerged in its new form, that knowledge of the cosmos was no longer sacred. All I suggest the architects of the 3rd Degree did was to take that knowledge, convert it to allegory and metaphor in a new theatrical tale, and offer it as a new level of initiation in addition to the two that already existed. Thus the past was preserved in such a way as to carry the earlier knowledge, but was detached from its factual basis. It was offered to the new membership without any explanation as to its origin, so that each brother could draw his own understanding from what he was shown.

That is precisely the purpose of allegory, and therefore the term 'denied' is perhaps not entirely the right word. Hidden – yes, but not out of a desire to deceive. Rather it is to preserve the past forever, hidden at the centre of a semi-secret society that was modelled on the mystery schools of the ancient world.

Having studied the constellation of Orion in considerable depth, I have come to believe that those first Freemasons used minute details about its position in relation to the zodiac, and its interaction with the sun on the solstices and equinoxes, to link the Hiramic legend to his alter ego Osiris. The constellation has many characteristics which link it to the movements of the sun, and its shape and movement through the sky also exhibit characteristics which link it to very precise elements of the Hiramic legend, way beyond the raising of the candidate that had initially drawn my attention.

In particular, I was to discover that its position relative to the signs of the zodiac at this particular time in the 26,000 year precessional cycle of the heavens means that it interacts with the sun in some startling ways, and on dates which were already considered important to both Masons and to the pre-Christians who venerated the pagan gods. The key to the puzzle was not immediately obvious, however, and it was some months before I first identified Hiram in the constellation, but when I did, everything fell into place with breathtaking speed.

CHAPTER 23

ORION, SHOWN HERE as he was perceived in ancient times, was known as the Hunter of the skies, and references to him can be found in the earliest myths of many cultures around the world. Due to his

position straddling the celestial equator he is directly overhead at the earth's equator, and can be seen from all places on the globe, so Orion can be said to be a truly universal figure. He consists of twelve or thirteen bright stars, arranged into the rough shape of a man with legs splayed and arms stretched out. The most noticeable feature of the constellation is the belt, formed from the stars Alnitak, Alnilam and Mintaka, which lie in an almost exactly straight line. Running down diagonally from the belt stars are three more that were traditionally seen as a sword. Above these, forming the shoulders of the Hunter are Betelgeuse to our left, his right, and Bellatrix his left. Below the belt are two stars that are either the feet or knees, again depending on the picture, named Saiph to our left and Rigel to our right. The stars fit well into the form of a man, and are far closer a match than most other constellations, many of which take a lot of vision to identify their beast or hero. This, then, is the Orion of antiquity.

The first interesting thing from our point of view is the geometrical layout of the stars within the constellation. There are three sets of three stars arranged geometrically within it, all in almost straight lines, and all roughly equidistant from one another. The belt stars are obviously the first set. Betelgeuse, Alnilam, and Rigel are another set that are almost precisely equidistant from each other and again are almost exactly in a straight line. The third set are the three which are very close together and form the sword which hangs from the belt, and are also equally spaced from one another. The belt stars also bisect the straight line between Betelgeuse and Rigel at roughly 90 degrees. It must be stressed that these are not precise angles and dimensions, but we are dealing with observational astronomy and not a computer calculation. These details may seem unimportant, but for an organisation seemingly obsessed with the number three, and which promotes geometry as the most exquisite of the sciences, the

constellation could have held a certain interest because of its geometrical series alone.

Other than these observations, which were admittedly not very much, I had not found anything else of interest during many cold nights spent staring into the inky blackness hoping for inspiration. Then very late one night the breakthrough came. It was around three in the morning, when, returning late from work and not ready for sleep I took the dog for a walk through the fields that surround my house. It had been cloudy all day so Orion wasn't on my mind as I walked, but then the sky cleared and the stars glittered into life. Orion had traversed three quarters of the sky and was not far from the western horizon. I had not seen the figure so far across the sky before, nor as close to being vertical, and that was why I hadn't seen it in this way previously. The stars Betelgeuse and Rigel were almost vertical, and the belt stars, which bisected the line between them, were almost horizontal, dividing the 'body shape' exactly where a belt would be. Then the image of Orion standing bolt upright rather than the Orion of antiquity with its

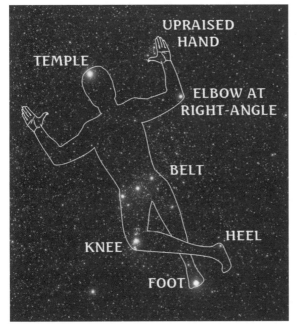

splayed legs struck me like a thunderbolt.

Betelgeuse was the head of the figure, whilst Rigel was the left foot. The sword stars became a thigh, running down to where the right knee would be in this new figure, and the star Cursa to the left was in precisely the correct place for the heel of the right foot. Taken with the knee, this meant that the figure had its legs crossed in the exact stance that Mithras' Torchbearers adopted to denote the crossing of the equinoxes in the Tauroctony that stood in every Mithraeum. It is also the exact stance adopted by Hiram Abif when threatened for the third and final time at the Eastern Gate of the Temple. Whilst in that position Hiram also had his arms raised, and then I noticed that the stars Bellatrix and Meissa could be reassigned to become the figure's left arm and hand, upraised and squared at the elbow - exactly like Hiram's.

I returned to the house to think over what I had just seen, but of course doubts soon surfaced. 'Steady on,' I said to myself, 'who do you think you are, drawing a brand new constellation of your own, just because it fits the picture?' But isn't that exactly what those writing an allegorical myth would do? Isn't that what those who created Mithras had done, inventing a new picture from the stars of Perseus and Taurus that told the story of Mithras killing the bull? The nature of that type of myth is precisely that it is made up, to illustrate a particular point of view. If the first Freemasons had sought a 'frame' on which to hang Hiram, and wished to include Osiris and the same veneration of the equinoxes that Mithras' Torchbearers displayed, then the constellation viewed this way would have fitted the bill perfectly.

Sleep was already beyond reach that night and my mind was too active to think of going to bed, so I connected to the Internet to see what I could find about Orion and Osiris, but I kept being drawn back outside to look at the star pattern. When I was inside I started to have doubts, but when I went outside again and saw the layout of the stars, the doubt dissipated and my conviction grew once more. The more I looked at the sword stars and Cursa forming crossed shins, the more convinced I became that it was no mere chance that Hiram crosses his legs in an identical fashion before being symbolically killed.

The more I concentrated on the peculiar posture of the candidate at that point in the Masonic ceremony the more contrived it seemed. No one questions the stance because the rest of the rituals are similarly obtuse and therefore it does not seem out of place, but focusing on it now in the wee dark hours, in the quiet of the still house, it seemed a truly preposterous position to adopt when facing attack, and the more I analysed it, the more bizarre it seemed. I had, of course, asked many brethren what they thought it meant, but the answer was always the same; a grimace, a raising of the shoulders and a slow shaking of the head. It's just one of those mysteries about the Craft which nobody understands. Although it made sense that the crossing of the legs in the 3rd Degree was symbolic of the stance of Mithras' Torchbearers and therefore a reference to the equinoxes, proof was a little thin on the ground. Could the stance of Orion be that proof?

I downloaded a good picture of the constellation from SKY-MAP.ORG and copied it into a drawing programme on the computer. Drawing the positions of the stars, I named them and then deleted the underlying bitmap image. I printed off a few copies of the layout and settled at the table with a pencil and eraser. Over and over again I sketched on top of the star pattern the outline of a man in the stance adopted by Hiram before his assault, eventually achieving some semblance of humanoid appearance. It precisely mirrored the body shape formed by the actual stars.

As the time passed I became more and more convinced that I had indeed discovered something, however unlikely it seemed at first. Eventually, my eyes gritty with tiredness, I decided to leave further fiddling until the morning and went outside for one last look at the stars. This was a full two hours after the skies had first cleared to show the almost upright figure, and the constellation had by then reached the western horizon. What I saw left me in no doubt whatsoever that Orion was Hiram. While I had known that the further west he goes the more upright he becomes, I was genuinely taken aback by the degree of precision the figure achieves when it reaches the ground. Rigel was just fading into the mist just above the horizon, and straight above it was Betelgeuse. The picture above is an outline of the figure laid over a picture of the actual stars, and shows how precisely the figure matches the constellation. The bodyline was a true vertical, bisected to an astonishing precision by the belt, which was absolutely horizontal. The thigh and knee fitted perfectly, and Cursa, the heel of the right foot, sat precisely where it should be also. The white overlay is precisely the position adopted by the candidate before being killed as Hiram in the 3rd Degree. I turned the drawing upright, and held it at arm's-length beside the stars. They matched perfectly, and in an instant I knew I was right, and my belief from that moment onwards was that those who had conceived the new 3rd Degree had indeed reassigned the stars of Orion to reflect elements from the original mystery that they wanted to represent symbolically.

The crossing of the equinoxes was the most obvious aspect of our thesis represented by the figure, because the crossed legs mimicked precisely the stance of the torchbearers in the Mithraic Tauroctony and would certainly have been the reason for the Masonic use of the constellation this way in the first place. The raised left arm squared at the elbow paid homage to the 90 degrees between the sunrises within the area bounded by the solstice square. I had also now discovered that when looked at from the perspective of this new layout, Orion is raised from a dead level to a living upright, becoming truly vertical as he reaches the western horizon at the end of his journey. And when he arrives there he stands on his left foot, resting the ball of his right foot on the ground, exactly as the candidate does in the Hiramic degree at the very end of his journey of initiation.

Although I was unaware of it at the time he cannot be seen to stand perfectly upright on the western horizon from every location on earth, and the reason I saw him so notably vertical was because I was near the latitude where he does so. To the far north he never reaches vertical at all, and in tropical regions he passes it and slopes backwards before reaching the horizon. The area where he can be seen to be vertical on setting is more or less coincident with the same latitudes as those of the solstice square, a fact that in itself is surely interesting to our quest. It truly was a revelation to discover that between the very lines of latitude that I suggest were considered special because the solstice sunrises form a true square, Orion can himself be seen to rise from the horizontal to a perfect upright.

If the above thesis was correct, then the situation presented an amazing linkage between the mediaeval mystery and the modern Craft. I already knew that the veneration of the solstices that was present in the original mystery could be related directly to the latitude of southern Scotland, and now it appeared that the Irish 3rd Degree could be linked with precisely the same area through the similarity between the stance of the candidate and that of the constellation of Orion.

I have put the cart before the horse as it were, by claiming Orion to be Hiram before I have offered any proof of the thesis, but I realise that the notions that I put forward in the following chapters will come out of left field, as it were. They will perhaps be better understood if the destination is known before the journey begins. Put simply, my suggestion is that Masonic origins lie in a confused tangle of astronomy, astrology, folklore, and pre-Christian understanding of the cosmos. Academic historians do not do folklore and myth, and as for astrology... I think not? And folklorists are not normally regarded as historians, nor indeed do they generally seek to substantiate the legends they gather in historical fact. In the thesis I offer as the origin of Freemasonry, myth and fact are mixed in equal measure. The architects of the Craft had factual historical truths they wished to promote; but as a vehicle to carry their story they used metaphors and allegories drawn from the myths and legends of the past, that exist in the fuzzy area between the astronomy of today and the astrology of yesterday. One cannot therefore stand in either the academic's or folklorist's camps and hope to see the truth. If those who conceived the rituals and symbolism of Freemasonry constructed their stories from folk tales, then it is in that direction we must look, if we are to have any chance of reaching a full understanding of the situation. To see the truth, one therefore has to walk the fence between the hard world of academic research and the fluffy world of folklore, and keep an eye focussed on each side simultaneously.

As I stood there that night looking at Orion standing on the western horizon I was convinced that I was right, but before I was to be able to discover just how close the relationship was, I had to understand why, and how, the ancients had woven their tales of the gods around the movements of the constellations in the heavens. And if I could discover that, I thought, I may have been able to understand how and why the first Freemasons did likewise with their allegorical Hiram.

Many early myths can be seen to have their origin in the movements of the heavens and the layout of the various constellations. We could fill a book with the tales of the ancient gods to illustrate this point, but that would be an unnecessary departure. Orion himself has many myths that can be seen to originate in the heavens, so we will restrict ourselves to him, and at least what we discover will be relevant. Many of the stories of Orion the mythical hero, whilst varied and disjointed, can be seen to be drawn from the positions of his heavenly representative and its movements throughout the year.

Perhaps the reason why the tale of Hiram I weave here has not been heard before is because no right thinking historian would look where I have looked. Astrology today is virtually a dirty word, so low has it sunk in our culture, but for the ancients it was the axis around which their world turned. Their priesthood studied the stars to predict the future and give advice on important decisions, and the movements of the stars gave rise to the tales of the gods. Modern researchers seek the safety of primary sources to provide a bulwark against criticism, but there are none to be found in ancient myth. Not a shred of any of the myths can be 'proved' in a normal historical sense, so it is perhaps not surprising that few will venture into the quagmire upon which they lie. But as we said earlier, if that is where the meaning of Masonic ritual lies, then it is there that we must look for its meaning.

Myth is not history – it is simply legend that tells a story. If one claims that Masonic ritual is truly based on ancient myth, how, then, can that proposition ever be proved? My answer to that problem is to highlight so many points of contact between the two that we reach a point of critical mass, where the sheer number tips the balance in favour of proving the argument. I feel that what is contained in the next few chapters goes way beyond the point of critical mass, but it will be for each reader to come to their own conclusions on that point.

What is important in this examination of the myths of Orion is not which of them may have been used as the basis of the Hiramic legend, though there will be plenty of evidence that they do, but that they demonstrate how the ancients constructed the tales of their mythical gods; and that this in its turn indicates how the architects of Freemasonry constructed theirs.

What follows is not Masonic lore, for the symbolism of Freemasonry is given without footnotes so that each brother can interpret what he witnesses as he sees fit. The theories about Hiram as Orion contained in the next chapter are therefore simply my own interpretation of the convoluted rites of the 3rd Degree, and contain possibilities that have never before, at least in modern times, seen the light of day.

CHAPTER 24

ORION IN ANCIENT times had many guises, but was most often seen as a powerful hunter, a giant, a great lover, or indeed all three rolled into one. He was regarded as the lord of the winter because of his dominance of the winter skies, and has attracted Man's attention since at least the Neolithic.

The constellation is mentioned in the Old Testament when God asked Job if he was able to 'loose the bands of Orion' ....In the language of the King James Bible; 'Canst thou bind the sweet influences of Pleiades, or loose the bands of Orion?' Job 38:31. The Hebrews called him 'Kesil,' or 'Fool,' and he was bound in the sky for rebelling against Jehovah. The constellation is also associated with Nimrod, an association that is of enormous importance to us, and will be more fully examined later. Already we have a reference to Orion being bound, and this has particular Masonic significance, because the 1st Degree initiate is led into the lodge room with a running noose called a halter around his waist and neck, and is then symbolically released before he is obligated.

We have already noted that Orion was prominent in Egyptian myth, and the Arabs had several names and identities for him, Al Jabbar, 'the Giant', and Al Shuja, 'the Snake' among them. It was not only the Arabs who identified him with a snake, as the Egyptians thought he assumed the shape of a snake when, as Osiris, he travelled into the dark recesses of the Underworld. Another interesting way the Arabs had of viewing the constellation, from our point of view, was as an accurate scale-beam. They saw the three belt stars as the pivot point of a set of scales, and this is interesting, as elsewhere we have seen the scales associated with the autumnal equinox. It is perhaps noteworthy that it is on reaching the western horizon that the three belt stars become horizontal, and thus like a scale-beam. Though we haven't yet looked in depth at the importance of the west in early myth, it is there that the pre-Christians believed the souls of the departed entered the Underworld.

The seamen who plied the seas of the ancient world saw the three belt stars as the Golden Yard-arm, and also viewed the constellation in its entirety as the great sailor or navigator of the heavens. This too is interesting, because the simplest icon for sea faring is the anchor, and the anchor figures heavily in Masonic symbolism. So big and easily identified was Orion, that sailors used him to find their bearings at night, and used his rising times to indicate the stormy season when it was not safe to put to sea.

The above are all different ways in which various early peoples viewed the constellation, but it is to the Graeco-Roman world we must turn for the most interesting, detailed accounts associated with it. In Greek myth he was the Great Hunter, who hunted by the banks of the mighty river Eridanus, accompanied by his two faithful hunting dogs. Orion lies to the side of the great sparkling ribbon of the Milky Way that the Egyptians equated with the River Nile and the builders of Newgrange associated with the Boyne, so the Greek myth placing him beside a river can be seen as a reflection of this. His two dogs are to be found in the sky too, where Canis Major and Canis Minor faithfully follow him across the sky every night. Canis Major, of which Sirius is the eye, lies below and to the left of Orion who for the Ancient Egyptians was Osiris. With his trusty dogs Orion hunted the various wild animals that surrounded him, and achieved quite a reputation for bravery. This reputation fed his ego, and was to lead to his eventual downfall, but perhaps it would be better to take his life story in order and start with his birth, which is perhaps the most Masonically interesting part of all.

Orion's birth gives us the first interesting link with Hiram Abif, in that he was traditionally believed to have been born in Hyrai, in Boethia, Greece. Not only is the name of the place suggestive of the name Hiram, but is claimed by Hesychius, compiler of an early Greek dictionary, to be from the Cretan word 'Hyron,' which, in addition to being very close to the name Hiram, means 'swarm of bees,' 'beehive,' or 'sisters of the beehive'.

This is extremely interesting when seeking to link the myth of Orion to Masonry, because the beehive is an immensely important Masonic symbol. Masonry exhorts its membership to work hard, that they may better play their part in society, and the industrious bee is offered as an example to follow. The hive also symbolises the lodge room, where though outsiders may watch Masons coming and going from it, what goes on inside, like the beehive, is hidden from view.

Bees had a deeper meaning and association in antiquity, and

that was as symbols of the portal to the afterlife. Bees and bee-keeping were prominent in Minoan civilisation, where a fermented honey-drink called mead, much older than wine, was used as an intoxicant to allow the priesthood access to the spirit world. Many types of hallucinogenic substances have been used the world over to permit access to an altered state of consciousness that in primitive times was believed to be the realm of the gods. By virtue of this intoxicating honey-drink, bees came to be seen as a bridge between the natural world and the spirit world, between the world of light and the Underworld.

Throughout the ancient Aegean world, bees were carved on tombs, and the Mycenean Tholos-tombs were even built to resemble beehives. The association of bees with the Underworld is very likely therefore to be the esoteric significance of the beehive in Masonic symbolism. So not only do we have the word Hyron from which the name Orion is derived being almost identical to the name Hiram, but the actual meaning of that word, 'beehive,' is itself prominent in Freemasonry.

The character of Orion also has considerable elements in common with Masonic lore. He was said to be not only a skilled blacksmith, but also a master builder. The obvious interest here is that in Orion we have two distinct abilities, smithing and building, both of which are replicated in the character of Hiram Abif. Orion was said to have built a marvellous underground forge for Vulcan on the Island of Lemnos, but his skill as a builder does not stop there. Not only did he build sea walls on Sicily to protect its ports, but also of immense importance to our seeking to link him with Hiram, Orion is also credited with building a temple to the gods on the island. Surely the fact that both Hiram and Orion were said to have built temples must be more than mere coincidence?

One of the myths relating to Orion's early life associates him with a woman named Side. The association seems to be mystical rather than a marriage as such, as 'Side' translates literally as pomegranate. There is no record of a physical assignation between the two, nor any offspring, nor indeed any place associated with their union, just that the two were associated in some unspecified way. The word pomegranate immediately sets Masonic bells ringing, because it is yet another one of the obscure symbols of the Craft.

In the Bible it is recorded that the two pillars that flanked the entrance to Solomon's Temple were decorated with pomegranates. The pomegranate also has associations with female sexuality, and has contributed in part to anti-masons' criticism of Freemasonry. Evangelical Christians are quick to claim that Masonry's use of the symbol is sexual, whilst at the same time ignoring the fact that the Old Testament books of First Kings and Second Chronicles are where the imagery actually comes from. I would suggest that the use of pomegranates in Masonic lore was drawn from the Bible to be a connection to the building of the Temple on an exoteric level, but on an esoteric level is yet another reference to Orion, and so whether or not the fruit had any particular significance to female sexuality in antiquity is therefore irrelevant. Masons, I believe, have included it in their symbolism simply because it is one of the details in the Bible's description of the Temple that can also be a hidden reference to the mythology they wish to commemorate. There are no sexual overtones attached to the pomegranate in the Scriptures, so why then attach them to Masonry's use of the symbol?

The word Side, or Sidhe, pronounced shee, has another connotation in lore in that for Celtic mythology it is the realm of the Dead - the Underworld. It is interesting, from a Masonic perspective, that one of the ways to access the Sidhe was by becoming lost - in the dark woods or in a mystical fog. One of the strongest themes that runs beneath the surface of Freemasonry is the search for that which was lost. This is in reference to the true secrets of a Master Mason which were lost to the world on the death of Hiram Abif. When we do not know what we are looking for but search regardless, we can be said to be lost ourselves. A recurring theme in Celtic myths is that in becoming lost the hero is in a sort of limbo, a 'liminal' place between light and dark, where he may be selected by the gods and taken to the other side to be groomed for kingship or some other role. We will come across just such a 'liminal' place later in our tale.

In another brief myth, which dwelt more on Orion's prowess as a lover than as a hunter, he fell in love with, and spent his time chasing, the seven daughters of Zeus. They are found in the Pleiades, the small cluster of seven stars that are just ahead of Orion in the sky, and which he will endlessly chase but never catch. Although there were seven sisters, the one he most sought was often absent, and in the Pleiades on the average night we see only six stars. When it is particularly clear, however, a seventh star can be seen, and this fact shows how precisely matched the myths of the ancient gods actually were to their inspiration in the heavens.

Another female in his life was princess Merope, granddaughter of Dionysus. Her father was King Oenopion, ruler of the island of Chios, and it was when Orion visited that island that he became infatuated with her. The king reneged on a promise to give Orion her hand in marriage, and one night, driven wild with passion, Orion tried to force himself upon her. The king was outraged and, waiting until the mighty Orion was drunk, blinded him in his drunkenness and threw him on the seashore. The blinded hero made his stumbling way to the island of Lemnos, to Vulcan's underground forge, which in other myths Orion himself had built. Vulcan took pity on the sightless Orion and gave him his own personal servant, Kedalion, to be his eyes and to guide him to the east where Helios the sun God would restore his sight. With the help of this guide, whom he carried on his broad shoulders, Orion arrived at the easternmost edge of the world, where the first rays of the rising sun cured him of his blindness. His sight restored, Orion tarried awhile in the house of Helios the sun God, where as each day dawned his skin grew paler until he was virtually transparent.

Having recuperated, Orion returned to the island of Chios to exact revenge upon King Oenopion for blinding him but could not find him, because the king lay hidden in a specially constructed underground chamber beyond the grasp of the vengeful hero. Although Orion strode up and down the island endlessly seeking him, his search for the king was in vain.

If we render the details of this story down to its bare bones, we can identify at its root the classic pagan tale of twin gods, one of whom rules the summer, one the winter. As recounted earlier in the myths of Nuadha and Bres, Llew and Goronwy, and the tale of Myrddin Wyllt, we find again the principle of twin gods who between them rule the year for six months each. In essence, these and many others were constructs to account for the fact that the sun passes into the Underworld, or technically the southern hemisphere, for six months of the year, so the lord of the winter was needed to rule in the sun's absence.

The constellation of Orion was perfectly suited to this role, because he is at the far side of the zodiac to the sun during December, meaning that he is prominent in the dark, mid-winter night sky. As such, then, he was in a position to rule the winter skies. The same division of the year into two halves is evident in many myths, and will be referred to often as we continue to investigate the meaning and purpose of this ancient symbolism.

The blinding of Orion in the tale is a metaphor for him passing into his period of darkness during the reign of the other God, and since we know Orion rules the winter skies, the other God must rule the summer, or in other words is the sun. Orion, after his blinding, spends time underground, in the forge of Vulcan, before continuing to the east where he has his sight restored, and from the earlier myth we know that it was actually Orion himself who constructed this underground forge, so it can therefore be seen as his own abode. When he returns to exact retribution on Oenopion after having his sight restored however, he cannot do so, because it is the king who has by then gone away, under the earth. This myth therefore places Orion under the ground, or more correctly in the Underworld, during the summer while Oenopion is above ground. During the winter the position is reversed, with Oenopion, or the sun, in the Underworld whilst Orion is in the ascendancy. We have between them, therefore, the twin gods who rule the year.

During the time he is away we are told Orion spends time in the house of the sun God Helios, and this makes perfect sense, because over the summer months of Orion's dark period, the constellation is in the same part of the sky as the sun. The myth further tells us that during his time in the house of Helios, Orion's skin becomes pale, almost becoming completely translucent. This is a very succinct and precisely correct description of what happens to the constellation in May and June, when the sun is exactly above him in the sky. Orion would then be completely invisible; indeed for two months, though he is technically in our vision every day, he cannot be seen at all. So the tale of Orion and Oenopion can be seen as yet another tale of two gods who between them rule the year, and is demonstrative of the ancients' division of the year into two halves.

In this Greek myth we have an identical metaphor to those of the Celts, and we can see Oenopion as the Samos - god of the summer, otherwise known as the sun, whilst Orion was the Giamos - god of the winter. In equating Hiram with Orion then, can we say that Hiram, too, is the lord of the winter, the dark twin of the sun. It also brings to mind the de-Christianising of the Craft that coincided with the introduction of the Hiramic legend. Where Jesus had previously been the winter solstice marker through his birth at mid-winter, and John the Baptist the summer, could the removal of Jesus from the ritual and his replacement with Hiram be seen in the context of Orion being the sun's winter counterpart in the Greek myth? Is Hiram then the sun's twin, and was his invention necessary to fill the gap left by the removal of Jesus as the winter solstice marker at the de-Christianising of the Craft? Where Jesus had been the symbolic head of the mystery in older times, did Hiram replace Jesus as a new, specifically non-dogmatic figurehead - a new composite character invented in the same way as the earlier gods of the mysteries had been created?

There is also a detail about the death of Hiram that adds to the idea that he is lord of the winter, and that is that his death in that capacity can be said to be at the hands of the sun. The three conspirators each carry a weapon of some sort, and it is interesting that both the first and second can be attributed to the sun, whilst the third can be said to be wielded by the sun. The first weapon is the twenty-four inch gauge or ruler, which is actually referred to in the ritual as being symbolic of the division of the day into twenty-four hours. As such, therefore, it is plainly meant to represent the daily revolution of the sun. The second conspirator uses a heavy metal square, already shown to be a reference to the sun on the two solstices within our two lines of latitude.

The third implement, the maul, cannot be shown to refer to the sun, but since it is being wielded by the Master who has been shown to represent the sun itself; it completes the ensemble of all three attacks involving allusions to the sun. Since I have sought to attribute the moment of the killing of Hiram to the passage of the lord of the winter into the Underworld and the assumption of power by the sun, it is obviously fitting that the sun be involved in all aspects of the overthrow of its opposite number.

Modern Masonry is today oblivious to these ancient meanings that rest in its rituals, so it is not difficult to see how outsiders, unaware of the symbolic nature of such actions and gestures as those outlined above would misread them, and think there is a more sinister reason for their continued use. It is no wonder, then, that those outside the Craft form their own opinions about what goes on in Freemasonry, and that those opinions are sometimes less than flattering to the order.

One of the main complaints Masons hear from those on the outside is about their use of blood-curdling oaths in their ceremonies. But as we can see, they do not refer to actual punishments at all, but are simply arcane references to the machination of the heavens. As laid out here there is therefore nothing sinister about those rituals at all, for they are simply theatre, structured to illustrate the ancients' veneration of the sun in identical fashion to the Greek myth of Orion and Oenopion.

Orion had another entirely different myth which is also very interesting, and in which his love life also contributed to his quite different death. Not only was he a great and powerful hunter, but he was also reputedly very handsome. Artemis, the moon goddess, herself a huntress of some renown, fell in love with him, and became so infatuated that she neglected her daily duty of carrying the moon across the sky in her chariot. Her brother Apollo, the sun-god became angry with her, and after a month of moonless nights, decided that her passion for Orion would have to be quenched, so he hatched a plan that would both deal with Orion and punish his sister for her neglect. One evening near sunset Orion was bathing far out to sea, with only his head visible above the water, a mere dot on the horizon. Apollo pointed the distant speck out to his sister, and challenged her to demonstrate her considerable prowess with a bow by hitting it. He surrounded Orion by dazzling sunrays that reflected off the water, deliberately blinding Artemis to what the distant speck was and leaving her ignorant of the catastrophic act she was about to commit.

The mighty huntress' aim was true and her arrow found its mark, piercing her lover's head, killing him instantly. It was only when the waves rolled Orion's body on to the seashore that she realised her mistake, and wept bitter tears for her dead lover. Distraught, she placed his body in her moon-chariot and carried it to the darkest patch in the centre of the sky where she fixed him for all eternity.

This myth, like the one of his unrequited love for Merope, also presents us with some interesting details that add to the view that Orion was the sun's dark twin. Orion, in his capacity as the lord of the winter, could be said to reach his nadir in high summer, in the same way that the sun reaches its lowest point on the winter solstice. During June, when Orion is at his weakest, he sits invisible in the daylight, just under the sun. The myth tells us that it was sunset and Orion was on the horizon, and also that the sun's rays dazzled Artemis so that she could not see what she was shooting at. This would indicate that the sun was setting in the west at the same time as Orion was bathing. The time of the year when both are together is June, when if Orion could be seen, he would sink into the sea in the west with the sun directly above him. If he had sunk beneath the waves until only Betelgeuse, his head, was above the horizon, the setting sun would only be a matter of a few degrees above that star and would certainly dazzle anyone looking west at the time. So this myth shows us that he was killed in June, the lowest point of his yearly cycle. By dying in June, he follows the example of the other group of myths which have deities dying at their nadir, their least powerful moment of the year.

It should also be noted here that although it was Artemis who delivered the fatal blow it was still with the connivance of Apollo the sun God, and so though he did it by proxy, the lord of the summer still 'killed' the lord of the winter, as we would expect he should. It is also telling that Orion was killed by a blow to the head, as Hiram was too. As the constellation sets in the west, Betelgeuse, the head, is the last star to disappear. As the constellation was regarded as having 'died' with the final glimpse of the last star, the fact that only Orion's head was visible as he died, is again indicative of the astral origin of the myth.

The final snippet of myth about Orion also deals with his death, in another version of the tale, and it too is indicative of the role played by the stars in his life's story. We have already noted that he was a fine hunter of some renown, and it was because of this great skill that he boasted that he could rid the entire world of wild animals. His bragging reached the ears of the Earth Goddess Gaea, and she could not countenance such a threat to the balance of nature, so she sent the lowliest of creatures, a scorpion, to kill him, which it achieved by stinging him on the heel. As he died he asked that after his death he be placed in the sky with the stars, and that the scorpion that killed him be placed as far from him as possible, so that it would never have the chance of stinging him again. As noted before, constellations were thought of as dying when they set and being born when they rose, so it is interesting that it stung him on the heel. Orion would 'die' when he reaches the western horizon, and if he were perceived as an upright figure, then he would be standing on the western horizon when he died, and in such a position the scorpion would have been able to sting him on the heel as the myth records. It is not only my 'rearranged' figure that would be standing of course, because all the various ancient figures would have been also. What is interesting about this myth for our thesis is that Orion was standing when he was killed, because in the 3rd Degree Hiram is standing too.

The idea of it being a scorpion that kills Orion comes yet again from the position of the constellations relative to each other in the heavens. Directly opposite the constellation Orion, on the far side of the sky, is Scorpius, the scorpion. Because they oppose each other, Orion sets as the scorpion rises and is thus killed by it.

The idea that Orion dies on setting was to become important later when I started to examine the movements of the constellation in regards to the rituals of the 3rd Degree. It was starting to appear that Hiram, in being identified with Orion, was indeed the lord of the winter, dark twin of the sun, and since we are seeking to link Hiram with Osiris it is interesting that the Egyptians' god of the Underworld was also regarded as the sun's dark alter-ego. Although I earlier suggested that the Masonic pavement, with its never-ending pattern of black and white squares could have referred to the equinoxes, it could also refer to the relationship between the lord of the summer and his counterpart the lord of the winter, one of which rules the light half of the year, the other who rules the dark in a never-ending cycle. This is, of course, merely another way of expressing the same thing.

In conclusion I would reiterate that having looked at the myths of Orion for any hint of relevance to Masonry in general and the character of Hiram Abif in particular, I was taken aback by the sheer number of connections I found. I had formed the opinion that the introduction of Hiram was as the winter solstice marker in place of Jesus who had been removed during the de-Christianisation process that had taken place just before Hiram appeared in the ritual. In the earlier mystery, Jesus and John the Baptist would have been the solstice markers at opposite ends of the year, John representing the midsummer sun, Jesus the winter. Even in established Christian dogma the two were six months apart in age, so Christianity's inclusion of details that had previously been pagan may account for this fact.

More importantly than any of these actual details, the study of the myths of Orion had shown how the ancients structured the tales of their heroes around the rising and setting points of their constellations relative to other celestial bodies - above all the sun - and in particular that Orion had been killed by the sun in several separate myths. What I then had to do was try to get into the minds of the architects of the 3rd Degree, to see if they had created the myth of Hiram to reflect similar themes.

By this stage I was working on the principle that although Osiris was the ultimate identity of Hiram Abif, it was actually as Orion that he found his way into Masonry. This was necessary because the mystery was in the process of being opened up to a much wider audience and it was imperative that Hiram's identity as Osiris be completely invisible. If there had been a mediaeval mystery tradition at the root of the Craft, then what had previously been contained in the secret levels at the core must have been re-packaged, and given 'up-front' in symbolic form to the whole membership. In the past it would have taken many years to achieve the knowledge in the highest degrees, but in modern Masonry the average member will have achieved all three degrees within a year of joining. The innermost knowledge is therefore imparted long before the member has proved himself as 'worthy' – in a symbolic sense, of course - to hold it. There was nothing stopping someone joining out of mischief, simply to gain the knowledge and then leaving to broadcast it far and wide. It was for this reason that the true meaning of the knowledge was disguised, so that in the event of the rituals themselves being broadcast, as indeed they were within a decade of 1717, the meaning remained inviolate. The only way to achieve this and maintain Osiris' identity as the figurehead of the new version of the tradition would be by having the Osirian references pointing obliquely at Orion

rather than towards the known myths of Osiris. This placed the first
screen between him and his audience, because if there were no elements
of the known Osirian myths included in the Hiramic legend then it
would be unlikely that Hiram's true identity as him would ever be
discovered. And if someone like me were to speculate that such was the
case, the fact that all was allegory would mean there would be no way
of proving the case. The truth would remain inviolate forever, therefore,
exactly as its architects intended. The only way the truth would be lost
would be if the rituals were changed, for then they would have lost their
essence. It is for that reason that the Craft maintains the illusion that its
symbols are secret, for by doing so they can continue to use the arcana
of the past as handed it by its forbears.

Having cast my eye over the Graeco-Roman myths of Orion, I
realised that those myths themselves were not the complete basis of the
Hiramic legend either, but this was perhaps to be expected, because
Hiram was a composite character that was primarily the builder of
Solomon's Temple. So now it was time to re-examine the legend of
Hiram Abif in minute detail, to see if it would reveal similar
cosmological significance as the original Graeco-Roman tales of the
gods of that era.

To understand better the relationship Orion had with his fellow
constellations I turned again to the computer astronomy programme,
which would allow me to see the exact locations of the stars at any time
in the past, present, or future, and would give me precise rising and
setting times of celestial bodies and the distances and angles between
them. All references, unless stated otherwise, are based on the viewer
being at the latitude of Edinburgh – the heart of the solstice square.

CHAPTER 25

IN THIS CHAPTER we will look at aspects of the constellation of Orion that find an echo in Freemasonry's 3rd Degree. We will discover that many aspects of its appearance and behaviour resonate with the mystery of Hiram - and some in particular, appear to form the basis of the entire myth.

It was the geometric layout of the stars within the constellation itself that had first attracted me to look in detail at Orion. The original mystery had included details of the crossing of the equinoxes, and the most noticeable aspect of the redefined Orion was that he displayed this by having his right leg crossed over his left. The figure of Orion viewed this way therefore incorporates the sun crossing from one hemisphere to the other by having his shins crossed like the Mithraic torchbearers. He also has his left arm raised, squared at the elbow, in reference to the sun's square at the latitude of Edinburgh. What this new figure adds to the ancient beliefs, then, is the veneration of the special relationship between the sun and the earth at the latitude of Edinburgh, and gives us the reason for the siting of the mystery in Scotland. Before we get into the detail, we will look at the constellation in general terms.

A dead level

The most interesting geometrical aspect of the constellation is that the belt-stars become perfectly horizontal to the naked eye as they set on the western horizon. The picture shows just how precisely horizontal the belt looks when it sets when viewed from Edinburgh, and I think this precision, that can be termed 'dead level', is one of the more important aspects of the constellation. I had already noted that the three stars were horizontal on setting with my own eyes, but it took the precision of the computer programme to show how accurate the alignment truly was.

ORION'S BELT SETTING IN WEST

72 degrees

The computer also gave me the angle they rise at, which was almost as interesting as the setting. The three stars are not exactly in a straight line, even that much can be seen with the naked eye, but the very slight angle that separates them was the first of many eye-openers I was to discover about them.

ORION'S BELT RISING IN EAST

The first star to rise is Mintaka, followed nine minutes later by Alnilam, the centre star of the three. The angle they rise at is 72 degrees to the horizontal, which in itself is interesting because it is the same as the angle between each of the five points of a pentagram; the shape traced in the sky by that other significant body in Masonry, Venus. When Alnitak, the third star, rises yet another nine minutes later the angle between it and the first, Mintaka, is 69 degrees, which whilst not being significant in itself, brought me to the realisation that the difference between the two angles is three degrees. If one were wishing to attach the new Masonic 3rd Degree to Orion, then surely it's most prominent three stars forming this angle, and that it is the 3rd star that is offset by three degrees, would be enormously significant.

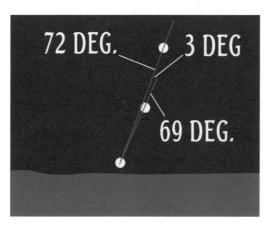

It is also a fact that the stars rise at 72 degrees and are horizontal when they set. This means that during the time all three stars of the belt are visible, they turn by exactly 72 degrees – the precise angle between the points of a pentagram and exactly the number of years it takes for one degree of precessional shift.

Thirty-three degrees

I had noted previously that the constellation rises due east and sets due west, and it was whilst checking exactly where it does rise that I noticed just how precisely on the cardinal points it actually is. The third of the belt stars, Mintaka, sits almost exactly on the celestial equator. Even when examined on a computer screen, it is incredibly

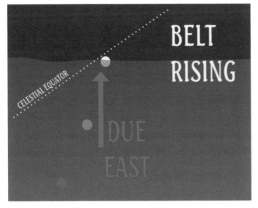

close to the line at a mere 0.6 of a degree off. This means that the belt in particular, and therefore the figure as a whole, arcs across the very centre of the heavens, rising due east and setting due west. Since the east has been venerated for thousands of years because of the equinoctial sunrise, the belt of Orion rising in that exact spot would be significant. More precisely than any other celestial group, then, Orion can be said to be a man from the East, which is exactly what Hiram is taken to be in the Craft.

If we cast our minds back to chapter 3 we will remember that the celestial equator is at a particularly interesting height above the horizon in the area covered by our thesis. At Aberdeen, which is the northern boundary of the phenomenon of the sun's true square, the celestial equator, at its highest point on the meridian, is 33 degrees above the horizon. When I mentioned this, then, it was to make the point that the sun, as it travels along the line of the celestial equator on the days of the equinoxes, was 33 degrees above the horizon.

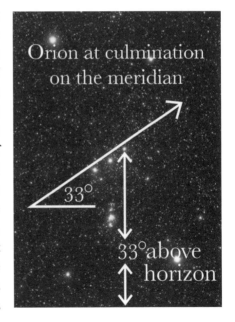

Mintaka, the third star in the belt, rests to all intents and purposes on the celestial equator, so that star is therefore also 33 degrees above the horizon at its culmination in the south. This is therefore two links between the heavens and 33 degrees, and though the 33 degrees of Freemasonry is are relatively recent, it is a link none the less.

Whilst checking that Mintaka did indeed travel along the celestial equator each day, I then noted yet another instance of 33 degrees in the constellation, for at the moment the belt crossed the meridian, it was also at an angle in the sky of 33 degrees. The picture on the previous page shows both occurrences of 33 degrees in the constellation's attitude in the heavens. We must ask ourselves, then, if the adoption of the number 33 as the ultimate number of degrees in Freemasonry was simply chance, or was it a complex, multi-layered reference to the height above the horizon of the celestial equator.

Orion, the celestial equator and the sun

The celestial equator is a notable line for another reason relevant to our quest, and gives us our best proof yet that Orion does indeed lie behind the persona of Hiram Abif. As noted above, the interesting point about the celestial equator is that the sun travels along it on the two equinoxes. The celestial equator is earth's equator extended out into space, and depending on whether it is summer or winter, the sun is either above that line or below it. In the northern hemisphere the day after the spring equinox is the first day the sun is aloft for more than twelve hours. The visual effect of this is that the sun's path is now higher in the sky than the celestial equator. The sun's passage across the sky gets higher and higher each day until Midsummer, when it reaches its peak and then starts to drop. By the autumn equinox it is again on the celestial equator for a single day before dropping into the southern hemisphere. It is on these two days - the days on which the gods of old entered and exited the Underworld – that the sun and Orion interact in a way that is alluded to in Freemasonry.

On the days of division, when the sun is balanced between the two hemispheres, it travels precisely along the line. Since Orion is on that line also, this means that Mintaka, or Orion's waist, passes along exactly the same pathway as the sun on those two special days, and when I looked at this with reference to the mystery thesis, I made possibly the most potent link yet between the rituals of the Craft and the interaction of the sun and Orion.

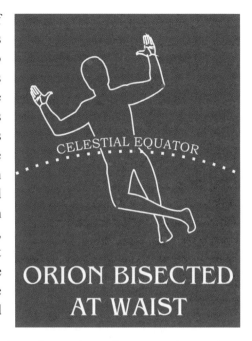

CELESTIAL EQUATOR

ORION BISECTED AT WAIST

I was brought back to the point made earlier about the method of execution of the third conspirator in the Hiramic legend. At the time I had mentioned that although the method of execution of the first two ruffians precisely mirrored the attacks they made on the Grand Master, the third assassin had killed Hiram with a blow to the head, yet afterwards suggested that he himself be sawn in half for punishment. The methods of execution had become the salutes in the three degrees, and it seemed to me that it was the salutes that were important and that the executions were merely the vehicle used to introduce those gestures.

As the constellation makes its way across the sky, it is exactly bisected by the celestial equator as has already been mentioned. The importance of this is that on those equinoxes, the very days the old pagan gods were overthrown and entered the Underworld; the sun's passage across the sky bisects Orion at the waist. The lord of the winter, then, could be said to have been killed by the sun on the equinox by being sawn in half, so there could hardly be a more concrete link between the movements of the heavens and what is depicted in the Masonic 3rd Degree.

Not only is the figure of the man bisected at the waist, but more precisely it is bisected at the third star of the belt. Could it be coincidence that the salute of the Masonic 3rd Degree is the drawing of the hand across the waist, bisecting the Mason's body, as the equinoctial path of the sun bisects Orion? Whilst this is done the thumb is squared to the rest of the hand. The squaring of the hand obviously refers to the square of the sun, so the sun correspondingly becomes the agent of death in the gesture. Indeed the thumb is squared in all three salutes, not only bringing the sun into all the salutes, but links the sun, through that nuance, with the death of the three conspirators.

If we look at some of the older rituals used, they are even more specific about the point about the drawing of the hand across the abdomen. The exposure pamphlet of 1761, 'Three distinct knocks,' says on page 44. '*Oh that I had my body severed in two, one part carried to the **south**, the other to the **north**'*. This statement from the third conspirator actually attaches the idea of north and south to the bisecting of the waist, which is very pertinent to Orion who stands in the sky with the upper half of his body in the northern hemisphere of the sky and his lower half in the south. Although I have referred to Irish ritual throughout, some of the Scottish versions of the 3rd degree salute are even more telling, in that although the hand is drawn across the abdomen in identical fashion to the Irish, it is done twice in rapid succession. Since the sun's path bisects Orion's middle on two days of the year - the two equinoxes - the Scottish salute is perhaps closer to reality than the Irish in this respect.

To recap the significance of this point because I think it the most important yet - we have the salute for the 3rd Degree bisecting the waist, and we find that the third star in the belt, which I equate with the same 3rd Degree, is the precise place where the path of the sun on the equinoxes, the celestial equator, bisects Orion on those days. We even have the hand that is drawn across the abdomen forming a square by the thumb being held at right-angles. If the square does indeed allude to the sun as I have suggested throughout, then in the salute we actually have the sun/hand bisecting Hiram/Orion at the waist. Surely this must constitute proof of some sort that Orion is indeed Hiram, and can be no mere coincidence.

Three degrees

It is an open secret that Freemasons know each other by 'secret handshakes,' but how they can be considered secret since their publication in the 'exposures' of the 18th century and many other times since is anybody's guess. The secret handshakes are referred to in Masonry as grips, and it is during the initiations, whilst kneeling on the steps of the altar, that the grips relevant to each degree are shown to the candidate. The grips take the form of pressure on the knuckles, and there are three different pressure points that identify the first three degrees. The grips vary slightly between jurisdictions, but in Irish ritual, which has been our basis throughout, the pressure points extend from the first knuckle to the second. In the 1st Degree, pressure is applied to the knuckle of the forefinger. In the 2nd Degree it is applied to the hollow between the first and second knuckle, and the 3rd is on the second knuckle. When I searched for significance in this particular notion I came across a reference in orienteering to working out one's bearings in the landscape without a compass.

By extending your hand to full arms length to use as a scale, different parts of it can be used to gauge degrees on the horizon. The fingers splayed out cover twenty-five degrees, whilst the closed fist covers ten. And from the point of view of our study... 'Extend your fist to full arm's length. The distance covered between the end knuckle and the second knuckle is about three degrees'. And from another site, this time from that of Harvard University... 'Hold your fist extended at arm's length. Your first two knuckles are about 3 degrees apart'.

Surely it can be no coincidence that Masons use those two knuckles as indications of their three degrees, when they also mark three degrees on the horizon.

I then carried this realisation into my examination of Orion, and discovered that the knuckles held at arm's length against the belt of the constellation lined up precisely with the three stars, with each star marking exactly the pressure-point that denoted the Masonic grip. When I saw that the two knuckles which signify the three Masonic degrees were three degrees apart when

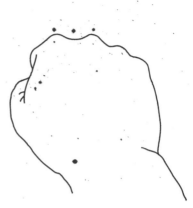

viewed this way, and were also found in the angle of separation of the belt stars of the constellation that I am attaching those same three degrees to, I became convinced that I really had stumbled upon the spiritual notions these allegories were intended to portray.

Orion's square

From looking only at the three belt stars, we will now widen our study and look at the constellation as a whole. The figure I had taken as representing Hiram could not in any way be described as a regular, symmetrical shape, and so I thought there was no way the overall figure could be seen as geometrically perfect. But as with so many other aspects of this enigmatic figure, I was to be proved wrong when I actually looked.

It was because one of the stars of the belt sat on the celestial equator that I knew that the figure rose in the east. But when it rises it is lying almost flat, and therefore is much wider than it is when it

reaches the western horizon and has become upright. I was, however, in a particularly methodical mindset when I was at this point in the research and had resolved not to let any stone remain un-turned. I set the sky on the computer to the precise moment the first star, Betelgeuse, rises, and noted its angle from the north, (all subsequent angles are taken clockwise, from north being zero.) I found that Betelgeuse rises at 76.42 degrees, and that was duly noted. I then reset the sky to show Rigel, the last star, rising, and noted the angle to be 104.36 degrees. The difference between these two sight-lines gives an angle on the horizon of 27.94 degrees, illustrated in the sketch above, which I will call its rising footprint. This footprint is also centred to an astonishing degree on due east, with the middle point of the two being at 90.49 degrees - due east being 90.

I don't quite know what I was hoping to find with this exercise, but I then pointed the cursor towards the west, and set the computer to show the constellation as it set. When upright, it looked to be a little over half as wide as it was when recumbent in the east, and I dallied with the possibility that perhaps the relationship of the rising footprint to the setting one would be near the Golden Ratio – 1:1.618 that is often referred to in Craft symbolism. That would have given a setting footprint of just over 17 degrees, and would certainly have interested anyone looking for geometric significance in the figure, but I was way off in this, because the setting footprint was nowhere near my hoped for proportion of the rising one.

Although Betelgeuse is the first to rise, the rotation of the figure

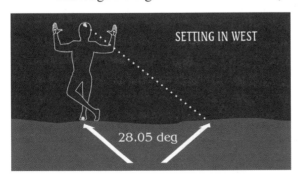

as it traverses the sky means that it is Rigel that sets first, and setting the screen for the precise moment of its setting, I noted it as 255.08 degrees. I then changed the time to show the star

Betelgeuse setting, and noted the angle as 283.13 degrees. As I subtracted the setting point of Rigel from that of Betelgeuse I could not believe my eyes when I arrived at an angle of 28.05 degrees, only 0.11 of a degree different from the rising footprint of 27.94 degrees. I thought I had obviously made a mistake somewhere along the line, because there was no way a tall figure could give the same reading as a wide one, so I checked everything again. The answer was the same the second time, so the fact was blinking up at me from the computer screen - Orion rising horizontal was the same size as setting vertical, so he is within a tenth of a degree of an exact square, despite twisting through almost 90 degrees during the process. Masons talk of being raised upon the square, and here in the heavens Orion can be said to do just that. And as the rising is centred on east, the setting is also centred to an astonishing degree on west, the centre-point of the setting points being at 269.33 degrees, with due west being 270.

What I was looking at was a figure of a man which outlines an almost perfect square on the ground as he rises from the horizontal to the vertical, and this happened in the same area where the sun forms a perfect square on the ground with its rising and setting points on the solstices by its movements over the year. I was starting to be in awe of this geographical / astral phenomenon, which seemed to link every one of the original aspects of the veneration of the sun with the figure that also happened to be the basis of many of the pagan god-men in antiquity. I was starting to understand why this figure became the basis for Hiram Abif.

I was truly stunned by the figure's geometry, but couldn't figure out how it achieves such a feat until I did a little maths. It is because of the angle at which the celestial plane is tilted to the earth's rotational plane, which in turn means that at the latitude in question any body that lies in the centre of the heavens will not rise straight up out of the ground, but will 'slide' up to the right at an angle, in this case of roughly 23 degrees. Likewise it will do the same on setting, sliding sideways down into the ground at the same angle. Because the figure is wide and squat when it rises, the constellation rises quickly from Betelgeuse to

Rigel, but when it sets it is tall, and takes far longer to disappear from first to last. This means it has more time to 'slide,' further, and covers a greater linear distance across the horizon than its width would suggest. By an amazing coincidence, the complex interplay of time, distance and angle combine to mean that the rising covers almost exactly the same footprint as the setting.

It is similar to the fact that although the sun is four hundred times farther away than the moon, it is also four hundred times bigger, and so when they line up during an eclipse they appear to be almost exactly the same size. This is a mere quirk of circumstance, but must have appeared divinely inspired by ancient Man. By the same reasoning, then, the curious squareness of Orion must also have seemed sublime to those who noted its passage across the sky and who sought to link it to the movements of the sun at the same latitude as the sun itself forms a square on the ground.

The three-runged ladder

To focus on the three belt stars once again, I did a little digging on them too, to see if they themselves held any particular interest for ancient society, and yet again what I found added to the picture. Space

does not permit much detail here, suffice to say several ancient cultures, such as the Dogon people of Mali, West Africa, viewed the three belt stars, as they emerge in the east at the steep angle that they do, as a stairway to the realm of the gods. The Milky Way, which runs past Orion in the night sky, was seen as the great river of the heavens, teeming with knowledge, and Orion was thought to guard that knowledge. The three-runged ladder of Orion's Belt could therefore be climbed to gain access to that sacred information.

It would be perhaps too much to claim that they might have been the inspiration for Jacob's Ladder in the Old Testament, but that is nevertheless how they were viewed by some ancient civilisations, who believed that their shamen ascended the three steps to gain enlightenment from the gods, no doubt whilst they were under the influence of some hallucinogenic substance or other.

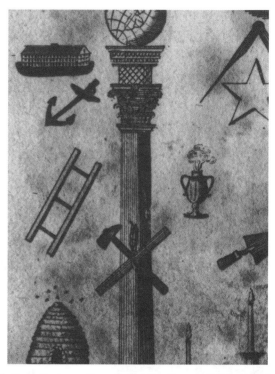

Many early Masonic objects are literally covered in a hotchpotch of symbols, and in many instances depict a ladder with three rungs. Those rungs often have three letters, F, H, and C, representing Faith, Hope and Charity, but again, those letters will be an instance of using well-known symbols exoterically, to carry an inner, esoteric meaning. To the un-informed viewer the three-runged ladder is a simple vehicle to carry the three letters that are the reason for the motif. I would suggest, however, that it is the three rungs of the ladder that are the true purpose of the emblem, and that the F, H, and C are merely a facilitator, to give it purpose. The picture above is a close-up of a typical 19th C. Masonic document and includes the ladder on its own without the letters, suggesting, surely, that the letters are superfluous.

The three steps of the altar

To carry the symbolism of the three steps further, whilst being obligated and being given each degree, the candidate kneels on one of three steps that lead to the altar. In the 1st Degree he kneels on the first step and so on, so it can be said that as his knowledge increases he ascends the steps. It is whilst in this position that he is given the symbolic knowledge, and more importantly perhaps, the handgrips of each degree, the handgrips being spread across the three knuckles that are three degrees apart. Whilst purely symbolic, Masons can therefore be said to ascend the three steps of the altar in search of enlightenment in precisely the same manner as the shamen of old ascended the three steps of Orion's belt in their own pursuit of higher knowledge. Many Masonic buildings incorporate three steps to their entrances, or to the dais on which the Master's chair rests, so do we see in that too the ascent of the three stars of Orion's Belt?

To summarise, the candidate kneels on a progression of three steps whilst receiving knowledge, and it is in those positions that he is given the handgrips that signify each level. In ancient times the shaman figuratively ascended the three stars of Orion's Belt, regarding them as three steps in the search of knowledge. Those stars are to all intents and purposes three degrees apart, as are the knuckles that denote the handgrips the Masonic candidate receives on the three steps of the altar. Circumstantial it may be, but the evidence was certainly starting to pile up.

The winding stair

Taking the idea of the belt stars being a ladder and extrapolating it a little farther, we can tie it to yet another enigmatic symbol of the Craft. The idea of a winding stair is very strong in Masonic lore, though it does not, on the surface, seem to convey any particular lesson. In legend, masons ascended the winding stair which led to the middle chamber of the Temple where they would receive their wages. Just why the stair has to be winding isn't made clear, though if referring to the belt stars, it actually makes perfect sense.

We have already seen how, as the night progresses, the constellation twists around as it passes towards the west. The belt stars start off in the east at the steep angle of seventy-two degrees, and become horizontal by the time they reach the western horizon, almost making a quarter turn as they arc through the southern sky. If they are regarded as steps at all then they must also be regarded as a winding stair, because they 'wind' or 'spiral' as they cross the sky. Masons regard themselves as travelling towards the east in search of enlightenment, and that would indicate starting in the west. The constellation is precisely in the west when the steps are horizontal on the ground, so would become the bottom step, rising as it regresses towards the east. The workmen's wages, which they receive at the top of the stair, are obviously symbolic, and can be seen as the knowledge that is imparted through the initiations.

By ascending Orion's winding stair then, they can be said to pass from the west to the east in search of knowledge or enlightenment. To relate this directly to the lodge room, the candidate is kneeling on, and ascending, the steps at the west side of the altar, and he is facing east when given that knowledge. It is also a fact that before the candidate is placed on the steps of the altar he begins his journey in the west of the room, and takes three specific steps eastwards along the ground to bring himself to the aforementioned altar steps. Are those three steps representative of three belt stars lying flat on the ground as they set in the west? I earlier suggested that the three belt stars represent the three degrees, with the third, Mintaka, representing the 3rd Degree. It is a fact that in the ceremony as each of the three steps is taken, the salute of each of the three degrees is given. This, too, does not dissuade us from the possibility of my suggested link.

The passage from west to east is portrayed here through the movements of the constellation, but is actually derived from the sun. The sun is reborn every morning in the east, but it must fade and die in the west in order to be able to rise again. It must also spend some time in the dark, in the 'Underworld' before it is able to emerge replenished. It cannot appear in the east, however, unless it first disappears in the west, so its own path towards enlightenment starts in the west. To carry this into its allusion in Masonry, Man must first pass into the Underworld in the west and spend some time in darkness before emerging enlightened in the east. This is precisely what happens in the 3rd Degree.

Slipshod

The next item to take our attention is another strange aspect of the degrees whereby the candidate is led into the lodge room with his heels bare. Moccasin type slippers are provided for the occasion, and the socks are pulled back off the ankle so that the heels are exposed. This is referred to as being 'slipshod,' and though strange, does not seem any stranger than other details.

During the ritual, the candidate is informed that he is so attired because the Hebrews used to take off a sandal to seal a bargain. Since the candidate's request to become a Mason, followed by his acceptance into the lodge can be seen as a bargain, the reference to finalising a deal makes sense. As with so much else in Masonry it appears that the Hebrew reference is allegorical however, and I feel that the true reference yet again relates to Orion.

If we look at the way the right foot sits in such a stance, with only the toe and the ball of the foot touching the ground, any sandal that was worn would fall away from the sole of the foot, as illustrated in the figure above. This would leave the foot with the heel bare, or in Masonic-speak, slipshod. If one observes a

candidate in the stance indicated here, as he is before being symbolically assaulted, then the moccasin slipper does indeed fall away from the foot exactly as shown in the drawing, and because the sock is pulled back, the heel is exposed. In the constellation arranged as I have it in this thesis, Cursa, the heel, is one of the stars that highlights the cross-legged stance. Is the candidate's exposed heel therefore derived from that star?

The Charge of Nimrod

We now, however, come to what can be considered inalienable proof, not only that the thesis is right, but that the tradition existed in the days of the purely operative stonemasons before speculative Freemasonry came about. That proof lies in the Charge of Nimrod, by which the operative craft was governed - for the persona of Nimrod is regarded by many as being based on the constellation of Orion.

This charge is much older than speculative Freemasonry and can be traced back to at least the 1620s. It was a document that laid out a fulsome list of instructions for the conduct of working stonemasons. The choice of Nimrod as the focus of that charge is curious, because although he is traditionally thought of as the builder of the Tower of Babel, he is generally regarded in a slightly dark light, and even as God's adversary. This therefore makes him an odd choice to front the ritual observances of the stonemasons. In being linked to the constellation of Orion, Nimrod shared that rebellious streak that Orion also possessed. God said of him, in connection with the building of the Tower of Babel… 'I made Nimrod great - but he built a tower in order that he might rebel against Me.' (Talmud, Hul. 89b) God then sundered the workmen one from the other to frustrate the building work, causing each to speak in different tongues. This did not cause Nimrod to change his conduct however, and he remained an idolater. Indeed, the more we look at the tales about this character, the less suitable he seems to become the one to whom a charge of good conduct is directed.

Though not actually named in the Bible, Nimrod has since the earliest times been portrayed as the builder of the tower of Babel. Being a builder would certainly have made him appealing to the mediaeval stonemasons, and this argument is generally advanced, but why not use Solomon as did the later Freemasons? When we consider that Nimrod was based on the constellation of Orion - the constellation upon which Hiram is also based - the picture becomes altogether clearer. There is one particular aspect of the constellation that I have identified in the Craft, and is also unmistakeably present in the Charge of Nimrod.

Computer astronomy programmes are marvellous tools, but I was to discover that not all the stars that one can see on a clear night appear on the screen. The observation I now make centres on the star Meissa, which I had attributed to  being the upraised left hand of the figure, for it was not one star, but three. The re-drawn figure as I have depicted it has both arms up, although of course only the left side actually has a basis in the stars - but with both arms raised, the stance of Orion is still incorporated.

In Masonic ritual the arms are raised several times, but there is one time when only the left is raised. This is when the candidate is being obligated in the 2nd Degree. Kneeling on the second step of the altar, he raises his left hand as though taking an oath in court. The instruction is quite specific that the thumb be held at a right angle to the rest of the hand, forming a 90-degree square. It is presumed that this is another instance of a right angle simply being shoe-horned into the ritual without reference to anything specific, but a closer examination of the night sky shows the true reason for inclusion of this gesture at this point. I didn't see it straight away because only Meissa shows up on the computer programme I used, but one particularly clear night when the stars were brighter than usual, I noticed that Meissa has two more stars

very close by, and taken together they form a passable right angle. The angle even points the right way for the thumb, i.e. towards the head. I have illustrated the hand overlaid on the stars in the figure above, and indeed this can also be clearly seen in the context of the full constellation in the photograph on page 253.

As mentioned earlier, the placing of the thumb in this position is also incorporated into all three salutes of Freemasonry. In the 1st Degree the thumb is specifically held at a right angle as the hand is drawn across the throat. In the 2nd, when the left hand is raised in identical fashion to the stance of Orion, the thumb must also be held rigidly at 90 degrees. In the 3rd, when the hand is drawn across the abdomen, the thumb must be similarly squared with the rest of the hand. In all these cases the correct posture of the hand is to hold the thumb in the way mentioned – and is simply another unexplained aspect of the curious rituals of Freemasonry. I had suggested earlier that squaring alludes to the sun, and that is no doubt the intention, but here in the stance of the constellation of Orion, we can see another reason for the gesture – because Orion himself stands with his own thumb squared.

The above is a very close correlation between the rituals of Freemasonry and the stance of Orion in the sky as re-interpreted by the thesis, and is not vague but is quite specific. The connection becomes particularly interesting when we examine the contents of the above-mentioned Charge of Nimrod, for in it we find the candidate having to place his hand in a very specific way…'The sign is given by placing his left arm and hand, **with thumb extended**, in a perpendicular position pointing upwards, and his right arm and hand, **with thumb extended**, in a horizontal position…' This is precisely the same as is carried out in the Craft to this day. That it can be attributed to the stars of Orion in such a specific way, in a document that refers to Nimrod, who was Orion, means that the constellation was unmistakeably at the core of the operative stonemasons' rituals too, and pushes the esoteric back to the days before Freemasonry came to the fore.

The above is a very definite link to the past, but it is much more important than that in terms of our thesis. The fact is that the link is a gesture that is attributable to this new reading of the stance of Orion in the sky, and therefore substantiates the re-assignment of stars that form the thesis. And the fact that this is from a written source from the past is surely teetering towards the paper proof required by academia.

The other aspect of the stonemason's gesture was holding the right arm horizontally across the stomach with the thumb squared in similar fashion as it was in the upraised hand. This is the salute of the modern Craft's 3rd Degree and is truly fascinating, because when modern Freemasonry emerged in the 1700s it had only two degrees; not three. The 3rd appeared in the late 1720s, and is therefore thought to be of modern invention. Academic historians claim that the salute of the 3rd

Degree is simply derived from the position of the right hand in the Charge of Nimrod, but it is not as simple as that. I noted earlier that although Hiram has both arms up at the moment of his slaying, the constellation only has the left arm up. Where, then, is the figure's right arm? It does not appear outside the bodyline, but it could be accounted for if it were across the abdomen as depicted in both the modern 3rd Degree and the operative masons' Charge of Nimrod. We can therefore redraw the figure of Orion with his right arm squared across the front of his body, bisecting him at the waist as shown in the sketch on the previous page, and note that the position of his forearm, like all the other body-parts mentioned, is highlighted by stars.

The full significance of this bisecting of the waist will not become apparent until the next chapter when we discover how pivotal it is in the geometry of the heavens. For now we will simply note that the gesture is derived from the constellation. The fact that it can be seen to have an esoteric meaning and is found in the 1600s is also proof that though the 3rd Degree was only given an outward face in the 1720s, it must have been pre-existing in some form or other before that time. I suggested earlier that a tradition had existed from long before modern Freemasonry appeared, that carried teachings that were hidden from the world under layers of initiation. I also suggested that as the Craft developed into a more open fraternal society in the 18th Century, that that deeply esoteric knowledge was re-packaged, brought out of the shadows, and converted to allegory so it could be given to all. The trail of this gesture of the squared thumb back to the days of the operative Craft through the Charge of Nimrod is surely proof of the existence of that path.

Having now substantiated Orion in the thesis, we will now look in more depth at the constellation, for we have not yet looked at its position in relation to other celestial bodies, particularly the sun, to see what relevance can be drawn from those relationships. In the next chapter I will demonstrate that almost every aspect of the death and raising of Hiram is drawn directly from these relationships, and that Hiram, like Orion before him, was killed on the equinox.

CHAPTER 26

WE WILL START this exercise with an observation that has already been made, and that is that Hiram was killed while he was standing up. If the constellation of Orion can be said to die on setting, then standing upright is precisely what he is doing when he sets in the west. But what of his rising in the east? Can anything be drawn from the ritual that surrounds Hiram's raising? From the ritual outlined earlier it will be remembered that Hiram was buried outside the Eastern Gate, and so because he was raised from that temporary grave, we can regard him as being raised in the east, exactly where the constellation rises.

The most notable thing about the rising of the constellation is the emergence of the three belt stars one after the other. If we look at the ritual we noted earlier on page 234, there are three attempts made to raise Hiram's body. Two craftsmen attempt but fail to raise the stricken Grand Master before the third succeeds with his special grip. I would suggest that the three attempts are a theatrical device to split the raising into three parts deliberately to refer to the emergence of one belt-star after the other.

Moving to the attack in the Temple, we again find the number three in the attempts to kill him, and I would link these incidents also with the three belt stars. This time, however, I would say that the belt stars are representative of the three ruffians as well as the attacks on the Grand Master's person. My reason for suggesting this is because of the place and manner of their later discovery. They were discovered at Joppa, to the west of Jerusalem, and if Hiram was Orion, who 'died' on the western horizon, that is where the stars would be found.

In identifying this aspect of Hiram's dying with the west, we are starting to move into a territory that we will shortly explore, and that is the ancient pagan belief about being born in the east and passing into the Afterworld in the west. This is a concept ultimately derived from the sun, which 'rises in the east to open and illumine the glorious day', and fades from view in the west, ending the day and heralding darkness. The quote above is drawn directly from the opening ceremony of the lodge room, and is spoken in response to the question '...where is the Master's place in the lodge?' The full answer is '... in the East. As the sun rises in the east to open and illumine the glorious day, so the Worshipful Master presides in the east, to open the lodge, to rule and govern it with good and wholesome advice and instruction...'

So the ritual has the three conspirators in the west, but it is so much more explicit than merely having them at that cardinal point. They are found on the coast, as far west as they can go. They could have been found in a forest or a house, but the seashore is specifically mentioned. Having them discovered on the seashore is so much better than anywhere else because it yet again ties in with a specific aspect of the constellation of Orion.

In the first place the seashore can easily be counted as the utter west for the purpose of the legend, being the westernmost extremity of the land, or where the sun sets. Then in the second place, if we cast our minds back to the Orion/Oenopion myth we will remember that Orion was thrown onto the seashore when he was blinded, which we have already seen is a metaphor for his 'death' and passing into the Underworld. This associates Orion's passage into the underworld with the seashore - and the seashore, between high and low water mark, was important in myth as a 'liminal' place; being neither land nor sea, where the powers of the gods were neutralised. Considering the usurping of Orion by Oenopion that the moment signifies, the inclusion of the seashore is obvious. Though the fragmentary myth of Orion does not specifically record that seashore as being in the west, the fact that it was can be deduced from Orion then making his way to the east to be cured of his blindness. Orion's other death-myth, where Artemis was tricked into killing him, also places him in the west, just off the shore, at the going down of the sun, so on two counts the usurping of Orion can be said to be related to the western seashore.

There is also another very pertinent reason for the choice of the seashore for the discovery of the conspirators, because it introduces the concept of them hiding in a cave, which, by its nature, is underground. The wording of the ritual refers to the search party hearing voices '...as if emanating from the ground', and that it was only on inspection that the cave entrance was discovered. When Orion arrives at the western horizon he is bolt upright. He then slides into the ground whilst still in an upright position, and when only his head is visible, the three belt stars are below the horizon, or for the purposes of the myth, are underground. This equates very precisely with the three conspirators' voices emanating from the ground. The last part of the figure to disappear is Betelgeuse, the head, and that is why the final, fatal blow is to Hiram's temple. At the moment that star disappears from view the constellation can be said to be dead, and at that moment in the ritual the still upright Hiram falls dead on the ground.

This, then, is why the third conspirator, whilst killing Hiram with a blow to the head, asks that he be sawn in half for punishment, because by changing the method of execution, two separate aspects of the constellation can be incorporated in the ritual - the fact that Orion shares the celestial equator with the sun on the equinoxes and is thus bisected at the waist, and also that the last star to disappear is Betelgeuse - the head, signifying the instantaneous death of the constellation in an upright position.

In some of the other Constitutions, and indeed some of the early references in the 'Exposures' of the 18th century, Hiram is killed at the

Western Gate of the Temple. That places him in the west, and as the gods were thought of as passing into the Afterworld in the west, this makes perfect sense. In Irish ritual however, which has been my basis throughout, he is actually killed at the Eastern Gate. At first this seemed a problem, as it appeared to contradict the death in the west, but after a little thought I realised that as had been the case so often in my quest, the reason was sitting there staring at me.

In versions placing Hiram at the Western Gate of the temple he would have been facing the west when confronted by the conspirator outside that gate. The constellation however, on reaching the western horizon, stands facing back to the east as it sets with its arms raised and legs crossed, and to achieve this in ritual, Hiram has to be at the Eastern Gate, where looking out he would indeed have been facing east. I conclude from this that in early versions of the myth, before Orion became enmeshed in it, Hiram was killed at the Western Gate to fit in with the pre-Christian principle of dying in the west leading to rebirth in the east, but once Orion had been adopted as a template, the stance of the constellation in the sky dictated that the location be changed to the Eastern Gate.

To sum up this important point then, when Orion dies, or sets, he is **facing east**, he has his **arm raised**, his **thumb at a right angle forming a square,** and his **legs crossed** making him **slipshod**. When the candidate, who has assumed the role of Hiram dies, he is also **facing the east**, has his **arms raised**, his **thumb held at a right angle**, his **legs crossed**, and is **slipshod**.

In addition, the wording of the ritual is again suggestive, for though the Master 'presides' in the east, and the Junior Warden is simply referred to as being 'in' the south, the Senior warden 'stands' in the west – the only one of the three associated with this word. Since the constellation can only be considered to 'stand' when it reaches the western horizon, the allusion is therefore strengthened. Surely all this is beyond coincidence?

We can finally, now, come to see how much symbolism is incorporated in the right hand with thumb extended being held across the abdomen as outlined above. Since the rituals of the operative stonemasons that preceded the introduction of the 3rd Degree by many years also carried the gesture, it can no longer be argued that they were not possessed of esoteric secret knowledge of the cosmos.

I thought the above was quite a convincing explanation for the origin of the Hiramic legend, and was quite pleased that what I had pieced together fitted the Masonic legend so well, but there was to be one further discovery in this train of thought that put the icing on the cake, as it were. If Hiram is indeed lord of the winter, then we would expect him, like Orion, to be killed by the sun, and to pass into the Underworld at the equinox. We saw this earlier in the path of the sun bisecting his waist on those days. Adopting the cross-legged stance before being killed is certainly indicative of the equinoxes, but I wondered if I could find anything more conclusive than that.

It took some time, but I finally focused again on the fact that on the two days of the equinoxes the sun travels along the celestial equator, which is the same line that Orion passes along every day. This means that on those two days they follow precisely the same path across the sky – two objects on a circular track through the heavens. Where were they in relation to each other on those significant days I wondered? I knew that on the winter solstice the sun and Orion are at opposite sides of the sky and that they are together on the summer solstice, so I turned to my computer programme to find out where they were on the equinoxes. It was when I looked at this aspect of their geometrical relationship in the sky that it all started to make sense.

On the spring equinox the sun travels along the celestial equator - the same path as that taken by Orion every single day. The immense significance of this to our quest is that seen as two objects on a circular track, they are exactly 90 degrees apart on the celestial equator, as shown in the figure above. Yet again we have geometry linking the two objects in a way that is significant to the other relevant factors. The 90 degrees is the angle created by the sun on the Edinburgh line, and now we see it again in the angle between Orion and the sun on these special days. When the 3rd Degree Mason bisects his abdomen with his thumb squared, we can now see that he does so because the sun is square to Orion on the

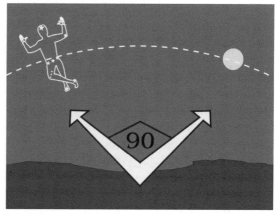

day of the equinox on which Hiram's death happened. The significance of this, however, goes way beyond this simple fact. The following timings are approximate, depending on where on the earth the viewer stands relative to their time zone.

On the 21st of March the sun rises around six in the morning, and Orion, six hours behind it, rises when the sun is at its highest. Orion can therefore not be seen until the sun sets, because it has arisen in daylight. The first time Orion can be seen that day is when the sun dips below the horizon at six in the evening, and when this happens, Orion is exactly on the meridian. Masons refer to noon as High Twelve, but to understand the Hiramic myth we need to see High Twelve as a location in the sky rather than a time. High Twelve can also be seen as the meridian, where the sun and indeed all celestial bodies attain their highest point, and can be seen as their most important moment in the day. So on the spring equinox, the day on which the ancient gods were born, Orion's first appearance of the day places him on the meridian, or at his most powerful. Can this moment be seen as his birth? It happens as the sun sets, so can we also see this moment as the sun's figurative death?

In primitive times the equinoxes were the days on which the gods changed places, and in identifying Orion as the lord of the winter we find that on the spring equinox he is positioned to attain his highest point in the sky simultaneously with his opposite, the sun, setting, or more correctly dying. If taken literally, the lord of the winter would die at the spring equinox rather than the sun, but the 3rd Degree incorporates both dying and raising simultaneously. The myth is also a conflation of more than one mythical idea, as we will see in the following chapters, and is perhaps even an intermingling of both gods of the year into one. Not only is this ripe with symbolism, but the separation between the two on the celestial equator on that day is exactly 90 degrees, enabling the figurative birth that is the raising to be classed as being 'on the square.' When Masons refer to being 'Raised upon the Square,' then, that is therefore a metaphor for their rebirth from the Underworld at the equinox, when the pre-Christian gods of old were traditionally re-born.

Having shown how Orion/Hiram is 'born' on the spring equinox we will now look to the other equinox to see how it too is referred to in the ritual. The 21st of September is the mirror-image of the spring, and the sun is then six hours behind Orion, which means they are again exactly 90 degrees apart on the celestial equator. Their positions in the sky are now the reverse of what they were before and now we have Orion rising first, around midnight. The sun does not rise for another six hours, so during this time Orion is visible as it climbs towards its zenith on the meridian. When it reaches that point the sun breaks the horizon and lightens the sky. Orion then becomes invisible in the blue sky of daylight. The constellation's appearance on the meridian in spring which I suggested could be seen as Orion's birth is now matched in autumn by his disappearance at the same important spot - the meridian. Could his obliteration by the light of the sun be seen as his death? But was the constellation not regarded as dying on setting in the west and not on the meridian?

If we advance another six hours the invisible Orion then reaches the horizon at the same time that the sun attains its zenith on the meridian. Orion then dips below the horizon, or dies, at noon - the precise time that Hiram is killed in the legend of the 3rd Degree. This happens at the exact moment the sun reaches its most powerful on the meridian. Both these deaths are at noon - one when Orion is at High Twelve, the meridian - the other actually at the hour of noon. Orion can therefore be said to die on the autumn equinox, killed by the sun, in exact mimicry of the ancient pagan twin gods, who each ruled the heavens for half the year. Reinforcement of this is that in Masonic ritual, as we saw earlier, it is the Master who plays the role of the third of the conspirators, the one who actually delivers the fatal blow to Hiram Abif.

I then realised that the scheme I have just laid out, of Orion the constellation being killed twice, could be reflected in the fact that in Masonic ritual Hiram has two burials; one under rubbish in the Temple, signifying a partial burial when Orion is rendered invisible by the rising of the sun; and the more permanent burial outside the city walls signifying his actual setting on the horizon?

In this chapter I have sought to show that Hiram being killed is an allegorical representation of the death of the pagan God-men of the ancient world and their passage into the Underworld. From the outset I have also claimed that the ceremony is somehow representative of the ancient Egyptian burial ceremony in which the dead Pharaoh became Osiris and passed his divinity to his son who became Horus. Such a ritual is thought to have occurred in the Great Pyramid of Khufu at Giza. According to the theory of Robert Bauval in his book The Orion Mystery the narrow passage that has become known as the southern 'air-shaft', in the Kings Chamber, was directed straight towards the belt stars of the constellation of Orion as they culminated on the meridian during the era of the pharaohs. The ground-plan of the three great pyramids mimics the layout of the three belt stars in the sky, which adds considerable weight to Bauval's claim, but is not universally accepted by Egyptologists. Research which I am working on in that field at the moment, and which will be included in my next book, tends to agree with Bauval that the passage is more correctly a star-shaft than an air-shaft, and does indeed refer to the three stars of Orion's Belt, even if I do not agree with his dating for the link with the constellation.

So rather than merely being for the ingress of air, it appears that the shaft was a sacred portal to the stars, up which the soul of the deceased pharaoh travelled on his way to the Duat - the Underworld he would thereafter rule. The constellation of Orion must therefore have been regarded by the pyramid builders as representing the 'other side' so it is surely intriguing that Masonry has used the constellation in a similar way.

By this stage in my investigations I had formed the opinion that in undergoing the raising ceremony of the 3rd Degree the candidate metaphorically became Horus. It is after all, on becoming a Master Mason that one becomes known as a 'son of the widow,' and in Ancient Egypt, the young son of the Pharaoh would not have been considered fully divine until his father's death, whereupon he would have become Horus simultaneous with his father becoming Osiris. Are Entered Apprentices and Fellow Crafts being equated with the young, mortal sons of the living pharaoh, and are they being prepared for the time when they will assume the mantle of Hiram in the 3rd Degree, where on their figurative death and subsequent raising they will become, symbolically of course, Horus the son?

It was with this in the back of my mind that I was to venture into the investigation of the substituted Master Mason's word, to see if it too could be linked to the ideas mentioned above. In that search I discovered that this time the relevance did not lie in faraway Egypt, or in the lands that surround the eastern end of the Mediterranean Sea. This time they were attached to the home-grown myths of the ancient Celts and pre-Celts who inhabited these islands before us, the very Bronze-Age people who I believe first identified the land of the solstice square.

CHAPTER 27

AS MENTIONED EARLIER, the giving of the Master Mason's Word is the axis around which the entire Craft revolves. There are many higher degrees than that of the raising of a Master Mason but set beside the antiquity of the first two and the elements symbolised by the third, these higher orders are relatively recent additions to the fold and are therefore not being assigned particular relevance to our quest. They may well be laced with more details that have been mined from the same mother-lode as the Craft degrees, but a close study of the nuances of their rituals will have to wait for another day.

What I have discovered of the rituals of the first three degrees has not merely come from reading them once or twice in a book - it has come from nineteen years of watching them being repeated over and over again on the lodge room floor, whilst all the time studying them for their subtle nuances. The point here, perhaps, is that no amount of study into early documents will explain the rituals as I have here. Nor indeed will any historian who is not a member of the Craft ever be able so 'see' the significance of the rituals, however academic his or her methods.

Masons who have attained higher degrees are always quick to point out that those higher bodies are 'side' orders and not actually higher orders, and that the pinnacle of one's Masonic career is being made a Master Mason. If that is so, and I believe it is, then the word used to make one a Master Mason must carry a lot of esoteric significance indeed.

Various words are used, or have been used in the past, for the substituted Master's Word. The pamphlet *Shibboleth*, one of the exposures printed as early as 1760, says on page 34... 'and then whisper softly into his ear, MAHHABONE; but the more general word is MACBENAC'. In another exposure printed in 1808 entitled *Three Distinct Knocks*, we find, 'and whisper in his ear, and say MAHABONE; that is, almost rotten to the Bone, which is the Master's Word'. Elsewhere we find the words given variously as MABONE or MAHABONEY.

In modern times, spelling has been standardised and set in stone, but in the mid 18th century spelling varied widely between regions and was not as rigid or consistent as it is now. It would be expected that different regions would have different spellings for the same word, and so the variations on Mabone are probably all one word, and we will take them as such. The other word, Macbenac seems unrelated to the first and we will treat it as a separate word. What we have then, are two different words which can be said to have been used as the substituted Master Mason's Words; Mabone and Macbenac.

Of the two words it is Mabone that is most interesting, and is very much in line with the division of the year into its light and dark halves. It shares one particular detail with the Masonic 3rd Degree ceremony that proves beyond doubt that the derivation I offer here is correct.

The other word, Macbenac, is very straightforward, for when taken in its Gaelic form, it can be split into its constituent parts – 'mac' meaning son, and 'benac' meaning blessed. It therefore means blessed son. When we examine the meaning of the word Mabone, we will see that blessed son is a very apt companion for it.

In the course of this research I have had to cast my net into some very deep pools indeed, and it very often came up empty. Every now and again, however, something snagged in the webbing that deserved further study, and the word Mabone was one such thing. Many Masonic historians suggest a Hebrew root for the word, whereas John Robinson, in his book *Born in Blood*, suggests an origin among the dispossessed Templar Knights. He links the 'bone' part of the word to the French 'bon' meaning good. He also suggests that fugitive Templars-turned-pirates were the origin of the 'maha' part of the word, and drew it from the pirate town of Mahadia on the North African Mediterranean coast. He reasoned that if the Templar pirates had been well received in that port they could have referred to it as Mahadia-le Bon, Mahadia the good. He himself admits in the text that the notion is quite speculative, and says that the word had defied all his attempts to uncover its origin in the French language, so his suggestion is not made with any great degree of conviction. I would totally agree with him that some refugee Templars may well have taken to the seas as pirates in the aftermath of their order's destruction, but I think the reason he could not identify the French origin of the word is that it is not French.

It was whilst researching the autumn equinox that I discovered that the pagan celebration of that day is called Mabon. I immediately made a note that this was its ancient pagan name, though I was troubled, because it seemed so obvious that those writing a deeply veiled reference into the ritual would never have used something that was so easily identifiable. I later discovered, however, that in thinking of this as ancient I was wrong. It turns out that the ancient pagan name for the autumn equinox did not find its way into the written record, and that the word Mabon was a modern attachment by neo-pagans of the name of an old pagan god to the celebration, in an effort to give the resurrected festival an 'old' significance. This means that when Masonic ritual was written in the first quarter of the 18th century, the word Mabon would not have existed in popular culture like it does today, but would have been an obtuse reference, trawled from the obscurity of a long forgotten myth. It is only in our own, modern age that the word Mabon was raised from anonymity to prominence. So where did the word that the neo-pagans used come from, and why did they choose it?

On seeking the background of the god Mabon I found him to be a Celtic god from the Welsh pantheon. It was when I looked into the attributes of the god in this myth that I realised that it could be no mere coincidence that the word Mabon was so similar to Mabone, the substituted Master Mason's word. To recap, I had earlier suggested that the raising ceremony of the 3rd Degree symbolised the moment when the dead Pharaoh passed his mantle of divinity to his son. When I discovered that Mabon is a Welsh word meaning 'Great Son,' and that this great son was born on the spring equinox, I needed to look no further into the myth to be convinced that I was on the right track.

What I had previously pieced together from the raising ceremony indicated that the candidate, in assuming the role of Hiram, was metaphorically transformed into Horus, the son of Osiris, and I had now discovered that the word whispered into the candidate's ear at the most critical moment in the ceremony is the Celt's word for 'great son'. That was only the start of the links however, and I was soon to find that the rest of the myth of Mabon fitted perfectly into the thesis that in dying and being raised the candidate does indeed become the Great Son.

If Graeco-Roman myths are patchy, then Celtic myth is even more so, because the Celts' oral tradition meant that they did not overly concern themselves with correctness and the faithful recording of detail. As the stories of the gods meandered through the peoples of Europe they changed, altered over time to suit those who absorbed them. Long before the myths of the dying and resurrecting God-men of the Middle East made their way into the West, carried there by the Roman legions and other waves of immigrants, similar notions had been long since been settled in the hearts of the people. The tales of these Ancient European gods later became conflated with similar gods from the East, and formed a patchwork of hybrids that were all slightly different, but many of which conformed to the same basic template. This means that the general gist of many of these stories contains the same elements as others, and in many of them the same division of the year into light and dark halves is evident.

Understanding of the gods changed through time, and scraps from one time and place often conflict with snippets from another. The Celts were never a literary people like their counterparts in Greece and beyond, and their oral tradition does not make it easy to pin down with any accuracy the tales of their mythical gods. Preserving stories orally is though, in the long run, actually a far safer way of preserving them than committing them to writing. Little was written down in ancient times, and of what was, very little survived. Original texts are virtually non-existent, and what we have are often simply quotes of quotes of quotes.

The myths and legends of the Celts were not written down until relatively recently. They had been passed down orally through countless generations until the art of storytelling started to fall into disuse in the 19th Century. Though the demise of the oral tradition was largely brought about by the rise of the written word, the written word was also its saviour.

The very richness of the Irish storytelling tradition itself gave birth to the literary movement led by men like Joyce and Yeats, and women like Lady Augusta Gregory. Fascinated by the legends of the past that they knew were fading, they gathered those ancient tales around the hearths and door-steps of the ordinary folk, and recorded them on paper, many of them for the first time ever. All across Europe people did likewise, taking the time to live among the ordinary folk, listening to the tales of the fireside, and saving them for posterity.

Today, archaeology has in many cases given a basis in fact for stories that were handed down orally for perhaps two thousand years before finally being written down. That is a truly wondrous thought, and demonstrates not only how well the oral tradition husbanded those tales, but how ancient notions could survive among ordinary, semi-literate people, until emerging into the light - long, long after their relevance faded from the world.

The Mabinogion, a collection of early Welsh mythology, records the tale of Mabon ap Modron, which translates as 'Great son of the Great Mother,' the mother in question being Mother Earth. Mabon was also seen as a Celtic version of the sun God Apollo, sometimes known as Maponos, and was known, tellingly for Masons, as the Son of Light, for they sometimes describe themselves in similar terms. The druids appear to have had him as the Divine Child who is within us all, this too indicating the suitability of this tale for grafting on to the Hiramic legend. Whilst he himself was equated with the light half of the year or in other words was the sun, his mother was regarded as the keeper or guardian of the Otherworld. Yet again, then, we have the light and dark halves of the year being ruled by different deities.

One part of a myth has the newborn Mabon stolen when he was three nights old and taken into the dark underworld. Another snippet suggests that the dark underworld was in fact his mother's womb and that he took the sun with him into the darkness. This carrying of the sun with him signified that the imprisonment was temporary, and that he would shortly thereafter rise again into the light. The ancient Celts believed that over the winter months, when night was longer than day, the power of the sun resided in the roots of the plants and remained imprisoned there until the length of the days once more exceeded night. In spring the previously lifeless plants returned to life, and in doing so released Mabon from his underground prison. Whilst a prisoner in his mother's womb, Mabon's strength, or more correctly the sun's strength, was restored in that nurturing environment, and it was this detail that left me in no doubt that the architects of Masonry had deliberately grafted Mabon on to the other myths that form the basis of the 3rd degree.

In Masonic ritual as outlined earlier, when the candidate is 'killed' and symbolically buried in the centre of the lodge room floor, a gold set-square is placed on his chest before the sheet he is lying on is wrapped around him in symbolic burial. I have elsewhere linked the square to the sun through its rising points on the solstices. Gold has also been revered by many cultures, not for the commercial value we place on it today, but for the fact that it never tarnishes and when polished glitters like the rays of the sun. A gold square, then, would be doubly significant in reference to the sun.

According to Masonic myth, the gold square is placed there at that point in the proceedings so that afterwards the recovery party will realise that it is indeed the body of their fallen Grand Master that they have found. As I have said so many times in this narrative, this has to be seen as only the exoteric explanation of the event – the peg on which the esoteric is hung. I would suggest that the underlying, esoteric reason is that the candidate, whilst buried under the ground, or perhaps more precisely in the Underworld, carries the sun with him, to indicate that the sojourn is temporary and will later lead to re-birth, exactly as happened with Mabon.

To reiterate the importance of this myth for Masonry, we have a Welsh god who dies at the autumn equinox and departs for a time into the Underworld carrying the sun with him. He emerges into the light six months later at the spring equinox, reborn as the 'Son of light,' or the 'Great Son of the earth'. In Masonry the candidate dies on the equinox whilst playing the part of Hiram Abif and carries a gold square on his person whilst temporarily buried, before being raised as a Master Mason by having the word for the Welsh god known as 'the great son' whispered in his ear. The gold square is lifted off the candidate's chest when the cloth is finally thrown back, thus the sun is released from its underground prison with the raising of the new Master Mason.

When I said earlier that I thought that perhaps Hiram as the lord of the winter should have died at the spring equinox rather than in the autumn, maybe that aberration can be explained by the presence of this other myth which records Mabon as being killed in September. This linking of a deity who ruled for half a year with the word on which the Master Mason is raised simply cannot be ignored by the Masonic historian. As noted before, any one of these observations on their own can be dismissed as a flight of fancy but when they are counted with others as I have done here, there surely must come a time when they constitute proof that the overall thesis is right. The use of the word

Mabone in this way, in this part of Masonic ritual, is strong evidence indeed that Mabon is indeed the esoteric basis for the Master Mason's Word.

Considering the above meaning of the Master Mason's word, the other word Macbenac, then, in meaning blessed son, carries an identical allusion to the Great Son of the earth that was Mabon.

In identifying the symbolism of Masonry as referring to a matrix of old-world deities, each of which embodied the same principal of splitting the year into two halves and having a separate god rule each half, I felt I had found what I believed was the meaning behind the Masonic 3rd Degree. The original discovery of the equinox and solstice veneration in Masonic ritual had perplexed me at first, simply because I could think of no reason why those days should have been important enough to have the rituals written around them. On deeper examination, however, I had discovered that the death of Hiram and his subsequent raising was a representation of the handing of authority from one deity to another. It now seemed that the importance of the equinoxes was that they were the days on which that changeover took place, and was the reason for the rituals of the lodge room being focused around the ability to pinpoint those days. In choosing the sun as a symbol of deity, how better could the rituals allude to that concept than to have them structured around the identification of the equinox, the day the sun triumphs over the darkness of winter.

A Masonic object that suggests that this is indeed the case can be seen in the picture on the next page, which is of an artefact in the Scottish Grand Lodge Museum in Freemason's Hall, Edinburgh. It appears to be a whiskey decanter, and carries the name D. Dunnet, Lodge No. 42. There are six separate items on it; an x-shaped cross mingled with a set of scales, a pillar with globe atop, a ribbon tied in a bow from which is suspended another x-shaped cross, another pillar with globe, and finally the Agnus Dei. Below these items is an equilateral triangle with twelve candles arranged around its perimeter.

At first it may seem like a random jumble of various Masonic symbols without any particular reason for them being selected and grouped as they are here. But in terms of the thesis suggested here for the underlying allusions of the symbols of the Craft, there could be no more succinct and complete gathering of emblems than those on this object.

The first notable thing is that there is a rhythmic pattern of cross and pillar denoting equinox and solstice time about, the way they happen during the year. The first cross is entwined with the scales of Libra, so this can readily be identified as the autumnal equinox. Then we have a pillar, already identified as one of the solstices, followed by a small equinoctial cross that is hanging from a thread. We then have another solstice-pillar followed by the Agnus Dei that alludes to the spring equinox. We mentioned earlier that the Agnus Dei and the Scales in a Masonic context were complementary symbols, and here on this object we find an example of that union. At the bottom of the object there is an equilateral triangle with twelve lighted candles that I suggest alludes to twelve full moons during the year.

The artefact therefore depicts the solar year as recorded by our ancient forbears, with two solstices, two equinoxes and twelve full moons. The globe on the left pillar has the line of the zodiac sloping upwards, indicating the sun travelling through the signs as it heads towards its zenith on the summer solstice. The second globe shows the line of the zodiac sloping downwards as the sun heads towards its nadir in December. The middle cross, which I suggested was to achieve balance in the picture, is interestingly suspended from a ribbon, the suspension alluding to the axis of the heavens noted earlier and elsewhere illustrated as bunched fingers holding a string, or here in the picture below as a cherub holding a plumb-line. This is from the warrant of Lodge No. 754 Coleraine, and dates from 1792.

The equinoctial cross as an emblem can be said to represent the union of the two forces that were known to govern the heavens in ancient times, being the intersection of the two planes of movement of the celestial bodies on the equinoxes, and therefore celebrated that day of union and balance. In suspending an equinoctial cross on a string it is given the ability to rotate, which is precisely what the slow revolution of the heavens does around the Axis Mundi with precession, gradually moving the crossing point of the two planes through one zodiacal sign after the other.

The emblem of the suspended cross at the centre of the artefact is therefore an accurate depiction of the phenomenon of precession, and displays that knowledge allegorically exactly as the Mithraic Tauroctony does in Perseus killing the Bull of Taurus. In the Tauroctony the torchbearers signified, with their crossed legs, the crossing of the equinoxes that demonstrate the first two forces, and the killing of the bull introduces the third force. In the above Masonic emblem we have the first two forces represented in the x-shaped cross itself, and the third force added by the suspension of that cross on a thread.

In the way that the Tauroctony was a visual and very visible representation of the greatest secret of Mithraism which was shown to all but only explained to the few, this deeply symbolic Masonic emblem is likewise on show to all, but would only have been understood by the highest members of the mystery.

CHRIS McCLINTOCK

THE CRAFT AND THE CROSS

PART FOUR

THE ROAD TO ENLIGHTENMENT

THE CRAFT AND THE CROSS

CHAPTER 28

I STARTED THIS odyssey because I was convinced that there was more to Masonic symbolism than meets the eye. Born from that belief was a determination to understand the rituals of the lodge room and to answer the ultimate Masonic questions, 'what is Freemasonry?' and 'where did it come from?' My first findings uncovered an undeclared veneration of the sun underpinning almost every aspect of the Craft – a fact often mentioned by others, but never given purpose. I believe I have set that veneration of the sun in context, and can therefore speculate on the path down which the mysteries of Freemasonry arrived at the 18th Century. We will now speculate on that hitherto unknown path.

We will start the tale in Ireland in 3200BCE with the building of Newgrange. The people who built this megalithic temple of the sun must have watched the movements of the great burning disc that gave them life for generations before committing their beliefs to stone in such a monumental way. Though we otherwise know nothing of them, we can tell from the orientation of the entrance that the new-born sun on the winter solstice and the division of the year on the equinoxes were uppermost in their spiritual lives. Those people disappeared after a thousand years, and the next people to follow their lead were the Celts and their druids.

Those newcomers had their own panoply of gods and goddesses, and those deities too were based on the movements of the sun. The sun formed a cross with its rising and setting on the solstices, so the sun's cross was venerated long before Christianity appeared with its new interpretation of that sacred symbol. The druids who held the sun as an object of veneration were literate and were accomplished astronomers; recorded by Plutarch as a race of Magi living on an island near Britain. They were also an ascetic priesthood who wore white mantles and carried wands of yew. Those wands were their bachall, the basis of their power, and if akin to the wands carried by Masonic deacons, were for marking the sun on the landscape. Since the power to predict eclipses, comets and the like called for pin-point accurate recording of the calendar, the staffs that marked the sun would therefore have been vital to the druids' powers. In the thesis presented here modern day deacons with their wands are vital players in the lodge room ritual, and are an interesting corollary to the skills of the druids.

The ancient poem, The Mystery of Amergin, is about a druid of that name. In it are the words, 'I am the beam of the sun…Who is he who announces the ages of the moon? Who teaches the place where falls the sunset?' If the druids were the first to teach where falls the sunset, is Freemasonry the last?

Those druids ruled the Celtic lands spiritually up until the advent of Christianity, and in Ireland, and probably elsewhere too, those priests of the sun first intermingled with, and then became monks in, the new faith that swept Europe. It is now thought that they were absorbed into Christianity rather than being overthrown by it, and that St. Patrick only achieved the success he did because he readily embraced their beliefs rather than trying to replace the old with the new. Did they leave behind all they had previously held dear? Or did they carry their beliefs with them into Christianity?

History tends to favour the latter, for there arose in Ireland a strain of the faith quite divorced from the Christianity that came to dominate Europe. By the time Christianity had settled itself on Rome, and was strong enough to reach out to strangle the pagan religions of the continent, Ireland was already on a separate path. That path was still Christian – but it was Christian with a twist of paganism. The Celtic Church was born.

This union of the old with the new created a hybrid Christianity that was at considerable odds with the burgeoning Church throughout the rest of the Christian world. This all happened during the Dark Ages so history was not recorded as it was during the mediaeval period. Although the druids faded from the scene as Christianity arose, their memory lived on in the tales of the bards and the songs and poetry of the troubadours. It was in these tales that knowledge of the druids was preserved, and the bardic tradition that held that knowledge survived in the Celtic lands long after it had elsewhere disappeared.

Though the Culdees were Irish, they were also closely connected to the emergent nation of the Scots, for they were part of the migration of peoples across the Irish Sea to the west coast of Scotland in the 5th and 6th Centuries. With them went St. Columba, who left Ireland forever in the year 563 to take his church to the Picts.

The Irish never were subject to the 'civilising' influence of the Romans and as a result may have preserved ancient ways that elsewhere faded under pressure from outside influences. After the fall of Rome in the 5th Century there was a gradual migration from the northeast corner of Ireland into Argyll and Kintyre, a landscape which had similarly remained outside the influence of Rome, forming the kingdom of Dalriada that spanned the narrow channel of water between the two halves of the British Isles. Through time, the High Kings of Dalriada subsumed the Picts and became the Kings of Scotland, and it was one of their number who saw the cross in the sky at Athelstaneford and gave us the Saltire as a symbol. King David I in the 12th Century, who gave the Templars their headquarters and built the abbey to house the Holy Rood, was also descended from those same Scots–Irish settlers.

The Culdees were their church; indeed those who occupied the highest positions in the movement were closely connected to the royal houses of both Ireland and Scotland. They existed for seven centuries outside the bosom of the Mother Church as an ascetic, monastic movement that was ruled by a hereditary, married priesthood. Even in the copious writings that record the life of St. Columba himself we find him performing miracles, walking on water and raising the dead - closer to the behaviour of the shamanic druids than that of a Christian priest. Christian history tends to play down the doctrinal differences between the Culdees and the mainstream Church, but we know that there must have been considerable divergence because the Venerable Bede was very hostile to their ways, and records his outrage that they held his religion as being 'of no account at all.'

It is often cited that the main differences between the Culdees and the mainstream Christian Church were their tonsure and their date for Easter. These may seem trivial, but both are deeply rooted in the pagan past. The regular Christian tonsure was the 'pudding bowl' we see in Christian art, where the top is shaved, leaving a rim around the head. In contrast, the Culdees shaved the front half of the head from ear to ear over the crown, in the style of the druids of earlier times that is thought to be in honour of the rising sun.

The date of Easter was another bone of contention between the two sides. It is a movable feast, and its calculation has been noted elsewhere, but the date used by the Culdees was different to the one used by the mainstream Church. On the face of it this may seem petty and unimportant, but when we realise that the Celtic dating allowed for the inclusion of prominent pagan dates within the festival period and ensured that the festival of rebirth took place bathed in the bright light of the full moon, we yet again see the part the pagan past played in the Celtic church. To quote Dr. Bob Curran again from the Complete guide to Celtic Mythology, '...prominent among the festivals was that of the moon-goddess Eostre who gave the festival its name. The Roman church claimed that this was proof that the Celtic church had wanted all along, to return to paganism...'

Having looked briefly at the Culdee Church in Scotland, it would perhaps be timely to trace it backwards in time to Ireland – where I suggest that particular strain of Christianity first absorbed the pagan veneration of the sun into its doctrines. We saw earlier that St. Columba, on leaving Ireland, first lived in a cave on the shore of Loch Caolisport. That cave lies exactly in the centre of the area where the sun forms a true cross on the solstices, and we mused that he may have left Ireland to go in search of the true cross of the sun. For this to be true, we would have to find evidence that he was aware of the right-angle formed by the sun on the summer solstice in the land of his birth.

The thesis was well advanced when I first sought evidence that this was the case. What I found has enormous implications for the thesis presented here, for whilst looking at Columba's story in Ireland, I discovered irrefutable evidence that the Culdees did indeed incorporate the sun into their understanding of the Christian cross. This is perhaps even more important than the origin of the Saltire from the sun's cross at Athelstaneford, for it provides a credible basis for the emergence of that emblem two hundred years later. It also provides a well-laid foundation for the rest of what is contained in the thesis regarding the absorption of the pagan veneration of the sun into early Christianity and its survival into Freemasonry.

CHAPTER 29

WE EARLIER NOTED that St. Columba was born in Gartan Co. Donegal and that this was within the solstice square. At first that was the only importance I had attributed to him but it was not until the full impact of the Culdee contribution to our story became clear that I thought of looking a little deeper into the Irish part of the saint's story.

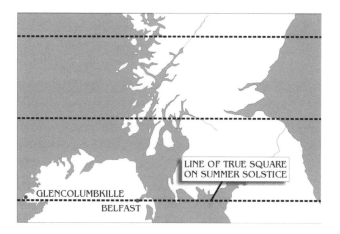

One of the sites in Ireland associated with Columba is Glencolumbkille on Donegal's most westerly peninsula. The name comes from the Gaelic, *Gleanncholmcille*, and means the 'glen of the church of Columba'. When I applied myself to looking at the site in detail, the first thing I noted was that it lies on the same line of latitude as Belfast, and this is of enormous importance, because Belfast marks the southern extremity of the solstice square.

To recap how the square is delineated, it is because there is no place on earth where an exact, measurable-on-a-computer-simulation, true cross is formed by the sun on both solstices. At the latitude of Belfast the rising and setting of the sun on the summer solstice is indeed an exact 90 degrees, but the winter solstice is a couple of degrees off being square. At Aberdeen the reverse applies, with the winter solstice being exact and the summer slightly off. Mid-way between these is Edinburgh, where the cross formed by the four points on the horizon, although not precise according to our modern mindset, is nevertheless the truest the cross ever gets on earth, and would be true for those using primitive tools. Since Columba's mission in Ireland was right on top of the line where perhaps the most important of the 'true' right-angles - that of the summer - is formed, I thought a visit to Glencolumbkille might produce evidence that the square formed by the sun was important there. In all it took three years to identify what I am now going to relate, for Irish summers are not usually kind to those wishing to see the sun on particular dates.

Columba in Ireland

Glencolumbkille is in one of Ireland's most remote and picturesque valleys, being at the end of a broad peninsula that juts out westwards into the Atlantic, and is separated from civilisation by a broad upland moor of tufted grass interspersed with occasional bog cotton. The valley can be said to have only a westerly aspect, being open towards the setting sun but closed in by steep slopes on the other three sides. It is hemmed in by the imposing Glen Head to the north that ends in a dramatic headland in the north-west corner of the valley, and the bulky mass of Slieve League to the south. Though steep-sided, the bottom of the vale is relatively flat, and as we would expect, the church associated with the site sits on a low mound in the centre of the glen. The valley is littered with remnants of the past; standing stones, cairns and holy wells - each of which is marked with numbers and the words '*stad turas Chomcille*', or 'station of Columba's pilgrimage'. There are fifteen in all.

Though these are ostensibly Christian sites, it will become evident as we examine the nature of the stations that they would have been important long before Christianity appeared in the valley, which again bolsters the argument that the early Christians took over pre-existing sites and Christianised them. It is also interesting that St. Columba, Ireland's second favourite son after Patrick, was drawn to this valley, where legend has it he cast out a horde of demons too powerful for even St. Patrick himself to defeat. Was the strength of these demons a reference to the strong pagan veneration of the sun, and was the site considered special because it lay at the latitude where the sun gives a true right angle? Those were the questions that were in my mind as I wound my way down into the valley from the east three summers ago.

The stations are all numbered, and modern pilgrims tour the sites on June 9th, Columba's holy day, having set rituals to perform at each location. The first of the standing stones I encountered is right in the middle of the village at a crossroads, and as soon as I saw it I knew that the markings could be related to the right angle of the sun. It is marked station 13, and sports a circle containing the cross that perhaps could simply be seen as the Christian cross, and indeed will be by those pilgrims who follow the journey of Columba. I do not argue that the intention of those who carved it was indeed to portray the Christian cross, but as with other instances contained in this book, there is more to the symbol than meets the eye, for it was drawn to embrace the pagan past as well as the Christian future.

The enclosing circle is a reference to the sun, and when we look at how the cross in the centre of the circle is constructed, it is with four back-to-back right angles. Since the sun, within the boundaries of the solstice square, outlines four right-angled squares on the ground, there could be no more straightforward way of linking the two crosses – of the sun and of Christianity – than is done here. But there is much more to this stone than this first observation, for if we trace downwards we find two more very curious markings. In themselves they are not curious, for they are simply cup and ring marks that are found on ancient stones all over the Celtic world and are generally taken to represent the sun or stars. What is curious is that they are on a stone that purports to represent the Christian cross.

The stone is a piece of very thin schist, which while eighteen inches wide, is no more than three inches deep. This gives it a very definite alignment, so I set down my compass to see its orientation. I was less than surprised to see that the faces of the stone were aligned SE-NW. This meant that it was aligned towards the place where the sun rises on midwinter's day, and also where it sets on the summer solstice. When we add the amalgam of solar symbols on this stone to its orientation, can we see the veneration of the sun as the true meaning behind the symbolism?

From the position of this stone my attention then fell on the aforementioned church that stood on a low mound a hundred yards west of where I was standing. The church stands within a boundary wall that I was later to discover delineates a sanctuary that may date back as far as 3000BCE. This dating is from a souterrain, or underground passage, that runs under it from east to west, and was a common feature in many ancient sites. The west end of this chamber is actually the first station on the pilgrimage trail, and whilst being inside the grounds of a church may make it seem normal for those who follow the trail, it is a very curious start indeed to the pilgrimage tour of a Christian saint. Standing at the opening to that 5000-year-old underground structure I was struck by the oddity of its being revered within the Christian tradition, but there was to be much more in a similar vein as I worked my way through the other sites on the pilgrimage trail.

At the east end of the graveyard stands another stone, the last of the fifteen stations of the Turas, so the pilgrimage starts and ends in this graveyard. The stone is too weathered for any sense to be made of it, but as I looked at it my attention fell on a nearby headstone which had a small round face carved on it. It is pictured here and is plainly the sun, with sunrays arrayed across the top of the face. As I looked around me I counted no less than a dozen graves with exactly the same motif – carved in precisely the same way on each. These were 19th Century graves, so did not pertain to the ancient past, but still indicate the subliminal persistence of the ancient motifs. I laid out the compass to check the alignment of the church and found it lies east-west with its entrance to the west, like almost all churches. Whilst looking along the wall of the church my attention was drawn to another standing stone, on top of a mound that was about ten feet high, precisely due west of the church. This was the second station on the pilgrimage trail.

When I arrived at it, I found it carried very curious symbolism indeed, which left me in no doubt whatsoever that the sun's right angle played a part in the spirituality of whoever erected it.

The stone itself is flat-faced and round-topped – about six feet high and eighteen inches broad. It is thin, like the first mentioned stone, and is no more than three or four inches thick, giving it too a definite orientation. It is decorated on both sides. One side is badly weathered, but the other is very clear, and like the stone in the centre of the village, those markings again suggest the square of the sun. Seen here in the picture, the inscribed design has three sets of four right-angled squares, themselves arranged into squares. At the centre of each of the sets is another square. This was remarkable, considering that this valley is at the exact latitude where the sun gives a true square on the summer solstice.

I expected it to be aligned east-west, in line with the church, considering it lay on the church's axis, but on setting my compass beside it I discovered that like the stone at the crossroads, it is very precisely aligned on a NW/SE axis. As will be noted below, stones can have two alignments – one in the direction of the broad face, and the other the way the thin edge points. It is the broad face that I refer to here. If one stands in the position from which the photograph was taken, one is pointing towards the place of the setting sun on the summer solstice. Likewise if one stands behind the stone looking the other way, one faces the rising of the sun on the winter solstice, though the bulk of Slieve League would obscure the view until long after first-light. When taken with the orientation of the stone and its standing on the latitude that gives a true right-angle, the squares and right-angles on it are certainly suggestive of my offered meaning of the symbolism. And if not my suggested meaning, then to what else could these squares and right-angles refer?

My time was limited on that first day, and I had to leave without seeking out the other stations of the Turas. A few days later, when reviewing my general photos of the area, I noted a feature on the landscape that I had missed that first day - a notch in the north west corner of the valley. As noted in an earlier chapter about the Boheh Stone in Co. Mayo, many sites became sacred and had stones raised at them because they were vantage points from where solar phenomena were visible. This usually involved a feature on the horizon, that when the sun reaches it, denoted a particular time of year. In the case of the Boheh Stone it was from there that the sun 'rolling down' the side of Croagh Patrick was visible.

When one stands at this pilgrimage station in Glencolumbkille and looks along the axis of the stone, one is looking straight at a very

notable notch on the horizon, seen in the picture here. The v-shaped notch is to the north west of the stone – where the sun sets on the summer solstice. This means that as spring turns to summer, the setting sun marches to the right across the horizon, across the whole open west end of the valley, and would reach a standstill on the summer solstice, somewhere near the notch.

On the day on which the true square is formed, therefore, the sun would set in line with the orientation of this stone. The first stone I had encountered at the crossroads, though a hotel now blocks its alignment, also points towards the same place on the landscape, so that was two stones, that had similar markings, which both pointed to this same place on the landscape. There were twelve more stations in the Turas to be explored, and though some were holy wells and cairns that probably wouldn't carry symbolism, there may be more standing stones that did. I resolved to revisit the valley on the next summer solstice, and if weather permitted, to verify my observation that the sun did indeed set in this corner of the glen.

What I discovered in the intervening months was that though the sites were thought to be truly ancient, the standing stones themselves were not pre-historic, but were indeed erected during the sixth century when Columba himself ministered there. This means that the symbolism on those stones is undeniably Christian, and this had enormous implication for my thesis. If I was right that the stones venerated the sun in some way, then the fact that that they were erected at the behest of St. Columba or those who followed him demonstrates something of their mindset. Those who seek alignments in the landscape generally find them in ancient stone circles and lines of megaliths that have stood on lonely, bleak hilltops since the Bronze Age. Here at the heart of one of the most Christian sites in Ireland we find similar alignments, but from within the Christian era, and from within the Christian mindset.

When I returned to the valley on Midsummer's Day 2007, I was armed with an extremely enlightening book, *Gleanncholmcille, a guide to 5000 years of history in stone*, by Michael Herity, that gave a history of the Turas and a map of all fifteen sites. I found another two standing stones with markings similar to the two I had found earlier, and both were as interesting as the first, for they were also aligned to the same spot on the horizon.

The first one I found on this occasion was station 14. It was edge on rather than facing Glen Head, so it actually faced northeast rather than northwest - sunrise on the solstice rather than sunset. This stone was also thin and blade-like, and when viewed edge on, as in the picture, it pointed straight to the point on the horizon where Glen Head met the plain. Its different alignment was perhaps a deliberate attempt to include the point where the sun rises as well as where it sets.

Standing stones were sometimes used to indicate more than one alignment, and often a row of stones will give two orientations - one along its length encompassing all the stones – the other by the alignment-plane of the individual stones themselves. If taken as a group, the standing stones in Glencolumbkille all point to the north-west where the sun sets, though the stone at Station 14 is different from all the others and actually aligns at 90 degrees to the others, where the summer solstice sun rises.

The markings on the stone were also interesting, for as depicted in the sketch on the previous page, the cross is formed yet again by four right angled cut-marks placed back to back inside a circle. This was similar to the cross on station 13 at the crossroads, but whereas that one could be read as a simple cross with a line through it, this one actually had the right-angled shapes separated from each other, highlighting the L-shape.

The next stone, Turas 9, was the most interesting yet, because not only was it aligned to the same place and carried the same mix of symbols, but it was pierced with a hole at the centre of its cross. With the stone being yet again aligned to the same point on the horizon, the headland was dead-centre of the view through the hole, as can be seen clearly in the picture below. This, in itself, was indicative that the purpose of the stone was indeed

to venerate the setting sun on the solstice, but when I examined the carved detail on the stone, it became even more pertinent.

The cross is again encapsulated within a circle, and is as depicted in the drawing on the left. The arms of the cross end in squares, and at the centre of the cross is another square, placing it central to the cross. The hole was centred on that square, and since it gave a view of where the sun that forms a square sets on the day it forms the square, this gave the most telling hint at the true meaning of the symbolism yet. At sunset on the summer solstice, then, the sun itself shone through the square at the centre of the cross, showing, surely, from whence that symbolism originally came. Local folklore also suggests that couples became betrothed by entwining fingers through the hole, and also

that heaven could be glimpsed through the hole if the viewer was 'right' with God.

On considering the big picture of all these stones taken together, though all the symbols are different, they are all based on circles, squares and L-shaped right-angles, grouped in different ways to form crosses. From the point of view of this thesis, then, the intention was clearly to link the circle of the sun with the right angle it forms, and to use both of these to form the Christian cross.

Unfortunately the weather deteriorated during the day in 2007, and dark clouds had rolled in from the Atlantic well before sundown. There was to be no solstice sunset to confirm my findings that year, but thankfully 2008 was to deliver an excellent view of the sun going down over the valley of Columba, and when I saw it, it was far more telling than I could ever have hoped.

From the point of view of a naked-eye observer, the sun actually stands still for seven days at solstice, so I had a window of a week to see a setting sun. The glen was a two-and-a-half hour drive away, so a photography trip was not to be entered into lightly. As the date approached I kept an eye on the weather forecast and perhaps serendipity again played a hand, for it was the solstice itself that offered the best likelihood of a sighting. On the eve of solstice 2008 I packed my camera gear and headed off with hope in my heart towards the west coast. I arrived at Station 2 with less than fifteen minutes to spare, and was pleased to see the sun approximately where I thought it should be.

Five minutes later I had the camera on the tripod, though the sun was too bright to see the actual disc, and was simply a dazzlingly bright patch of sky. The sun appeared to be a good bit higher than the notch where I thought it would set, but I waited with bated breath as the brightness lessened as it neared the dark outline of rock. I zoomed the camera to full magnification and took a series of pictures as it disappeared from view. When I looked at the pictures on the computer screen later I was awestruck by what I saw, for the sun sat right on the corner of a noticeably square outcrop of rock.

Setting upon the square

As the month of June passes the sun would climb higher and higher up the slope of Glen Head, and on the solstice itself, the very day on which its rising and setting are separated by 90 degrees in this valley, the golden orb settles itself on top of this massive square boulder that not only gives a perfect silhouette of a right angle, but one that is horizontal on top and vertical on its side. If the ancients were aware of the sun's right-angle at the location, the sun setting against this particular stone on the solstice would surely have been significant for them. Bearing in mind the importance of the sunset in ancient Man's spirituality, the words of the ancient poet Amergin come again to mind '...*who teaches the place where falls the sunset?*'

The daytime picture of the headland on page 347 shows the peculiar squareness of the boulder better than the black silhouette above, and indeed highlights another square boulder, even bigger than the first one. It is just down the slope from the first, and is perhaps equally as significant.

The day of Columba's pilgrimage is the 9th of June, and commemorates the day he died on Iona. June 9th is twelve days before the solstice. In those twelve days the sun rises just over half a degree up the sky towards its zenith on the solstice. The sun-disc is half a degree wide, so this means that twelve days before the solstice the sun would have been half a degree, or one complete sun-width, lower than when the above photograph was taken. This would place the sun right on top of the lower, larger square rock on June 9th. Was the date truly Columba's death, or was it recorded as such to mark his symbolic passing into the next world in the west with the setting sun on this second square rock? We have seen that the stories of saints like Brigid were constructed around pagan references, so why should we not contemplate the same possibility for Columba?

The tales of his is death, like those of many heroes, was laced with many remarkable occurrences, not least a pillar of light seen from many miles off. There is a natural phenomenon called a sun-pillar, which can be seen under certain sky-conditions just after sunset as a vivid orange line of light reaching up into the sky. The picture here was taken of one just after sunset near Arbroath, Scotland in April 2008. Recording that such a pillar of light attended his death was obviously a fanciful inclusion to attach significance to him, but nevertheless associates his death with the setting sun.

It was also recorded that when he died alone at the altar in his chapel on Iona, a great light shone from him, illuminating the interior and causing the chapel itself to glow. Again we have symbolism akin to the setting sun, and we must remember that the association of death with the setting sun had been a very common theme in antiquity. Even today we remember fallen soldiers at the going down of the sun. It is significant then that the real setting sun on the day he was reputed to have died was in such a notable place. The details of his death, and indeed his life, are typical of those recorded by devoted followers, and one only has to read the 7th Century Life of Columba by Adomnan to see this. All manner of miraculous events and abilities are included, from calming storms to turning water into wine and raising the dead. These are obviously fanciful claims, and we must remember that the feast days of many early saints were the Christianising of the pagan past, so recording his death as being the 9th June could well have had an allegorical purpose – and that purpose appears to have been to attach his passing to the sun setting on that great square block in the Glen of Columba, on the date that pilgrims still honour to this day.

Demon's Rock

In concluding the tale of Columba in Ireland, there is one final point to mention, and that is about how he brought Christianity to the valley. A hundred years earlier Saint Patrick had chased the demons off Croagh Patrick in Co. Mayo - a reference to the sun rolling down the side of the mountain. Banished from Mayo, those demons gathered in the valley of Glencolumbkille. When Columba came to this place he found that they had shrouded the valley in a thick, impenetrable fog. They also caused the river that meanders through the valley to become a fiery stream that barred passage across it.

The mention of the river is very interesting, for it lies towards the north side of the valley, along the base of Glen Head, and opens out into a wide estuary as it reaches the sea. This river is intriguing on two counts, for in the first instance it separates the high place where the sun sets on the solstice from the rest of the valley. This high mound can be seen below the headland in the picture on page 338, and is known today as Beefan. It is behind Beefan that the sun sets on the solstice. Had this been a sacred area to the ancients, then this river creates a natural boundary for that sanctuary space.

We also secondly have these demons turning the stream into a river of fire – barring passage over it. Around the time of the solstice the reflection of the setting sun in the valley would have turned the river a fiery red – particularly where it enters the sea as a broad estuary just below Beefan. So yet again we have the setting sun being referred to obliquely in myth, in similar fashion to the death of Orion at the hands of Artemis where the setting sun dazzled her.

Michael Herity, in his aforementioned book about the valley translates the myth thus… 'And of the river that forms a boundary to the north they made a fiery stream so that none at all might go across it. And whoever should touch of that stream little or much, he should die immediately.' The above points are minor, obscure details in the overall tale of Columba, but like the rituals of Freemasonry, when examined with a particular mindset, the true origin of those details can finally be revealed.

Columba refused to be cowed by these powerful demons, and strode off into the fog to do battle with them. It is where he defeated them that is the most telling of all the points to date, for when he had chased them up on to the mound of Beefan, he cast them down from the high cliffs on to a rocky islet that is to this day called Demon's Rock – *Screig na nDeamhan*. The place from which he threw them off the land is reputed to be exactly at the stone the setting sun touches on the solstice. Could we expect better corroboration of the true meaning of a myth than this?

He finally chased them off this rock into the dark waters of the Atlantic by throwing at them his bell and a green stone that had previously been given to him by an angel. After the demons disappeared beneath the waves forever, he asked God for his stone and bell back. This God granted, and they rose up out of the water in a glow of fire and fell at his feet. This last detail is perhaps the best of all, which I will quote directly from Michael Herity's book and must be read in consideration of the picture on the previous page. 'And Columcille blessed that land whence he had banished the evil spirits. And he bestowed thereon the right of sanctuary from that time. And he left the stone as a chief treasure to do marvels and miracles'.

This can be none other than the above square stone on the headland that the sun touches as it sets on the day of the sun's greatest power. And in this tale we have the purifying and Christianising of a location that had previously been the abode of demons (those pagans who venerated the sun) and was ever after a sacred Christian sanctuary.

We must also remember that the demons who resided in the valley of Glencolumbkille had previously been banished from Croagh Patrick in Co. Mayo. That mountain had previously been called Cruachán Aigle – Eagle Mountain – the mountain of the summer solstice sun. And here we find those same demons being banished on the summer solstice in Co. Donegal. It is often said that a grain of truth lies at the heart of every legend, and here the certainty of that saying is proved conclusively.

The stories of the ancient pagans had shown their awe for the sun, and Christianity, rather than impose its own belief system, simply stripped the pagan flesh off those myths until only the bare bones were left. They then re-vitalised the skeleton of the past with Christian tissue, which hid its true origin for one and a half thousand years. The skeleton still remains, however, for it was that which made the Christian tales of Patrick acceptable to the pagans he sought to convert. By dissecting the Christian legend as I have done here, however, the ancient past can be seen again in all its glory.

I had established a southeast-northwest sightline between the standing-stone at station 2 and the place where the sun sets on the summer solstice. Whilst standing on the hill at Beefan, just under the square stone upon which the sun sets, I looked back to photograph the stone at station 2 in the middle of the valley. My view was obscured by a hill on which was situated St. Columba's Chapel, yet another station on the Turas. About thirty yards away from the chapel, on the highest part of the hill, was a cairn topped with a rudimentary stone cross.

It was directly in my sightline to station 2, so I thought it might be yet more confirmation that the entire valley's mythology was structured around the setting sun. The photograph above is of the cairn looking northeast to the square stone. Also in the picture is fellow researcher Robert Bashford, pointing to station 2 directly behind me in the centre of the valley, the great step in the slope directly behind him. This third site on the same line confirms beyond doubt that the purpose of the stones of the valley of Columba was the veneration of the solstice sun.

On the same raised platform as these other features lies St. Columba's Chapel; a low ruin with only the entrance door now discernable. This building is no less intriguing than the other places mentioned, and likewise aligns with the massive square rock upon which the setting sun alights. Just in front of the doorway is yet another cairn topped with a very rudimentary stone cross. All align with the headland, and in doing so corroborate all the other alignments we have noted. Is it possible that if the building was still intact we would see a window on the far wall that would permit the light from the setting solstice sun to shaft through the open door and illuminate the cross on the cairn?

I am, I believe, the first person in modern times to look north-westwards from the sacred sites of the *Turas Chomcille* and regard them as places from which the setting sun was venerated in pre-Christian times. Albert von Szent–Gyorgi said 'discovery is seeing what everybody else has seen, and thinking what nobody else has thought.' That is all I have done, and what I found proves that the veneration of the sun from those primitive times was not only extant during Columba's time, but that he absorbed it into his own faith. When I first ventured to Gleanncholmcille three years ago looking for evidence that such was the case, I never dreamt that what I found would be so overwhelming.

The veneration of holy wells, cairns and standing stones in Ireland, and the rituals that are performed at them are perhaps difficult for those from far-afield to comprehend. Beefan, the raised area where the demons were overthrown has five stations of the Turas within its bounds. One is the aforementioned St. Columba's Chapel. The pilgrim walks around the outside three times clockwise, or as it was traditionally referred to, sun-wise, whilst praying. He then enters, and lying down on a flat stone known as St. Columba's Bed, he swings his prostrate form around three times sun-wise. At station 3, there is a small round stone that is passed around the body three times sun-wise whilst invoking the Holy Trinity. The Trinity brings a sliver of Christianity to the ritual, but is only the thinnest of veneers, for the number three was sacred long before Christianity claimed it as Christian and foisted a new meaning on an already existing sacredness. Taken in their totality, the quirky aspects to the rituals performed at the Turas are so far removed from anything within Christianity that they simply have to be carried over from the pre-Christian past.

In concluding our look at Columba in Ireland, we have investigated the world in which he lived and have found much to interest us. It is a fact that Freemasonry today carries arcane references to the square of the sun, and uses that square as a metaphor for God. The carvings on the standing stones in the Glen of Columba suggest that the square of the summer solstice sun at that location was older than Christianity, and was blended with the true cross of Christianity in that remote valley. If we are tracing the tradition that became the Craft back in time in search of an origin, we can perhaps see this as the most defining moment in our quest. As such, then, perhaps Saint Columba can be seen, in a very loose way, as the first Freemason.

In all of this we have not been dissuaded from our thesis. Indeed on the contrary, we leave the Irish part of Columba's story bolstered in the opinion that he was indeed cognisant of the sun's right-angle on the summer solstice, and that he may well have travelled to Scotland in search of where not only the midsummer sun drew a square on the ground, but the midwinter sun did as well giving the true cross.

Columba in Scotland

We earlier mentioned St. Columba's cave, where he is reputed to have lived for a time before settling on Iona for his base. That was not, however, where he is first recorded as landing. It is reputed that he first landed at the very tip of Kintyre, at Keil, near Dunaverty. There is a pair of footprints on a rock there that are supposedly where he first set foot on Scottish soil. Though Dunaverty is very remote I felt a visit to photograph the footprints was nevertheless necessary.

On finding them on top of a high outcrop on the seashore my jaw quite literally dropped open. One could expect the footprints to be aligned in the same direction, as they would be whilst standing naturally. The footprints of Columba are not, however, side by side as one would expect, but are at right-angles to each other.

This was a truly enlightening discovery.

If we cast our minds back to chapter two we will recollect the position Freemasons stand in whilst Standing to Order. In a stance unique to the Craft, the feet are placed at right angles to each other - a stance that refers to the right angle of the solstice sun. Here on Kintyre is a carving that places the feet in an identical stance. I had just discovered that Columba left Ireland aware of the right angle created by the sun on the summer solstice, and this carving in Scotland associates him with the very same right angle, in a stance that is identical to that used in the Craft to this day. Perhaps Columba was the first Freemason after all.

It is actually even more telling than this, because the left foot in the carving is the one that is placed in the hollow of the right. If we look again at the Masonic foot-positions we find that this is standing to order in the 2nd Degree. Inasmuch as this study has shown, this refers to the sun on the summer solstice. When this is done in the Craft the candidate is facing the east, and the right footprint on Kintyre is facing due east.

Second Degree

Summer Solstice

NE corner

There is a disputed claim that the second, left, print in Kintyre was added in the Victorian Era, which on the face of it would nullify the suggestion that the stance has esoteric significance. I tracked the source to a pamphlet, The Ancient Churches and Chapels of Kintyre, reprinted in the 1950s from an article in the Campbelltown Courier. EBay offered a copy for sale and I had it in my possession within two days.

The claim that the second footprint was added in 1856 was related to the author of the article by one David McArthur in 1935. He claimed that seventy-nine years previously, as a child of five years, he sat by his grandfather, Daniel McIlreavy, as he carved the second print.

His grandfather may have done something to the rock, either reshaping the stone to make it more foot-like, or adding the (wrong) date that is thought to be more recent, but it is unlikely that he added the left foot.

In Scotland there are various, similar footprints on rocks that are in every case of one single foot. The most notable of these is at Dunadd, the ancient capital of Dalriada near Kilmartin in Argyll. This no doubt adds credence to the suggestion that there was only one footprint at Keil, but in Ireland there are at least three sets of Columba's footprints, in Derry and Donegal, and in every case there are two prints. What is more, they are specifically attributed to Columba, as are the pair in Kintyre. The single footprints in Scotland are not associated specifically with the saint, and this, I believe suggests that the recollection of the eighty-four-year-old David McArthur was dimmed by the years.

The second picture is of the prints without the author's feet obscuring the view. As can be seen, the second, allegedly added print is more than half missing. It is highly unlikely that the rock has crumbled to such an extent in a hundred and fifty years, so either Daniel McIlreavy carved only a portion of a print over rock that wasn't there, or more likely, it was carved in antiquity when the rock was whole and all he did was add the date to strengthen the saint's link with the area. Indeed as can be clearly seen, he could have cut a whole footprint had he moved the left foot further back towards the right one.

Until now there has been no great importance placed on the right-angle formed by the left foot at Keil, therefore few have taken an interest in it, but considering the other discoveries we have made about St. Columba's purpose in going to Scotland there can be little doubt that the carving is an immensely important part of the tale.

We have referred throughout to them being Columba's footprints, but of course they did not miraculously appear in stone to mark the saint's passage. What they are, however, are evidence of the ritualistic beliefs of the past that were simply Christianised in the 6th Century by Columba, in the same process as has been shown throughout. We don't have any way of dating them, but it is thought by some that they may have already been over a thousand years old when the saint associated himself with them. Their very existence also proves that what is done in Freemasonry today was first done a very long time indeed before Christianity came to Britain.

After arriving at the southern tip of Kintyre, Columba is then associated with the cave in Loch Caolisport mentioned earlier. That cave lies precisely on the Saltire line, where the true cross is formed by the sun, and further hints that the phenomenon was known to him. Like the footprints, the cave's significance would also have predated his arrival. We are too far removed in history from those days to know his purpose, or indeed if he did actually live in that cave, but the mere fact that his name is associated with it is all that matters.

Having arrived at the centre of the solstice square the next time we encounter the Saltire line is in the 8th Century, when St. Andrew's name was invoked before battle. Enough has been written of that to remove the need to repeat it here, suffice to say it is the second time the line appears in a way relevant to our quest.

Columba was the foremost figure in the Celtic Church, and that movement existed in Scotland until the 12th Century when it was finally overcome. The push to bring the Culdees under control was more about politics and economics than piety, and as Constantine had earlier forced

Christianity on to his peoples in an effort to unify his empire, a similar situation existed in 12th Century Britain. Where the cell structure and lack of hierarchical control in the mystery schools of the east set them apart and precluded their becoming the state religion that Christianity did, the same can be said of the Culdees, for their similar structure was isolationist and clannish, and placed them outside the governance of the mainstream Church. This resulted in the Culdees being forced out of the picture to give way to the more universal and therefore more politically suitable version of the faith. From what is contained in this book it is apparent that though the Culdees may have faded from the world nine hundred years ago, some aspects of their teachings never entirely disappeared.

Uppermost in the drive towards the consolidation of Roman Christianity in Scotland were Queen Margaret and her son David I, sitting between the Celtic, Gaelic-speaking past and the Saxon/Norman future, but as already noted, that drive was as much about economic control and governance as it was about a desire to spread the faith. It is obvious from the part played in the forgoing thesis by David I that he was deeply involved in the Christianising of the pagan motifs he inherited from the landscape he ruled. In encouraging Christianity was he truly pious, or was his desire to control his people, and the easiest way of achieving that was the accommodation of Culdee beliefs within Christianity? Whatever his true motives, in doing what he did regarding the sites where the sun had previously been seen as the true cross, he also assisted in the preservation of the old traditions.

Or perhaps his purpose was more proactive, and was actually to preserve the old ways in the face of the spread of Christianity? The rise of the Christian faith was unstoppable, so sooner or later the Culdees would be swamped under papal rule. Could King David I, who belonged to the same Celtic past as the Culdees, see the end of the old traditions coming and feel obliged to oversee their preservation? The Christian monks of St. Andrews may have begun the conversion of the true cross into a Christian symbol during his lifetime, but thanks to the king, the true story remained in the hills around Ballantrodoch with his grant of land to the new Templar knighthood, and in the abbey he himself built on the edge of Edinburgh.

The demise of the Culdees happened at exactly the same time as the Templars arrived in Scotland. The first Augustinian Friary was established at Scone in 1120, and that establishment signalled the start of the end of the Culdees. After ten years of trying to reform the Celtic Christians without success, an Augustinian community was 'planted' in St. Andrews to force change. That was around 1130 or thereabouts, and two years before that happened, in July 1128, the Templars appeared in Scotland.

Then within thirty years the tale of the Saltire as a Christian symbol emanated from St. Andrews. The rise of the Canons Regular coincides precisely with the demise of the Culdees, and without a doubt spelt the death knell of their way of religious life.

Their demise was not however instantaneous. In St. Andrews alone it took until 1144 to completely remove the Culdees from the cathedral, and that was only one of the thirteen sites that were subjugated. Realising they could not stand against the rise of the mainstream faith, did the Culdees actively seek out another home for their traditions, and did they find it within the Scottish Templar movement? As suggested here, those incoming knights had brought with them with them an understanding of the initiatory nature of the eastern mysteries, and their arrival at that time would have been seen by the Culdees as a gift from God in their time of crisis. If the Culdees were in possession of an alternative belief in the true cross as a sacred emblem, and their world was being swamped by the mainstream faith at that time, did they simply join the ranks of the new knighthood that also regarded the cross as an allegory? Did they swap the pure-white habits of their past lives for the pure-white habits with a red cross of the Templars? The transition was presided over by King David I, so was it therefore during his kingship that the two traditions that I have shown to be the basis of modern Freemasonry were married together?

It may be asked if the pacifist Culdees would have allied themselves with the war-like Templars, but the Templars did not become warriors as such for many years after their foundation. Their warmongering was also restricted to Palestine; their bases in Europe being little more than farms and mills. Many Templars never saw a battlefield during their entire lives, and anyway, as portrayed here it was not the Templars as a whole whom the Culdees would have originally allied themselves with, but simply a secret cabal at the core of the Scottish branch.

The marriage of ideas would have suited both parties, for from the eastern mystery's point of view it would have readily embraced the sun's cross of the Culdees as an allegory for the cross of Jesus. And from the Culdee's point of view, their imminent destruction would have left them two options – die out and allow their beliefs to pass from the world, or join the burgeoning ranks of the new knighthood and preserve their teachings for those who came after. In making this transition they were maintaining their beliefs at the very heart of the church, which was exactly where they believed those teachings should be.

The Scottish Templars were a formidable host for the new, merged teachings from east and west, and were well able to carry those teachings on for around two hundred years, until, of course, their own demise in the 14th Century. Whilst a sudden blow in France, it was two years before there was a half-hearted trial in Scotland, which was plenty of time for the followers of the tradition to fade away and find an alternative host for their labours. By the time a trial was held in Edinburgh there were only two Templars left in all of Scotland. I suggest that like the Culdees who saw their overthrow coming and 'jumped ship' to the Templar movement, the Scottish Templars themselves did likewise and jumped ship into the lodges of stonemasons working around Edinburgh, using the established lodge system to conceal their labours from the world. From then on the rites of the tradition took on the mantle of the stone-working industry, and were woven around the tools and working practices of that craft as they still are to this day. As the itinerant nature of their work took the lodges around the country, so the tradition then spread, in closed cells, throughout the British Isles.

As the years passed, the Mystery of Christ would perhaps have lost its impetus. More than anything else, the Reformation would have lessened its popularity, for there was no longer a single, oppressive religious doctrine in Europe. Once people had freedom of religious thought, the need for a secret mystery that offered just that would have been lessened. Coupled with that, the stone-carving industry that carried the mystery itself fell into steep decline with the advent of the clay building brick.

By the 17th Century the ancient tradition was perhaps down to a few percent of its original vitality, and only its allegories remained. They were still intact, however, simply because they had been preserved within complex rituals that were not intended to be understood – simply remembered. During the Enlightenment, the archaic rites were rediscovered and emerged into the light in a new form - as modern Freemasonry. A vital question is to what extent were the rites still understood, and how much meaning had been lost to the world? The answer to that seems to be that in different parts of the British Isles the level of understanding varied, and we will look at that situation in the next chapter.

CHAPTER 30

IN CHAPTER ONE I briefly mentioned that there was one body of Freemasons that seemed to have retained a clearer understanding of the meaning of the symbols than others. Those men comprised the Grand Lodge of the Antients and their story is particularly fascinating, so perhaps a brief comment on that institution would help our understanding of the situation as Freemasonry emerged.

Freemasonry announced itself to the world on the Feast of St. John the Baptist, 24th June 1717 when four Lodges met in the Goose and Gridiron alehouse in St. Paul's Churchyard London and formed a governing body to regulate at first themselves and then other local lodges. In doing so, they brought what had previously been a hidden tradition to the notice of the world at large. Ireland followed their lead eight years later in 1725 and Scotland followed suit in 1736. The emergence of Grand Lodges to organise the dispersed lodges into cohesive units was a considerable departure from what the Craft had been in the past, and from the available evidence it appears that London society sought something more akin to a gentleman's club than an archaic mystery school.

To think Freemasonry is a single entity is an error, because it exists as a raft of completely autonomous individual organisations called Constitutions, that have a similar relationship to each other as

Presbyterians have to Methodists or Baptists. Each of those denominations is Christian, but has its own way of working. As a result of this, Irish Freemasonry has no say whatsoever in how either the English or Scottish Constitutions conduct themselves, and vice versa. For the last couple of hundred years the three Home Constitutions have worked very closely together, but in the early 1700s, when modern Freemasonry emerged, there appears to have been no agreed stratagem to that emergence.

The Londoners made certain changes to the old usages, and these changes were opposed by Freemasons who were not affiliated to the Grand Lodge in London. A second Grand Lodge was formed to counter these changes, and took the name 'Antient' to show its purpose; 'antient' simply being an old-fashioned way of spelling ancient.

The Freemasonry that emerged in London was a different animal to that which emerged elsewhere in these islands, and leaned more towards a fashionable club than a repository of arcane knowledge. There seems to have been less interest in the arcana of the earlier Craft in London than in the outlying areas, because several intrinsic aspects of the rituals of the stonemasons were set aside by the London lodges, presumably because they were seen as mumbo-jumbo that were no longer understood. Because they sought to 'modernise' some of the old customs, this led to them being termed the 'Moderns'. In large part the Antients were formed to counter this abandonment of the past, and the modernising of the old ways.

Though the second Grand Lodge was formed in London it was largely organised by Irish Masons resident in the capital, and Irishmen played a disproportionate part in the movement. Of the Antient's first nine Grand Masters, at least six and possibly seven were Irishmen, and another Irishman, Laurence Dermott, was their chief advocate, serving as their Grand Secretary for nineteen years. The ritual they used was based on that of Lodge no 26, Dublin, which was Dermott's own Mother Lodge.

Dermott identified a list of ten points where the Grand Lodge of England had deviated from ancient practice, and discord about this rumbled for over sixty years before both Grand Lodges came together in a new body in 1813 - the United Grand Lodge of England. Though he did not live to see it happen, Dermott ultimately succeeded in his task, because all ten points on his list were addressed, and were reintroduced to the English working when the two bodies amalgamated.

Of the points of change, two were more important than the others, at least in terms of what has been discovered in this book. The Londoners had either discarded the use of deacons in the lodge room, or their use had simply disappeared before the speculative gentlemen came to the fore. As will be clear from the thesis presented here, the deacons with their wands and the part they play were vital to the ceremonies. The Londoners had also stopped yearly Master's installations, which, like the deacons' duties, were pivotal in the ceremony, for they marked the yearly birth of the sun.

There are several points to be observed from the situation vis-à-vis the Antients. In the first instance is the fact that the English had lost what can be considered intrinsic parts of the Craft, and this demonstrates that by the 18th Century, in London at least, the link with the past was more sundered than elsewhere. This is perhaps not surprising, because this was the era of the Enlightenment, of the throwing off of the ignorance of the past. London was the vanguard of this movement, and had been for some considerable time, so it is understandable that the urbane society that flourished there would have a very different take on the ancient Craft they inherited than would have been the case in outlying areas.

Secondly we know that the lack of understanding of those rites was not universal, and that others, represented by the Antients, still had knowledge of their original meanings. Current Masonic research is unaware of the importance this thesis places on the deacons' roles, so up until now the loss of deacons and yearly installations was perhaps seen as trivial. The thesis presented here has shown that the entire working of a lodge room is not a random series of invented references however, but combines to allude to a singular spiritual concept. All aspects were vital to that symbolic purpose, so the removal of any part, particularly the deacons, would have stripped the remaining rituals of their true significance and thus lessened their import.

The Antients wrought for sixty years to have the abandoned rites re-introduced to the English Craft, and this shows not only that they understood the subtleties of metaphor that this thesis has uncovered, but also that they were passionate about their preservation.

The premise of this book suggests that whilst modern Freemasonry can claim an origin in Scotland in the 12th Century, the older tradition from which it emerged originated in Ireland as a marriage of the sun's cross with that of Christianity. The Antients were demonstrably Irish; their ritual was Irish, their officers were largely Irish, and their chief advocate – Laurence Dermott – was an Irishman who left Dublin as a young man and championed the Antient's cause in London for the rest of his life. The push to retain the old customs was therefore largely an Irish endeavour.

Freemasonry in Ireland was, and indeed still is, a much more working-class institution than in London, where it was seen as the domain of the more privileged classes. This difference is still evident today, where even the ritual is decidedly different, for the working of an English lodge room is more detailed and embellished than the Irish which in comparison is earthy and unadorned.

We mentioned earlier the Celtic oral tradition and its ability to carry knowledge over vast timescales. Even today the Irish are known for their storytelling ability, and that stems from their Celtic roots. Is it possible that understanding of the esoteric rites of the stonemasons' lodges was preserved in the Celtic homelands while elsewhere it failed? Did their cultural propensity for storytelling predispose the Irish followers of the mystery to learn and memorize the convoluted wording, and thus preserve the archaic rites unchanged, whilst understanding amongst their more literate neighbours faded? Can we see the proof of this in the emergence of the Grand Lodge of the Antients?

If the Masons of Ireland better understood the ancient references contained in the obscure rites of the Craft, did they seek to counter the loss of important aspects of those rites in London? Was

Dermott's arrival in the English capital part of that strategy? Was he perhaps an *agent provocateur*, who went to London to maintain the rituals as they had been in the operative days, and prevent their dilution by the London gentlemen? Laurence Dermott was a giant in the Grand Lodge of the Antients, but the part he played in the early Craft has never achieved much recognition. That is in large part because it has never been conclusively proved that the Craft pre-dates 1717, therefore the point of the Antient's championing the old ways has not carried as much weight as it should.

As presented here however, by the time the Craft emerged it had existed as a mystery tradition for six hundred years, and preserved truly ancient knowledge of the cosmos. The modern fraternal society that emerged in the 18th Century was a long way away from the origins of the earlier mystery, and could very easily have lost touch with its past. In challenging the Moderns and forcing a situation that was only resolved two generations later by the reintroduction to English ritual of the elements that had earlier been abandoned, the Antients in general, and Dermott in particular, were instrumental in preserving that past.

This brings to mind the notion mentioned earlier that the 3rd Degree may have been written in Dublin and carried from there to Britain. This has never been proved, nor is it likely that it ever will, but it is nevertheless a point for debate. The thesis presented here certainly hints that such could have been the case, because if those who understood the truly ancient origin of the apparently meaningless rituals of the Craft were fearful that that past would be lost forever, they may have resolved not to let that happen.

The English Grand Lodge emerged in 1717, followed by the Irish in 1725. The 3rd Degree was written around 1728/9, very shortly after the Irish Grand Lodge was formed. As shown here for the first time, the legend of Hiram Abif was specifically written to carry allegorically what had previously been secret knowledge. In using that secret knowledge as the basis for a modern, allegorical myth it was preserved forever, and I would suggest that that was exactly its purpose.

It is a simple fact that the Craft existed before the Grand Lodges emerged into the light. If the London gentlemen unilaterally took it upon themselves to form a new, more open fraternity out of what already existed; perhaps that rush into the light was not universally accepted. The situation was exacerbated by the London gentlemen then abandoning aspects of the rituals which they attached no great importance to. If Irish Masons who continued their labours in secret for eight years after 1717 saw the tradition they held so dear in danger of being lost, was that the impetus for them to emerge into the light themselves, and at the same time introduce the legend of Hiram Abif to the Craft? For in that legend the entire ancient mystery tradition was preserved as deeply buried allegory, and its adoption by the emergent Craft would have guaranteed its preservation.

Fifteen years after the introduction of the Hiramic legend the situation had still not resolved itself, and Irish Masons in London still found themselves unwelcome in the capital's lodges. And although the new 3rd Degree had been adopted by the English Grand Lodge, the absence of the deacons and yearly installations still left the workings of the lodge room lacking coherence. The Grand Lodge of the Antients emerged out of that discontent, and to the author at least, the reason for its emergence is quite plain. If the London lodges could not be persuaded to retain the ancient landmarks of the Craft from within, then a rival Grand Lodge would have to be formed to address the problem. In challenging the Moderns' changes and forcing a situation that was only resolved two generations later by the reintroduction to English ritual of the elements that had earlier been abandoned, the Antients were pivotal in ensuring that the emerging Craft did not lose sight of its origin.

If the above interpretation of the Grand Lodge of the Antients is true, then Laurence Dermott, whilst undoubtedly seen by London 'Modern' Masons as a troublesome individual, was perhaps the most important of all the men who re-crafted the ancient philosophy from the 12th century, and made it into the Craft we know today.

CHAPTER 31

THE ANCIENT STORIES we have looked at in early myth were structured to venerate the sun and to make sense of why the dark ruled for half the year. They were brought into Masonry as a modern myth, I believe, to point obliquely at the sun as the ultimate symbol of deity so that each brother could honour the principle of God without coming into conflict with those of different beliefs.

It appears that the men of the 18th Century, who made Freemasonry what it is today, sought a fraternal society that whilst secular nevertheless endeavoured to promote godliness above all other virtues. How could godliness be secularised and stripped of its dogma, and yet be placed at the very heart of the new organisation those men promoted? Quite simply by placing a non-dogmatic symbol of God at the head of the new order. In as far as I have shown in this book, that symbol was the sun, and what a fitting symbol it was, standing as it did at the head of a tradition that predated the arrival of Christianity by thousands of years. How much more universal could one get than that? But in terms of the 18th Century, what purpose would this secularisation of religious belief have served?

The rituals of the Craft were stripped of all Christian symbolism in the 18th and early 19th Centuries. This could make a case for claiming that Freemasonry, in the days before it 'went public' was

Christian in nature. What is contained in this book proves that it most certainly wasn't, but it was religious in nature, and started out within the Christian Church as a suppressed Culdee doctrine.

The Mediaeval Mystery of Christ held Jesus as the figurehead of its outer mystery, so it would have seemed Christian for that reason. But on the blossoming of the Craft from a secret society to a semi-open fraternal society it no longer required that outer façade, so that aspect was ditched. In that process, the part played by Jesus in the earlier tradition was taken on by the newly invented Hiram, who carried the same allusion but was free from dogma. The de-Christianisation of the Craft that took place then does not therefore prove the Christian origin that many believe, but is merely the conversion of the sacred Mystery of Jesus into the secular mystery of Hiram, and the amalgamation of outer and inner mysteries into one. But why did those men deem it necessary to do this, to strip away the ostensibly Christian dogma that had previously existed in the stonemasons' lodges and replace it with a universal, non-dogmatic symbol of god?

Freemasonry as we know it today arose during the Enlightenment, when the world started to move away from the pulpit towards the science that gave rational explanations for what had previously been superstitions. Perhaps those men of the Enlightenment, many of whom were Freemasons, who drove forward the Age of Reason and replaced superstition with reasoned thought, recognised that faith in God was necessary for the cohesion of society, even though the scientific and philosophical movement they led undermined that tradition. Whilst faith has its merits, the divisions caused by overzealous devotion to dogma are the greatest cause of strife in the modern world. The evening news shows this almost daily, and it was so for the Freemasons of the 17th Century too, coming so soon after the bloodshed of the Reformation and counter-Reformation and the hideous witch-burnings that were still taking place in their own era.

The Reformation came about to correct perceived imbalances in the promotion of the Christian message within the Catholic Church, but the Puritanism that then emerged was just as intolerant as what had gone before. Was Freemasonry a reaction to the tyranny of all the established religions in forcing their beliefs on others? Is that why Freemasonry offered the concept of God as a universal symbol, in a secular fraternity unaffiliated to any church or specific religious system, and actively encouraged tolerance of the beliefs of others?

The Reformation was an 'in-house' religious affair, but one by-product of it was that the wider world suddenly had the freedom to express its spiritual aspirations in ways that would have been unthinkable half a century earlier. By removing the dogma from the concept of God, each adherent of Masonic philosophy could remain faithful to his own perception of deity, and yet join with brethren from all creeds in the pursuit of that which is best in human nature; charity, tolerance, assistance, and fidelity to his fellow man. All this was possible without arguments about which god was truer than another clouding his senses. The details of what each brother understood God to be could then be set aside and left up to his own conscience.

The symbols and allegories of Freemasonry are not occult, nor is Freemasonry a religion. What it is, though, is a secular fraternity that promotes moral responsibility, separated from specific belief in God, similar to the Scouting and Girl Guide movements. In being so it is neither a threat to Christianity nor a replacement for it, but is simply a way to encourage men to be better citizens. To join the Fraternity each candidate is simply asked to profess belief in God without any enquiry as to what God means to him. Therein, I believe, lies the very essence of the Craft, because God means something different to each and every one of us, not only between religions but even between members of the same faith. Personal faith is one thing; it is when we define the nature of our God and force others to conform to that definition that the problems start. Though those of a fundamentalist outlook will never agree, it is for this reason that the nature of God, in a secular organisation like Freemasonry at least, is better left undefined and up to the individual's conscience.

The simplest way of showing respect for God in the presence of others who may believe in a different deity, is by offering God as a universal symbol as Freemasonry does. There is no religious instruction in Masonry, nor is one man's god placed above another, indeed Masons are not even permitted to discuss religion in any way whilst at labour. In such an environment they can, as they themselves say, meet 'in harmony on the level and part on the square', without their own personal faith ever getting in the way of their bond with others. And that, I suggest, is the true purpose of Freemasonry, and the reason for its development at a time when the mechanisms of the universe started to be studied and quantified by educated men. That doesn't make Freemasonry anti-Christian. But it is non-Christian, a subtle but important difference. It is also non-Jewish, non-Hindu, non-Muslim and non-every-other-faith-that-has-ever-existed, so what is the relevance of saying it is non-Christian?

When Dr. Anderson wrote the Constitutions of the English Craft in 1723, he referred to Masonry as 'the religion on which all men can agree.' In terms of my suggested origin and purpose of the Craft, there could be no more succinct way of putting it than this.

If Freemasonry appeared to be Christian in its early days, as it does to many Masons, then I believe that was an illusion, deliberately created to facilitate its existence in a hostile religious environment. The fact that the mystery school started out within the Celtic Church, and closely aligned itself to Christianity during its first six hundred years, means that today looking back it is very difficult to tell them apart. And that is why the true origin has been such an elusive quarry. This, of course, gives those who suggest that the Craft was originally Christian plenty of scope to believe they are right, but if so, then they must account for the presence in the rituals of the non-Christian elements that I have included here. The close alignment of the Craft with Christianity also explains why today many Christians regard it as a religion in its own right.

The above, from its beginning in the Stone Age to the emergence of the modern Craft can only ever be a thesis, for history was written by the victor, and that victor was the Church. In the Church's history its saints were everything that was good in human nature, though the personal character traits needed to rise to the top of life's pile are rarely edifying. Likewise any who stood against the church stood against God, and as such were anathema; branded devils and demons. Those within the Church were not devious or dishonest in this, of course, for they really saw those outside Christianity as evil. When faced with the massively prevalent worship of the sun, they simply did what they had to do to convert the people to what they believed to be the true faith. Do we, however, really expect them to have recorded what they did to Christianise the past and why they did it? Do we expect the monks of St. Andrews to have recorded the truth about the true cross of the sun? Do we really expect them to have recorded that they had a difficult time converting the people from the veneration of the cross of the sun, and had to invent Christian connections with pagan symbolism? Would that not have been perpetuating that which they sought to suppress?

The idea that the cross was a symbol derived from the sun would have been heresy of the highest calibre if carried into Christianity, and would have been a notion that the church would have had to suppress at all costs. We should not be surprised, then, that history as recorded by Christian monks makes no mention of it. It is also interesting that both groups who are suggested to have carried the true origin of the cross as a symbol, the Culdees and the Templars, were both forcibly removed from the religious stage.

CHAPTER 32

IF HIRAM STANDS as a modern version of the myths of old that venerated the sun, it would be fitting to close with two observations from antiquity that are very relevant indeed to our thesis. The first is the myth of Cuchulain, the Hound of Ulster, for not only does his death reek of solstice details, but some of them are uncannily close to those of Hiram, and suggests a link between the two.

Cuchulain was the greatest of all heroes of the Irish cycle of myths. He is widely accepted as being the worldly personification of Orion, 'the Big Man' of the sky. Like a god that was locked into an upcoming handover of power, his death in battle was inevitable, causing much lamentation and fretting beforehand. In the days leading up to the battle he was found wandering on the seashore, between the high and low tidemarks in a place where his powers were diminished. This is identical to the liminal place mentioned earlier in connection with Orion's being dumped, sightless, on the seashore of Chios.

Measuring the solstices using gnomons is not an exact science. For three days before and after the solstice, the sun's shadow cannot be seen to move at all. It is the 3rd day before it can be confirmed that the sun has changed direction and initiated a new cycle, and that is why St. John the Baptist's Day is the 24th, even though it refers to the solstice three days earlier on the 21st. The 24th is the first day on which the sun can be seen to have reversed direction.

Cuchulain rested for three days in the village of Knockbridge Co. Louth before joining battle with his enemies. Let us say that this is a reference to the three days of the sun's non-movement that lead up to the solstice. Mortally wounded in battle, he did not wish to fall in the face of his enemies so he strapped himself to a huge standing stone in the vale of Muirthemne so that he would remain upright, even in death. He therefore died standing up, as does Hiram, again being suggestive of Orion being upright when he reaches the western horizon and passing below the horizon whilst still upright. So fearful were his enemies of him, that for three days after he went silent they dared not approach him. This is then the three days after the solstice that the sun continues to remain still. It was only when a bird settled on his shoulder that his enemies knew for sure that he was dead, and approached the warrior.

A further and fascinating detail is that Cuchulain was attacked three times, and it was the third attack that killed him. This is identical with Masonry's Hiram. Most tellingly of all, the final spear-thrust that killed Cuchulain pierced his abdomen, spilling his intestines out. The Masonic 3rd Degree salute refers to the cutting open of the abdomen, and that, in turn, refers to the sun's bisecting of Orion's waist on the equinox. This is surely indicative that the same thought-processes that created the Cuchulain myth during the Bronze Age were still to the fore in the 1720s, when the myth of Hiram was written.

The legend of Cuchulain has been around for perhaps 4000 years, as evidenced by his central role in the Táin stories. Being about bulls, they are stellar myths that relate to the Age of Taurus that started around 4000BCE and ended around 2000BCE. Considering the links between this ancient tale and that of Hiram, and the fact that they are derived from the self-same constellation, could there be a better link between those distant times and the modern lodge rooms of today? This not only confirms Orion as the basis for the Hiramic legend, if more confirmation is needed, but also that the legend of the architect of Solomon's Temple was designed to carry out exactly the same function as that of Cuchulain and countless other gods of the ancient world, the veneration of the sun.

Whilst on the subject of the veneration of the sun, we will now look a little closer at one of its most ancient manifestations, the sun-temple of Newgrange, for it carried exactly the same notions of deity that are present in Freemasonry.

Newgrange in Co. Meath has been mentioned several times before. It is about 30 miles north of Dublin near Ireland's eastern seaboard. Although the name refers to only one hilltop monument, it is sited among others in one of the most sacred and ancient landscapes to be found anywhere on earth. Known collectively as Brú na Bóinne, the 'palace or mansion of the Boyne,' the site encompasses about forty mounds including three major monuments, being Newgrange itself with its pure white quartz façade, Knowth, and Dowth. The last of these, Dowth, has not yet been fully excavated, and whilst Knowth has neither the striking quartz wall nor the sun-window of Newgrange itself, it is actually the larger and older of the two. Radiocarbon dating places Newgrange at 3200BCE and Knowth a few hundred years older. These are among the oldest structures on earth, and predate the Pyramids and Stonehenge by almost a thousand years. They even predate the arrival of the Celts by two and a half thousand years, so the symbols depicted within and around these monuments are among the oldest in the world.

One similarity all three mounds possess is that they align with points on the horizon relevant to the theory contained in this book; Newgrange towards the southeast, where the sun rises on the winter solstice, Dowth towards the southwest where the sun sets that same day, and Knowth east-west, where the sun rises and sets on the equinoxes. All three rest upon rings of huge kerbstones,

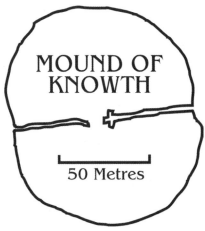

each stone about four feet high by six or seven wide, many of which are decorated with ancient runes or symbols. Because of their antiquity it is impossible to say for sure what the runes mean, but taken with the alignments of the passages within the mounds, an educated guess can be made.

Newgrange aligns with the sunrise on the shortest day of the year, allowing a pale amber beam to penetrate to the very end of the long passageway. Knowth is different, however, and is particularly interesting from the viewpoint of the symbolism of the Craft, because it aligns east-west, immediately bringing to mind the equinoxes.

The mound of Dowth, the third of these ancient temples, is different again and is aligned to the sunset on the winter solstice rather than the sunrise. The name Dowth comes from the Gaelic word 'Dubad' meaning darkness, so the allusion is obvious, being the darkness of the sunset on the winter solstice.

If we cast our minds back to chapter two we will remember that the candidate is placed, in the darkness of a blindfold, in the northwest corner of the lodge room. I equated the underlying symbolism of this action with the sun setting in that corner on the summer solstice. Though referring to summer rather than winter, the allusion in the Brú na Bóinne is the same.

If the darkness of Dowth is shown in its name and the going down of the sun, the other aspect of Masonry, the light that opposes the dark, is seen in the dazzling white quartz wall of Newgrange itself, aligned as it is with the rising of the sun. The light and dark of Masonry are therefore both present in the two mounds of Brú na Bóinne that were aligned with the solstice sun five thousand years ago.

Another question that must be asked is whether Orion is represented on the site, for as we saw from the myth of Cuchulain the constellation was known in ancient times? There is one particular kerbstone that includes marks that are commonly held to be the three belt stars of the constellation, and that is kerbstone 52. The picture here above is that massive stone, showing the sets of triple holes that are thought to be associated with Orion.

They are particularly interesting because whilst the overwhelming bulk of marks are merely scratched a few millimetres into the stone, the holes are about an inch deep, hinting that they were particularly important to the builders. As I have elsewhere shown Orion to be lord of the winter, governor of the dark skies of the winter solstice, and we have noted that both Newgrange and Dowth align to this day, is it in that capacity that the three belt stars are depicted on kerbstone 52?

There is one particular aspect of this enigmatic stone that not only suggests that the honouring of Orion is indeed its intended purpose, but hints very strongly that the constellation fulfilled a role similar to lord of the winter for those who built the monument.

It is undeniable that the purpose of the mound of Newgrange is the honouring of the sun on the winter solstice, and if we look at where Orion is on that particular day, it is right at the other side of the Zodiac to the sun. The precession of the equinoxes gradually moves the position of the constellation relative to the sun, but Orion would still have been dominant in the winter skies 5,000 years ago.

The two most important kerbstones on the site are K1 and K52. One has to climb over K1 to gain entrance to the passage, and so the symbols on it therefore refer to the interplay of the sun on that side of the mound on that significant day. K52 is

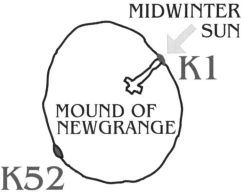

right round the back of the mound, exactly opposite the entrance to the passage. Is it mere coincidence that this stone, which is at the opposite side of the mound to K1, shows Orion which is at the opposite side of the Zodiac on the day the mound was designed to honour?

In being represented opposite the sun on the mound can this be interpreted as meaning that Orion for them fulfilled the position of lord of the winter, as indeed he did for many other ancient cultures? If so, then the choice of Orion for the mediaeval mystery that became Freemasonry has an ancient lineage. What is particularly intriguing is that Newgrange only started to give up its secrets in the 1980s, and indeed even today the theories about what the runes mean are many. Perhaps more than any other, the author Martin Brennan brought the astronomical purpose of Newgrange and other megalithic sites to the fore in his book *The Stars and the Stones* in 1982. It is intriguing, then, that a myth written in the 18th Century could be so closely aligned to the spiritual concepts contained in the 5,000-year-old symbolism of the Brú na Bóinne.

One final aspect of Irish mythology that shows an uncanny linkage to modern Freemasonry is to be found in the excellent book, '*Island of the Setting Sun, - In Search of Ireland's Ancient Astronomers,*' by Anthony Murphy and Richard Moore. Though they make no reference whatsoever to Freemasonry, they relate details about the river Boyne that are fascinating to our thesis.

The Boyne enters the sea near Drogheda Co Louth. The area's earlier name was Inbher Colpa, and was the end of the 'sacred way of the cow' as the river was alluded to. Inbher, like 'Inver', simply means meeting of the waters, but it is the word Colpa that is interesting to us. It literally means 'calf', which is understandable, considering that the name of the Boyne comes from the Cow-goddess Boann. How the area got its name I will leave to the authors. '…There are two distinct stories which tell how Inbher Colpa got its name. One recalls how a mythical monster was slain at Brú na Bóinne, and his bone, the story says specifically his shinbone (colptha) was washed out into the estuary…'

The mention of a shinbone immediately caught my attention, considering the crossing of the shinbone that forms the crucial part of the 3rd Degree ceremony. The second possible origin of the name is no less interesting, for '…it involves the arrival of the Milesian invaders in 1694BCE. Three brothers led the invasion – Eremon, Amergin the bard, and Colpe, the swordsman. Colpe was killed in battle with the De Dannan at the mouth of the Boyne, and was buried at Rath Colpa, beside the later St Columba's Church…'

It is generally regarded that the three Milesian brothers are an allusion to the three stars of Orion's belt, and of course the constellation itself was seen as the Great Swordsman of the sky. The authors continue with another interesting detail. '…The Colpe mythology consistently refers to a calf, although it is not immediately clear whether this is the calf of the leg or a young cow…The old Irish word Colpa has a number of meanings. It can mean a three year old calf and it can mean the calf of the leg, or shinbone'

The calf of the leg is also the shinbone which lies at the heart of the myth of the monster, so the allusion may well be the calf of the leg.

Freemasons are ridiculed for some of the more obscure things they do whilst undergoing initiation, and rolling the trouser leg up is one of them. Is the exposure of the calf an allusion to the mythology of Inbher Colpa?

So far we have encountered the shin-bone five times. The stance of Orion in the sky. The stance adopted by Mithras' Torchbearers. The stance of Hiram. The shin-bone of the mythical monster slain at Brú na Bóinne. And now the rolled-up trouser leg of Masonic ceremony. There are simply too many convergences among these themes for there to be no connection.

I met Anthony Murphy and Richard Moore recently to discuss their work. Perhaps most interesting of all is their discovery of Orion, or the *High Man* as they refer to him, in the layout of the landscape around Newgrange. Not only do the roads and place-names mark the shape of a great giant on the landscape, but the name of the area, Ferrard, comes from *Fir Ard*, High Man. And the High Man's shinbone is exactly at the great mound of Newgrange. Details of this huge figure can be found at their excellent website, mythicalireland.com, and though their work and findings are ostensibly unconnected with mine, they mesh so well together that there simply must be some substance to the figure of Orion they have discovered in the Irish landscape.

The scratched symbols of Man's early comprehension of deity found on the monuments of the Brú na Bóinne are among the oldest found anywhere, and pre-date the oldest stories in the Old Testament by almost two thousand years. If knowledge of them somehow survived the ravages of time, of the lives and deaths of men, of the rising and failing of empires, and found its way via the druids and the Culdees and into the mediaeval mystery started by the Knights Templar in the 12th Century which eventually became Freemasonry, then that is a truly momentous idea indeed.

And how fitting it is that Man's first endeavour to honour his perception of God in a permanent and lasting way, in the islands that would eventually give rise to that Freemasonry, was through the shaping and positioning of stones.

Truly the first Freemasons.

PART FIVE

THE FINGER

OF GOD

THE CRAFT AND THE CROSS

CHAPTER 33

FROM LOOKING BACKWARDS across the years to the earliest times in the British Isles, we will finish by coming right up to date, and looking at the modern Craft itself. I mentioned at the very start of the book that allegory would be mentioned often. Allegory has various purposes, from simple symbols that convey an obvious message that is readily understood to being truly obscure and multi-layered, needing additional information to get the true depth of what is intended. Knowing what we now do about the themes that Freemasonry is structured around, we will now look at possibly the most important Masonic document in existence – Anderson's Constitutions of 1723.

As the Craft emerged it took off across the world with dizzying speed. While it grew, so too did the need to regularise and formalise it, and the result was the book of Constitutions, written by Church of Scotland minister Dr. James Anderson. What we are now going to look at is the symbolism contained in the book's frontispiece, that appears below.

If we cast our minds back to the suggested underlying meaning of the Craft, it is that the pillars Boaz and Jachin symbolise the solstices and the gnomons needed to mark those days. Also that between the solstices lies the crossing of the equinoxes, where the sun passes from one hemisphere to the other. That the year is divided into light and dark halves and was ruled by twin deities and that as each new Master takes over the care of the lodge from his predecessor, he symbolises the handover of power from one of those deities to the other. Over all this the sun casts its rays, with particular reference to the square formed by the sun at Edinburgh.

Those principles, in their entirety, are embedded allegorically in the picture that is the frontispiece of the Constitutions.

Engraved by John Pine in Aldersgate Street London

On first glance we could be forgiven for thinking that it is simply an engraving that records the moment the outgoing Grand Master, the Duke of Montagu, hands authority in the form of the Constitutions of the Craft to his successor the Duke of Wharton, on St. John the Baptist's Day 1723, the year the Constitutions were produced. If we were to describe what we see in the picture we would note that two groups of figures stand between two rows of pillars that recede into the distance. At the end of the twin colonnade we have a masonry arch, through which the landscape diminishes to a vanishing point at the very centre of the picture. On the ground between the Grand Masters is a visual representation of Euclid's 47th Proposition, that demonstrates pictorially the mathematical law that when the squares of the two shorter sides of a triangle added together equals the square of the long side, then the angle between the two short sides will be exactly 90 degrees. Also included, and perhaps the most enigmatic aspect of the entire drawing, is the sun-god Apollo riding across the sky above in his fiery chariot.

Much has been written about this engraving, in particular the inclusion of Apollo. His presence has had many explanations, each having its own merit, but none allude to what is contained in this thesis. I would suggest that Apollo is simply a direct allusion to the sun itself and its daily progress across the sky. I earlier suggested that the Master Mason's Word, Mabone, stemmed from Mabon, the Celtic god. That deity was called by several names and was identified in Roman Britain with Apollo. If the figure in the picture is Apollo, then he is therefore also Mabon, the Celt's Great Son of the earth, the principle of which is enshrined in the raising of the 3rd Degree. The fact that he is travelling to the right also mimics the path of the sun from its rising in the east to its setting in the west.

Our attention is then drawn to the structure of the picture, and in particular the rows of pillars that march to the vanishing point in the centre. Coupled with the landscape beyond the arch that continues the lines to a point, this gives us a very definite visual x-shape that the entire picture is structured around. This x has been noted by others, but only in a geometric sense, and not in relation to the division of the year into its light and dark halves. There has been enough already written here about the x formed by the sun to need to elaborate further about its position in the symbolism of the Craft. In including it in such a prominent way in this defining document however, the first Freemasons are almost shouting its significance from the rooftops.

Another reference to the sun in the context of the thesis is Euclid's 47th Proposition, which illustrates visually the mechanics of what is more commonly known as Pythagoras' Theorem. The 47th Proposition occupies a curious place in Masonry, because whilst seen often as a symbol, it carries few if any symbolic connotations such as are found in other motifs. 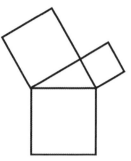 Its importance to the Craft is therefore unexplained, but its presence in this picture suggests how important it is.

Indeed Anderson goes even further in the text of the Constitutions themselves where he asserts that it is '...**the foundation of all Masonry'**. This is quite a statement about such a simple concept, but not if it is seen in the light of what I am suggesting here. The purpose of the 47th Proposition is, of course, to find a perfect 90-degree angle, and since the sun lays out a perfect 90-degree angle on the landscape that gave birth to the Craft, the Proposition can be seen as an allegorical representation of that phenomenon. It is only by understanding the mechanics of the right angle that the trueness of the cross formed by the sun in southern Scotland can be appreciated, and when Anderson states that the ability to find a right angle is the foundation of the entire Craft, we understand why that is so.

 Even the masonry arch at the far end of the colonnade carries symbolic meaning, for it too alludes to the sun. Whilst very simple, the plain, semi-circular arch has been used artistically to represent the passage of the sun across the heavens for thousands of years. Many ancient megaliths include the arch in specific reference to the sun. The arch included in the picture can therefore be seen as another reference to the sun, either generally in respect of its daily arc across the southern sky, or more particularly with the keystone added as it is, highlighting its zenith on the meridian.

If the x shape outlined by the perspective of the pillars is indeed a reference to the crossing of the equinoxes, this reminds us of the importance of those days in regard to the twin gods who governed the year. We could perhaps have expected to see the pavement upon which the figures stand laid out in the traditional fashion of black and white alternating squares that I suggest refers to those light and dark halves of the year, but it is not. The black and white may not be included in the pavement, but they are still present, though much more subtly, and in a way much more relevant to the scene.

If we look through the arch at the back of the picture we see an unnaturally symmetrical landscape that continues the perspective lines to the vanishing point. The scene is very definitely divided into a light half and a dark half, accentuated by the fact that each half is identical but for the lighting. The division between the dark and light is therefore centred upon the cross formed by the perspective lines, placing dark to one side of what I suggest is the crossing of the equinox and light to the other. There could scarcely be a cleverer way to include this cryptic reference to the junction between the light and dark halves of the year than as the engraver has done in the layout of this picture.

The picture goes even further in its references to the twin gods of the year when we allow our attention to fall on the group of figures that is the focal point of the entire scene. What is depicted here is the handing of authority from the outgoing Grand Master to the incoming one. I earlier suggested that the installation of the new Master of each lodge is symbolic of the changeover from one God to the other. Is the same allegory also standing silently behind the handing of the Constitutions from one Grand Master to the other?

Even their positioning on the engraving is significant, because the x formed by the perspective lines that delineate the equinox upon which the handover of power takes place lies right between them. Indeed the wisdom of using the dark and light halves of the landscape rather than the black and white pavement becomes apparent when we see that one Grand Master stands on the dark side of the division whilst the other stands in the light, and the Constitutions themselves lie right on the dividing line. This could not have been achieved had the black and white only been shown as a chequered pavement. It is significant also, perhaps, that the one receiving the Constitutions is in the light half of the picture, or in other words symbolises the passage from dark to light; the coming to power of the sun on the spring equinox. The very same symbolism is included during the 3rd Degree ceremony when the Master of the lodge kills Hiram, and here we find it in the frontispiece of arguably the most important Masonic document in existence.

So yet again the artists in the employ of the architects of the Craft have gone to considerable lengths to imbue every single aspect of their work with deeply buried esoteric references to embody as many aspects of the ancient veneration of the sun as possible, without being so blatant that their true significance would become common knowledge.

On the surface this engraving has a simple meaning, but if understood esoterically it records the Lord of the Winter handing power to the Lord of the Summer on the spring equinox. Remove our understanding of the esoteric elements that have been included however, and we only have an engraving that records the changing authority in the English Craft in the year the Constitutions were produced.

Many of the objects that carry Masonic emblems were the work of local craftsmen; delft jugs, bowls, medals, pendants, lodge banners and the like. We may see included a beehive, a wriggling snake, a square or Euclid's 47th Proposition, but many of those craftsmen in all probability did not understand the depth of the symbolism those motifs contained and merely copied them from other Masonic sources as part of the general mystique of the Craft. That argument cannot, however, be used for the frontispiece of the Constitutions, because that design emanated directly from a Grand Lodge, and contains precisely what the Craft's ruling body wanted it to.

Though not used in Ireland, Freemasonry in both Scotland and England uses boards drawn with symbols when conferring degrees. These have been mentioned before, and are known as Tracing Boards.

388

There is one for each degree, but the one that interests us here is that of the 3rd Degree.

It is covered in the symbols of the Craft and refers to the death and re-birth ritual the candidate undergoes in the 3rd Degree. On top of the coffin we see a pictorial impression of a pillared entryway that can be seen as a portal to the Afterworld. Rather than being in the darkness of oblivion, however, the veil at the end of the passage is drawn back,

allowing us to see a bright new day at the far end of the journey – again symbolic of the rhythm of light and dark. Is it a coincidence that directly above the entrance to the Underworld is a skull and crossbones, that according to this thesis represents the equinox? If the motif does indeed refer to the sun on the equinoxes as I have suggested, is it deliberately placed over the gateway to the Underworld to indicate the day on which that passage is effected?

Also on the board is recorded perhaps one of the most intriguing links yet to the thesis presented here.

On the coffin are three number fives, two at the top and one at the bottom, all three surrounded by the emblems that tell the story of the sun on the Scottish landscape. These numbers intrigued me from the first moment I set foot in a lodge room for they have no known explanation for their inclusion. As a result of my findings, however, I can at last reveal their true meaning.

The finger of God

The mystical poet William Blake's most enduring works are the words for the hymn Jerusalem, and his painting, 'the Ancient of Days', which depicts God as the Great Geometrician of the Universe, reaching down with a pair of dividers as though touching the earth. In terms of the thesis presented here, the sun reaches down to touch the landscape of Scotland with what can be considered geometrical precision.

Though I have not actually given it a value yet, the line of latitude that runs through Edinburgh, where we can consider God's finger to touch the earth and around which this entire tale revolves, is 55 degrees and 55 minutes north. If given as a three-digit number such as in a map reference, it would be **555**. And here on this board that is central to the Craft, that carries all the symbols that have engaged us for so long, are the numbers 555. Can there be even the slightest doubt that they refer to the location of the sun's true square?

Does this, then, not bring our story full circle, and prove that Masonry does indeed lie at the end of an ancient path such as I have laid out here? I have shown that at various times in history the same themes can be identified. Until the discovery of the true cross formed at latitude 555, none of these aspects of history has been linked as part of a single entity. The thesis presented here links them, and unites what is already known of the early Craft with the phenomenon of the sun's true cross, and includes what has only now been discovered about Freemasonry's complex allegories and symbolism.

Religion does not satisfy us on a scientific level, but neither does science satisfy us on a spiritual level. Life after death may seem ridiculous to many scientists, but the notion brings succour to the dying and those around them. We may be able to describe a beautiful sunset in technical terms, but would that description lift the soul as does seeing one? It would be a strange person who would derive pleasure from reading the sheet music for Beethoven's ninth, but listening to it can surely transport us to another place. Physical beauty in the human form might be measurable in terms of an equation of ratios, but true beauty is so much more than appearance. And what is love? Is love for a cat comparable to love of one's wife or husband, or one's child? For these and countless millions of similar reasons, both science and spirituality are needed in our world, but they are natural enemies. How then can they work in harmony?

Freemasonry offered those who could not believe in an anthropomorphic deity a secular fraternity that promoted moral and social responsibility, and allowed them to share in that fellowship with those who still remained piously attached to whatever God they wished. Freemasonry can accommodate both perspectives without conflict, and therein lies the very essence of the Craft.

So Masonry does not promote Christianity above other spiritual paths?

So what?

When today, forward thinking Christians meet with followers of other spiritual paths in ecumenical, multi-denominational services, and bow their heads with Hindus, Muslims, Jews and others in universal, corporate prayer, what are they doing and why do they do it? Surely it is because they see wisdom in bringing together those who simply wish to honour God irrespective of each person's individual perception of deity, and thereby showing respect for others? In doing so they seek to break down the horrendous barriers that exist in the world today by setting aside their differences and joining with other traditions in a symbolic, universal way. In doing this they leave their own particular dogmatic baggage at the door on their way in and pick it up again on their way out…Freemasonry has been doing just that for almost 300 years.

In one last postscript to the foregoing tale of the ancient, long forgotten veneration of the equinoxes and solstices, I would mention that without realising they have done so, almost everybody who reads this will have participated in the perpetuation of the practice on many occasions. Since the earliest times the convivial aspect of the Craft has been prominent in its ethos, when, after the labours of the lodge room, the brethren would traditionally partake of some refreshment. The proceedings were oft-times brought to a conclusion with a practice they called pile-driving where they would sing a song, whilst stamping their feet and joining hands with their neighbours by crossing their arms over their bodies. At the end of the song they would jump in the air and stamp their feet as hard as they could on the floor bringing their festivities to a close, hence the reference to pile-driving.

It will be obvious from the thesis of this book that the crossing of their arms across the body at parting, was, like the crossing of the deacon's wands at the opening and closing of the lodge, a reference to the crossing of the equinoxes. In the craft of building, the pile is what underpins the foundations upon which the structure is raised. Pile-driving in this symbolic context, then, alludes to that which underpins the Craft.

The exercise was common practice in the 18th century when the enthusiastic Ayrshire Mason Robert Burns was writing his poetry and songs. It was he who wrote down and popularised, with a few Masonic inclusions, the traditional song Auld Lang Syne, and over the years the singing of that song became part of Masonic culture and was sung at the installations of new Masters on or immediately after St. John the Evangelist's Day at the end of December. By introducing the equinox in the form of crossed arms to the celebration of the birth of a new year, the four significant moments of the great rhythm of the year referred to throughout as being central to the Craft's message could be honoured together.

The practice grew in popularity and eventually drifted to more general New Year celebrations, and though the pile-driving was reduced to the raising and lowering of the hands, in a movement that even today still mimics the driving of a pile, the practice came to be embraced by the entire world.

So when you next gather in a circle around the perimeter of a room and join hands across your body forming an x-shaped cross as you sing the immortal words '…for Auld Lang Syne'; pause a moment and contemplate the antiquity of your actions. Realise that in doing so you are perpetuating the memory of the division of the year into two halves, and are therefore paying homage, however inadvertently, to the symbolic veneration of the sun as carried out by the very first people to raise their eyes upwards and think of God.

In forming a circle you honour the sun, and in crossing hands with your neighbour you refine your tribute to the sun on the equinox. By 'pile-driving' that x with your neighbour you are celebrating with him or her one of the oldest spiritual concepts on earth, and venerating the crossing of the equinoxes in the never-ending rhythm of the cosmos of the ancient world. As repeated often here, original meanings are lost with the passage of the aeons, so you are not guilty of worshiping the sun, of course - or no more so at any rate than are Masons when following their own, arcane rituals.

Following archaic practices does something for the human spirit on a very deep level. In ancient times our forbears brought votive offerings to holy wells to give thanks for the miracle of clean, clear water welling from the ground. Today many still leave gifts of coins at such sites, even though the mystery of spring-water is geologically understood to be anything but miraculous. Adding our coin to those of others still satisfies an unknown need however, and that is because the urge to do so comes from deep within our sub-conscious. The rituals of

Freemasonry similarly tap into our consciousness way below the cognitive, and from what I have discovered of the meaning of those rituals, I believe this is because they carry allegorical references that have been part of our psyches for thousands of years, even though we have long since lost touch with those references. That is why Freemasons enjoy following rituals so detached from the modern world that outsiders believe the only reason educated men would partake in such curious rites is for personal gain, or sinister, anti-Christian purposes.

What has survived the millennia are not the 'secrets' that conspiracy theorists generally attribute to the founding of the Craft. What has survived are merely symbolic concepts that have been passed down the generations, that, because of their deep attachment to our psyches, provide a common thread through time. The advent of Christianity blurred the true meaning of those concepts by overlaying them with new interpretations. Freemasonry still carries those original, true meanings allegorically in its rituals however, where, though they are not understood on the surface, nevertheless speak to us on a deeper level. The Craft, I believe, is simply the post-Enlightenment way of carrying on what the Culdees and the pre-Christians carried in their own way in earlier times. The difference was that in earlier times it was sacred while in the 18th Century it was secular, and appealed to those who sought rationality over superstition.

We started this quest with two questions. What is Freemasonry, and where did it come from? If the above answers the question as to what Freemasonry is, can we then say when it began?

From the perspective of the thesis presented here, Freemasonry simply has no beginning, for like the mighty river that traces back through countless tributaries and feeder streams and becomes lost in a thousand swampy hilltops, the Craft is merely a variation of older traditions that similarly trace backwards in time, through various strands, divergences and unions, becoming lost in the miasma of ancient spirituality of primitive man. Though we can identify milestones in its development along the way, none of those was a beginning, but simply advancements along the pathway. Those milestones are only visible to us from the 17th Century onwards because before that it was a mystery tradition and therefore was invisible to the profane. And before that it was an oral tradition, and was similarly not recorded.

Put in this way then, the Craft is quite literally as old as Man. I earlier asked tongue-in-cheek if St Columba was the first Freemason, but in truth he was as far removed in time from the first Freemason as we are from him.

Freemasonry seeks to honour God in allegories drawn from the sun; allegories that are also woven around the crafting of stone. The stonemason uses the square to bring form to the rude mass of an un-worked stone. The Master Mason proves the work for incorporation in the structure with his own square, for if the work is not true the building will fall. But by what measure is the Master's square itself proven? At latitude 555 the sun gives the means to prove the Master's square, enabling the mason to build his structure true. If one wanted to link the symbol of God with the craft of building, where better to forge that link than at latitude 555?

The symbol of Christianity is the true cross. When rendered as the allegory outlined here, the true cross is also a true square. The square of masonry is therefore an allegory for the cross of Jesus, but in being an allegory, does not exclude from the Craft those whose religious beliefs do not rely on the Christian cross as a symbol. The Son of God, who is the focus of the Christian faith, becomes the Sun of God in Freemasonry – a subtle change in emphasis that renders god as a simple symbol, under which all men can meet to pursue high ideals, irrespective of their religious allegiance. So it is only now, at the very end of our journey, that we can appreciate the choice of title for this book – 'The Craft and the Cross.'

Of all Masonic practices, it is perhaps the raising of the candidate in the 3rd Degree that causes the most consternation to those outside the Order because it is imagined it to be a substitute for, or even a satanic mockery of, the Christian resurrection. As presented here, however, it is simply a theatrical depiction of the rhythm of the cosmos, of the changing of the seasons that has gone on since the very beginning of time, and will continue until the very end. It has nothing whatsoever to do with the Christian resurrection, and so does not profane that belief in any way.

I have made the point throughout that Christianity absorbed pagan ways and that this was how it converted Europe. Ireland was different however, and perhaps it would be more accurate to say that on that island at the edge of the world it was the other way round and that paganism took over Christianity and used that new faith to further its own ancient teachings. From the evidence presented here, Saint Columba was a druid who embraced the new faith and married the sun's true cross to that of Jesus.

And in that legacy lies the true origin of Freemasonry.

It was said of the bard Amergin '*I am the beam of the sun...Who is he who announces the ages of the moon? Who teaches the place where falls the sunset?*' In closing a modern Masonic lodge, the Senior Warden answers as to his place and duty...'*In the west, Worshipful Master... As the sun sets in the west to close the glorious day, so the Senior Warden stands in the west, to close the lodge at the will and pleasure of the Worshipful Master.*'

Throughout this quest I have sought to attach meanings to the symbolism of the distant past, meanings that have not previously been ascribed to those emblems. That Freemasonry has somehow preserved the true meaning of those symbols, when the world forgot them thousands of years ago, truly is something to contemplate.

Postscript

The tale related here is just the beginning of an immense historical tale that has remained completely hidden until now, and this book is only the first volume of what is expected to be at least a trilogy under the collective title SUN OF GOD. When the final draft of this was ready I believed that the tale I wove herein was complete, but as a result of a major discovery in 2008, which was only made possible by being in possession of the perspective granted by what is contained within these pages, I realised that the picture was a whole lot bigger than I had imagined. I alluded to this in the acknowledgements in relation to David Alan Ritchie. David has a book in the final stages of production that he has been working on for many years. I do not wish to steal his thunder by writing too much of his subject matter here, suffice to say that it dove-tails incredibly well with what is contained in The Craft and the Cross, and basically tells the same story from another perspective. In his own words he started with the answer and spent fifteen years looking for the question.

I am currently well advanced with the sequel to this book, which dwarfs this one in its implications to our understanding of history. The revelations it contains about what early Man knew of the phenomenon of the true square of the sun at Edinburgh, and what its discovery contributed to the development of civilisation, quite simply beggars belief.

Those revelations will have to wait to volume two of the series which will be called THE RHYTHM OF THE COSMOS; when we will discover exactly how and when ancient Man first became aware of the true cross of the sun, and how that knowledge that appeared at the very dawn of civilisation survived unchanged as the world developed around it, and is still carried to this day, completely unadulterated, in the most misunderstood fraternal society in the world – Freemasonry.

PHOTO CREDITS

Page 27   All Seeing Eye   Image reproduced by kind
permission of Portrush Masonic hall
Page 62   Mithras' Torchbearer   Yolanda McClintock
Page 108   Montsegur   Reproduced by kind permission of
Mr. David Allett, Auberge du Balestié, Ariège, Languedoc
Page 145   Newgrange entrance   Image reproduced courtesy of the
Office of Public Works
Page 148   Green Man   Image used by kind permission of
the Rosslyn Chapel Trust
Page 157   Boheh Stone   Robert Bashford
Page 158   Eagle lectern   Yolanda McClintock
Page 167   Tydavnet sun-disc   Image used by kind permission of
Monaghan County Museum.
Page 169   Boa Island figure   Yolanda McClintock
Page 172   Boa Island figure   Yolanda McClintock
Page 173   Carndonagh figure   Robert Bashford
Page 174   Celtic Cross Drumcliff   Yolanda McClintock
Page 178   Skull & crossed bones   Yolanda McClintock
Page 181   Chartres Cathedral   Yolanda McClintock
Page 182   Chartres Cathedral   Yolanda McClintock
Page 210   Tandragee Man   Reproduced by kind permission of
the Dean and Chapter of St Patrick's Church of Ireland Cathedral, Armagh.
Page 218   Temple Church interior   Yolanda McClintock
Page 219   Temple Church knight   Yolanda McClintock
Page 294   Masonic Charter   Robert Bashford
Page 320   Whiskey decanter   Image used by kind permission of
the Grand Lodge of Scotland Museum, Edinburgh.
Page 321   Warrant frame   Image used by courtesy of Lodge
754 Coleraine
Page 335   Sun face, Glencolumbkille Yolanda McClintock
Page 372   Mound of Newgrange   Robert Bashford
Page 374   Newgrange kerbstone 52   Image reproduced courtesy of the
Office of Public Works
Page 387   Tracing Board   Robert Bashford

The photographs of Orion are courtesy of the SKY-MAP.ORG website

SELECTED BIBLIOGRAPHY

An Account of the Chapel of Roslin 1778. Robert L. D. Cooper (editor)
Antiquities of the Irish Countryside, Seán P. Ó Ríordáin
The Arcana of Freemasonry, Albert Churchward
The Archaeology of Late Celtic Britain & Ireland, Lloyd Laing
Astronomy Before the Telescope, Christopher Walker (editor)
The Bible
The Bible came from Arabia, Kamal Salibi
The Bible – the Unauthorised Version, Robin Lane Fox
The Birth of Christ, Exploding the Myth, Colin Wilson
The Book of Hiram, Christopher Knight & Robert Lomas
Born in Blood, John J. Robinson
A Calendar of Saints, James Bentley
Cathair Na Mart vol 13, Westport Historical Society.
The Cathedral Builders of the Middle Ages, Alain Erlande-Brandenburg
Celtic Christianity, C. Bamford & W. P. Marsh
The Celtic Conciousness, Robert O'Driscoll
The Celtic Gods, Patrick McCafferty & Mike Baillie
Celtic Migrations, W. A. Hanna
Celtic Rituals, a guide to Celtic Spirituality, Alexei Kondratiev
The Christian Druids, John Minahane
Circles of Stone, Max Milligan & Aubrey Burl
Columba, Ian Finlay
Columcille, Mairéad Ashe Fitzgerald
Compendium Maleficarum, Francesco Maria Guazzo 1608
Complete Guide to Celtic Mythology, Dr. Bob Curran
Cracking the Freemason's Code, Robert L. D. Cooper
Cracking the Symbol Code, Tim Wallace-Murphy
Cruithin – the Ancient Kindred, Ian Adamson
The Dead Sea Scrolls Deception, Michael Baigent & Richard Leigh
Druids, Preachers of Immortality, Anne Ross
Early Christian & Pictish Monuments of Scotland 1964, H. M. S. O. Edinburgh
Early Christian Ireland, Márie & Liam de Paor
Early Christian Irish Art, Françoise Henry
The Early Church, Henry Chadwick
The Essence of the Gnostics, Bernard Simon
The Festival of Lughnasa, Márie MacNeill
The Freemasons, Jasper Ridley
Gleanncholmcille, a guide to 5000 years of history in stone, Michael Herity
God's Heretics, the Albigensian Crusade, Aubrey Burl
The Golden Builders, Tobias Churton
The Hiram Key, Christopher Knight & Robert Lomas

History of the Grand Lodge of Ireland 1925, Lepper & Crossle
History of Scotland (3 vols.) 1874, Thomas Wright
The History of the Knights Templar 1842, Charles G. Addison
The Holy Blood & the Holy Grail, Baigent, Leigh & Lincoln
Illustrated guide to Rosslyn Chapel and Castle 1892, Rev. John Thompson
Illustrations of Masonry 1770, William Preston
In Search of Scotland 1929, H. V. Morton
Inquisition, Robert Held
Intl. Encyclopaedia of secret Societies. & Fraternal. Orders, Alan Axelrod
The Invisible College, Robert Lomas
Ireland, elements of her early history 1921, J. J. O'Kelly
Irish Carved Ornament, H. S. Crawford
Irish Megalithic Tombs, Elizabeth Shee Twohig
Jesus, Last of the Pharaohs, Ralph Ellis
Jesus, the evidence, Ian Wilson
Jesus the Man, Barbara Thiering
Keeper of Genesis, Robert Bauval & Graham Hancock
The Knights Templar, Helen Nicholson
The Life of Columcille, Brian Lacey
Lives of the English Saints, John Henry Newman, 1836
Magi, the Quest for a Secret Tradition, Adrian G. Gilbert
The Malleus Maleficarum, Kramer & Sprenger 1596
Manual of Sepulchral Slabs & Crosses 1869, Rev. Edward L. Cutts
Megalithic Sites in Britain, Prof Alexander Thom
The Messianic Legacy, Baigent, Leigh & Lincoln
The Mythic Dimension - selected essays, Joseph Campbell
A New Encyclopaedia of Freemasonry, A. E. Waite
The New Knighthood, Malcolm Barber
Norse Myths, Kevin Crossley-Holland
The Origin of Satan, Elaine Pagels
Origins of Freemasonry, David Stevenson
Origins of the Mithraic Mysteries, David Ulansey
Our Ancestors – Scots Picts and Cymry, R. C. Maclagan 1913
The Passover Plot, Hugh Schonfield
The Philosopher and the Druids, Philip Freeman
Picts, H. M. S. O. Edinburgh
Prehistoric and early Christian Ireland – a guide, Estyn Evans
The Quest for the Celtic Key, Karen Ralls-Macleod & Ian Robertson
The Reformation, Owen Chadwick
Religion and Culture, Michael Foucault
Rosslyn Chapel, The Earl of Rosslyn
Rosslyn, Country of Painter and Poet, Helen Rosslyn & Angelo Maggi
Rosslyn and the Grail, Mark Oxbrow & Ian Robertson

Rosslyn, Guardian of the Secrets of the Holy Grail, Murphy & Hopkins
The Rosslyn Hoax?, Robert L. D. Cooper
The Sacred Mushroom and the Cross, John M. Allegro.
Sacred Sites of the Knights Templar, John K. Young
Scotland, Illustrated Guide to Ancient Monuments, H. M. S. O. Edinburgh
Scotland Through the Ages 1946, Michael Jenner
The Second Messiah, Christopher Knight & Robert Lomas
Secret Chamber, Robert Bauval
The Secrets of Freemasonry, Robert Lomas
The Stars and the Stones, Martin Brennan
From Stonehenge to Modern Cosmology, Fred Hoyle
Sun and Cross, Jakob Streit
The Sword and the Grail, Andrew Sinclair
The Táin, the Great Celtic Epic, Liam Mac Uistin
Talisman. Sacred Cities, Secret Faith, Graham Hancock & Robert Bauval
The Templar Revelation, Lynn Picknett & Clive Prince
The Templars' Secret Island, Erling Haagensen & Henry Lincoln
The Temple and the Lodge, Michael Baigent & Richard Leigh
A Test of Time, David Rohl
Turning the Hiram Key, Robert Lomas
The Twilight Pagans, Michael Sheane
Understanding Scottish Graveyards, Betty Willsher
The Unlocked Secret, James Dewar
Uriel's Machine, Christopher Knight & Robert Lomas
Warriors of the Wasteland, John Grigsby
Western Society & the Church in the Middle Ages, R. W. Southern

Index